THE CLASSICS
OF WESTERN
SPIRITUALITY

THE CLASSICS OF WESTERN SPIRITUALITY
A Library of the Great Spiritual Masters

President and Publisher
Lawrence Boadt, C.S.P.

EDITORIAL BOARD

Valentin Weigel

SELECTED SPIRITUAL WRITINGS

TRANSLATED AND INTRODUCED BY
ANDREW WEEKS

PREFACE BY
R. EMMET MCLAUGHLIN

PAULIST PRESS
NEW YORK • MAHWAH, N.J.

Cover art: Detail from *Saint John the Baptist Preaching*, Pieter Brueghel the Elder (ca. 1525–1569), oil on wood. Copyright Erich Lessing/Art Resource, N.Y.

The graphic elements reproduced on pages 71, 74, 76, 83 and 85 are from Valentin Weigel's *Vom Ort der Welt* (1613), and on page 166 from his *Der güldene Griff* (1616).

Book design by Sharyn Banks

Cover and caseside design by A. Michael Velthaus

Copyright © 2003 by Andrew Weeks

Library of Congress Cataloging-in-Publication Data

Weigel, Valentin, 1533-1588.
   [Selections. English]
   Valentin Weigel : selected spiritual writings / translated and introduced by Andrew Weeks ; Preface by R. Emmet McLaughlin.
     p. cm.
   Includes bibliographical references and index.
   ISBN 0-8091-4206-6 (alk. paper); ISBN 0-8091-0564-0
   1. Spiritual life—Lutheran Church—Early works to 1800. 2. Mysticism—Lutheran Church—early works to 1800. I. Weeks, Andrew. II. Title
BX8080.W335A25 2003
230'.41—dc21

          2003012901

Published by Paulist Press
997 Macarthur Boulevard
Mahwah, New Jersey 07430

www.paulistpress.com

Printed and bound in the
United States of America

✦ · ✦

Contents

Preface by R. Emmet McLaughlin   1

Introduction: VALENTIN WEIGEL (1533–1588)   9

Texts:

    I. *Sermon on the Good Seed and the Weeds* (ca. 1574)   51

    II. *On the Place of the World* (1576)   63

    III. *The Golden Grasp* (1578)   143

Notes   215

Select Bibliography   226

Index   235

To my good friends
James Van Der Laan and
Carl Springer
in gratitude for their encouragement

Translator of This Volume

ANDREW WEEKS is a professor of German literature at Illinois State University (Normal). He studied in Hamburg and Berlin and received an M.A. in German literature and the Ph.D. in comparative literature from the University of Illinois in Urbana. As a student of German intellectual history, Weeks turned his attention to a number of German authors who are often neglected because of their marginal status between medieval and postmedieval literature, among literature, philosophy, and religion, and between Catholic and Protestant confessions: Jacob Boehme, Paracelsus, Valentin Weigel, as well as the German dissenters, Spiritualists, and mystics before and after them. His research attempts to interpret the writings of these authors with reference to their historical contexts. Among the issues that arise in the relationship of dissenting authors to their times, two are of pressing relevance today: the problem of tolerance in the Age of Faith and the relationship between religious authority and natural or philosophical truth.

As a Fulbright scholar, Weeks recently taught the history of German mysticism at the University of Marburg and the German Spiritualists of the sixteenth- and seventeenth-centuries at the University of Szeged (Hungary).

Author of the Preface

R. EMMET MCLAUGHLIN is associate professor of history at Villanova University. He has published extensively on German Spiritualism in general and Caspar Schwenckfeld in particular. The spiritualizing tendencies of all the reformers led him to investigate what he terms the "spiritualistic trajectory" of Western culture, beginning with the Greeks. His works include *Caspar Schwenckfeld, Reluctant Radical* (1986); "Universities, Scholasticism, and the Origins of the German Reformation," *History of Universities* (1990); "The Word Eclipsed? Preaching in the Early Middle Ages," *Traditio* 48 (1991); *The Freedom of the Spirit, Social Privilege, and Religious Dissent: Caspar Schwenckfeld and the Schwenckfelders*, (1996); "Spiritualism," *Theologische Realenzyklopädie* (2001); and "Reformation Spiritualism: Typology, Sources and Significance," in *Radicalism and Dissent in the Sixteenth Century* (2002).

Acknowledgments

I would like to express my thanks to Dane Thor Daniel for his technical advice on cosmological questions raised by *On the Place of the World* and to Horst Pfefferl, editor of the new Weigel edition, and Bernard McGinn, editor of the Paulist Classics of Western Spirituality. Both editors assisted me with expert advice and scholarly information. Thanks are also due to the publishing house of Frommann-Holzboog of Stuttgart-Bad Cannsatt for generously allowing me to make use of the 1962 edition of *Vom Ort der Welt*, the 1977 edition of the "Manuscript Collection of Sermons," containing the sermon "On the Good Seed and the Weeds," and the 1997 edition of *Der güldene Griff.*

✦ • ✦

Preface
by R. Emmet McLaughlin

Although sixteenth-century Spiritualism, unlike nineteenth-century Spiritism, did not involve the shades of the dead, Valentin Weigel (1533–88), the last of the German Reformation Spiritualists, haunted the Lutheran Church. He threatened to hollow out the established church in Saxony and elsewhere by loosening the church's hold over the individual believer. Worse yet, Weigel was himself a minister of the church trained in Martin Luther's own University of Wittenberg. Weigel was thus a classic example of *trahison des clercs:* The defenders and upholders of the status quo are themselves the agents of its demise. Valentin Weigel, for all of his quietism, was truly dangerous to the church, and the church was well advised to ban his works and to pursue his followers.

However, Weigel offers the example of a Christian who embraced a more interior, heartfelt religiosity that dismissed externals as inessential but that did not turn its back upon the communal experience of religion or wallow in a thoughtless bath of warm emotions. He sought to infuse new life into repressive structures by using not only his heart but his head. In this he is a challenge to those who are satisfied with a faith without content and a love of neighbor that is vague and convenient.

SPIRIT AND SPIRITUALISM

In the wake of Luther's Protestant revolt against the medieval Catholic Church there soon appeared movements for whom

1

Luther was too conservative in both religion and politics. Although the Saxon reformer had led his followers out of Catholicism through his teaching of justification by faith alone and his exclusive reliance on scripture, he remained much closer to Catholicism than reformers such as Ulrich Zwingli (1484–1531) and John Calvin (1509–64). They objected to Luther's retention of a real presence of the body and blood of Christ in the bread and wine of the Lord's Supper. Others, such as Thomas Müntzer (1488/89–1525), expected the rediscovery of God's word to lead to a more Christian social order. The politically conservative Luther refused to draw any social implications from his religious discoveries. And he would appeal to the rulers of his day to take the church under their protection against both Catholics and those radicals whom Luther termed fanatics (*Schwärmer*).

However, the radicals refused to disappear. Zwingli and Calvin succeeded in founding a new branch of what George Williams called the "Magisterial Reformation."[1] Those more radical still, the "Radical Reformation" in Williams's terminology, divided among themselves into Anabaptists and Spiritualists. These groups were disenchanted with both Luther and Zwingli because, in the eyes of the radicals, both failed to draw the practical conclusions from their own principles. Additionally, the radicals were offended that the Reformation had not produced visibly better Christians. Instead, justification by faith alone seemed to discourage personal improvement and to encourage unchristian behavior. The Anabaptists separated from the established churches through believers' baptism to form purer churches in which to live a life of Christian discipleship based upon the gospels. That discipleship often espoused a thoroughgoing pacifism, a refusal to participate in the ordinary processes of government, and various forms of a communism based on love of neighbor. An essential part of that life was also the willing embrace of relentless persecution by both Protestants and Catholics.

The Spiritualists took a very different path. Spiritualists such as Müntzer, Sebastian Franck (1499–1542), and Caspar Schwenckfeld (1489–1561) saw the root of the Protestant malaise in the reliance on externals such as the sacraments, the church, and scripture. They argued that only the Spirit could directly inspire faith and remake the sinner into a true Christian. An inner Lord's Supper, an inner baptism, and an inner word all took precedence over outward rituals and the Bible, thereby rendering the latter superfluous. As a result, although the Spiritualists agreed with the Anabaptists that infant baptism was an abuse, the Spiritualists abolished the sacrament altogether rather than instituting adult (re)baptism.

However, the Spiritualists were divided among themselves based upon their understanding of the protean term *Spirit*.[2] For Müntzer, it was the biblical Spirit of God that had driven the prophets, punished injustice, and created a godly society. The result for Müntzer was an activist, utopian, religious and social agenda that ended in revolution. By contrast, Spiritualists such as Franck and Schwenckfeld operated with a conception of Spirit that owed more to Greek philosophy than to the Bible. Their Spirit was a Christian form of the immaterial Platonic or Neoplatonic mind *(nous)*. Far from inspiring action, the Spirit/mind beckoned within to find the ultimate truths and God, just as Plato had turned his mind to the realm of the forms or ideas. The material world, including the sacraments and the Bible, was not merely extraneous. It was the dualistic opposite of the Spirit/mind. As a result, all externals formed an obstacle to true knowledge and true faith. Sacraments and scripture were not merely irrelevant; they were by their very material nature opposed to the Spirit/mind and its works. Only Spirit-filled believers could safely use externals because they alone know the truth of which the externals are merely a pale reflection. Schwenckfeld would halt baptism and the Lord's Supper until the arrival of truly spiritual sacraments at Christ's second coming. Franck simply abandoned them as toys given to the infant church that could now be abandoned by mature Christians. Unlike Müntzer, therefore, neither Franck nor Schwenckfeld were driven to establish a new purified and just Israel. Nor did they court martyrdom. Rather, their goal was passive contemplation of the truth, and of Christ, within their own spirits. Weigel rather boldly lauded Müntzer, but he shared the spirit of Franck and Schwenckfeld.

Franck's influence is clearest in Weigel's skepticism. Franck's *Zeitbuch und Geschichtsbibel* (1531) had shown the incredible range of human opinion on things sacred and secular. It had also convinced Franck that the alternation of domination by one system or another revealed no discernible pattern, unless it was that truth did not usually prevail. The experience of the early Reformation was no better. The fissiparous tendencies of Protestantism had led to a proliferation of churches and sects, each of which laid exclusive claim to Christian truth. Franck's own religious odyssey from Catholicism to Lutheranism to Spiritualism had made him doubt the possibility of achieving a definitive theology. In any event, Franck concluded that the Bible itself was so full of contradictory teachings that God must surely have designed scriptures to drive believers in despair to consult the inner word. Weigel followed Franck this far, but not to Franck's conclusion that Christian faith was an experience rather than a doctrine, that is, that there can be no Christian theology. For Franck, all who claimed to "know," including Schwenckfeld, for example, were deluded. By contrast, Weigel's insistence that knowledge is in the knower rather than the thing known reflects Plato's solution to skepticism.

Weigel's position is similar to the less thoroughly skeptical views of Schwenckfeld, for whom the basis of true Christianity was an inner, spiritual "knowledge of Christ" *(Erkenntnis Christi)*. Weigel's Christology also bears a striking resemblance to Schwenckfeld's distinctive teaching on the "celestial flesh" of Christ. For both, the reception of a new, heavenly, spiritual body provided the foundation for faith in this life and for salvation in the next. Weigel's attitude toward the visible church is also closer to Schwenckfeld. The latter saw value in gatherings of Christians for mutual consolation and instruction, though he refused such gatherings the title of church and also denied that they could play any role in effecting salvation. However, there were Schwenckfelder communities in Silesia, and there were Schwenckfelder circles in South Germany. Schwenckfeld himself liked to attend services in order to hear the sermon. Interestingly, Schwenckfeld found a following among clergy like Weigel who were disaffected with the legally mandated church. Weigel's criticism of Schwenckfeldianism in his own writings may have an element of protective dissimulation, given the Lutheran Church's demonization of Schwenckfeld and his followers. With the appearance in print of Weigel's writings, he would replace Schwenckfeld as the premier heretical threat to the state churches of Northern Germany.

Spirit and Society

Weigel's devaluation of all externals in religion undermined the role and importance of the church. But it was the political corollary that truly frightened his critics. As with the other Spiritualists (excepting the revolutionary Müntzer), Weigel promoted not only religious toleration but religious freedom. Since the Spirit alone could grant faith, any attempt to impose a religious teaching was presumptuous and nonsensical. What is more, the use of force constituted an unforgivable breach of Christian charity. The arguments brought forward by Weigel and the others have become commonplaces, but in their time they were viewed by most Christians as unchristian and irresponsible. Clerics saw them as stratagems of the devil to undo all religion and decency. Sober men in the councils of government feared, with good reason, the social divisions that religious diversity would produce. The sixteenth and seventeenth centuries saw a series of devastating wars of religion. Looking to biblical precedent, both rulers and ministers also expected God to vent his wrath through war, disease, or some other punishment on societies that countenanced false worship and deviant belief.

But even more was at stake. In a process that historians label confessionalization, early modern states all over Europe identified themselves with one of the competing Protestant or Catholic "confessions." The state imposed a uniform code of belief, worship, and practice upon its subjects and presented itself as the guarantor of true Christianity. The result was an ideologization of the state that prepared the way for modern secular nationalism. While this alliance of church and state allowed Christian teachings to influence the policy and character of government, the church paid a very heavy price. Confessionalization harnessed Christianity to the fate of evanescent politics and "parochial" interests. God was on the side of one minor principality or another in struggles that impress the modern observer with their insignificance. Of course, much the same should be said of modern efforts to accord one nation the status of a new Israel and to invest its maneuvers for power and prestige with cosmic significance. Aside from the hubris involved, such presumption makes pitiless total wars out of clashes of interest or prestige.

The more immediate impact upon the church from its subordination to the state was a routinization and bureaucratization that sapped the living faith of individuals and communities. Spiritualism, like its seventeenth-century heir, Pietism, served as a remedy by loosening the ties to the larger community and focusing upon the necessity of individual commitment. One danger posed by both movements was that individuals or small groups would grow cold in their concern for others, especially the weaker members of society who burdened both the conscience and pocketbook of believers. Weigel's decision to remain within the state church maintained some measure of social solidarity. Another deficit of Spiritualism or Pietism was that such groups and individuals might so concentrate on a warm heart as to eclipse any intellectual confrontation with the demanding implications of faith. The result could be a thoughtless self-satisfaction that failed to appreciate Christianity's challenge to business as usual and dominant social structures. Weigel's demanding intellectual system was proof against such empty emotionalism.

SPIRIT AND SCIENCE

Spiritualistic dualism posed not only a problem for engagement in the social world but for the physical world as well. The disjunction between the material and spiritual realms freed the inner sphere from the dictates of physical reality, but at the same time it made problematic any relationship between the Spirit/mind and matter. The new science that developed in the seventeenth century benefited from the separation because it reduced physical phenomena to inanimate, quantifiable, and mechanistically describable events unburdened by transcendent meaning. However, the profound alienation of humans in modern culture now extended beyond human life and was applied to the physical universe as well.

Weigel addressed this challenge by drawing upon Paracelsus (1493–1541), a physician and speculative thinker who exercised wide influence in medicine, science, theology, and philosophy. Paracelsus and Weigel employed a complementary or, perhaps, competing notion of spirit that owed much to ancient medicine. This spirit was a very fine material substance that permeated living things and gave them life, heat, and movement. Alchemists claimed the ability to distill it from organic matter to produce various types of "spirits" (hence the use of *spirits* to refer to alcohol). This spirit substance comprised the animating Spirit/soul of nonhuman organisms such as animals and plants. It could serve the same function in humans by forming the lower reaches of a soul whose uppermost faculty was the immaterial Spirit/mind. In this theory the spirit/soul substance would serve as an intermediary between mind and matter.

Unfortunately, since matter and immaterial substance were totally incommensurate, no form of matter, however fine, could interact with the mind. Ancient Neoplatonists had multiplied endless mediators but had always confronted the same unbridgeable gap. At the root of the problem was the idea of immaterial substance and of an immaterial spirit. The acceptance of immateriality split reality irrevocably. While such a divide provided a moat behind which the individual could find refuge, it also left all other human beings and the physical universe on the other side. Engagement with the outside world was dangerous. Isolation, however, prevented community, love of neighbor, and actualization of the entire human individual.

Weigel sought to avoid some of the consequences of Spiritualism, but it is not clear that he succeeded. His Spiritualism actually relied on the state-imposed church as a counterweight to its individualistic trajectory. The eventual disappearance of state churches could undermine what remained of religious solidarity. And the triumph of scientific, social, and economic materialism marginalized the Spirit and threatened to rob it of all importance. What had begun as an effort to rescue the Spirit from contamination had resulted in its inconsequence.

During the seventeenth century, Spiritualism fed both Pietism and the early Enlightenment. Franck's inner word was equated with human reason. Schwenckfeld's inner Christ became spiritual friend who dwelt in suitably warmed hearts. Weigel was still able to combine the two, but his writings betray the unstable character of the composite. Spiritualism's days were clearly numbered.

Notes

1. George H. Williams labeled classical Protestantism "Magisterial" because of its reliance on the "magistrate" (*Radical Reformation*, 3d rev. ed. [Kirksville, Mo.: Sixteenth Century Journal Publications, 1992], xxix).

2. On what follows, see R. E. McLaughlin, "Reformation Spiritualism: Typology, Sources and Significance," collected papers, joint American-German conference "'Dissent' in the Sixteenth Century," Wittenberg, August 19–23, 1999, *Zeitschrift für historische Forschung*, supplement 27, 127–40.

Introduction
VALENTIN WEIGEL (1533-1588)

The writings reproduced in this volume for the first time in English translation convey spiritual experiences and conceptions of God, the human being, and the world that are both traditional and original. They articulate a distinctive voice in the chorus of the Protestant Reformation: the variant of its theological directions referred to by scholars as *Spiritualism*. Constructed as a type in contrast to Reformation-era *Baptism* or *Anabaptism*, Spiritualism refers to a form of dissent emphasizing spiritual or inner independence from rules, ceremonies, and the visible or organized church.[1] Where the Baptists cherished the sacrament from which their name derives, adhering to the letter of Holy Scripture and maintaining formal membership and exclusion, the contemporaneous Spiritualist was, as such, typically an individual rather than a member of a group (or, as a member, indifferent to doctrinal borders and accepting of kindred spirits of any other denomination). The Spiritualist deemphasizes the sacraments and the letter or history of scripture in favor of the free movement or anointment of the spirit. Weigel's writings are Spiritualist theory at its most articulate. As such, they complete a missing chapter in the history of mystical literature.

As an author, Weigel, like Pascal, is characterized by a profound appreciation of the spiritual implications of *relativity* and *infinitude*. Our world is dwarfed by the infinite abyss as a drop of water by the vastness of the sea. Since physical place is relative to the dimensions of the world and since the finite world itself can have no determinate relation to the infinite abyss, the relativity or indeterminacy of place in the physical realm transfers the point of absolute reference inward to the spirit. Weigel at times almost seems to anticipate Kant's interiorization of knowledge. However, we need to understand Weigel's thought without anachronism. To approach his vision in an informed way, the reader needs to know something about his life, the impact of religious conflict in his time, the manner in which he responded to doctrinal controversy by creating a synthesis of various philosophical and mystical sources, and the status of his thought in the tradition of German spiritual or mystical literature.

Historically, Weigel's writings are a product of the second half of the sixteenth century. The writings in this volume came into being between 1573 and 1578. Epochally, they reflect the transitional period between Luther's death in 1546 (or perhaps, more narrowly, the Peace of Augsburg of 1555) and the escalating inter-confessional rancor and strife that helped launch the Thirty Years' War (1618–48). Living between the heroic founding era and the approaching catastrophe of the Reformation, Weigel could gaze back at its pristine ideals and forward toward the prospect of a confessionally induced conflict of apocalyptic proportions. Two decades after his death, with the disaster of religious war on the horizon, the posthumous publication of Weigel's writings served as a prophetic warning of the approaching events.

In order to gain a clearer impression of the character of Weigel's era, we should therefore consider what went before it and what came after it. The Protestant Reformation had begun with Luther's enunciation of the *Ninety-Five Theses* in 1517. In the early 1520s the movement for reform rapidly spread throughout German territories, with resultant conversions, struggles, and sufferings. The popular movement for religious reform incited the Peasant Wars, a revolutionary insurrection linking religious reform and social justice. In 1525 the insurgent peasants were defeated and harshly punished. The same year was a significant turning point in the evolution of Reformation theology. Luther not only denounced the rebelling peasants and their leader, Thomas Müntzer, in 1525, but he also distanced himself decisively from the moderate Humanist Erasmus of Rotterdam, the militant reformer of Zurich, Ulrich Zwingli, and critical or radical reformers such as Karlstadt and Schwenckfeld. After 1525, their theological and social-political positions became alternative directions of the Reformation, parting from Luther's mainstream.

Despite the dissension that resulted within the ranks of the reformers, the main current surged forward under the leadership of Luther. Continuously embattled both within its ranks and without, the Lutheran Reformation and its adherents struggled steadfastly against every setback and peril until their status within the empire at last gained legal recognition in the Peace of Augsburg in 1555. During these same decades the Reformation was making headway in the Low Countries, France, Great Britain, and Scandinavia, as well as parts of Eastern Europe. The anti-papal movement for reform was giving rise to a cohesive and dynamic rival Protestant confession in Calvin's Geneva. Sensitive theological differences separated the Lutherans and Calvinists, to such a degree that by the end of the sixteenth century and in the seventeenth Calvinism was a more feared and hated rival to Lutheranism than Catholicism itself.

After 1555 a period of confessional consolidation began. The Council of Trent (1545–63) restored the unity and vitality of Catholicism. In Protestant lands the Lutheran or Calvinist confessions stood under the protection of territorial rulers who had a political interest in confessional cohesion and discipline. Confessional and political unity were threatened by the bitter and seemingly unending controversies in Protestant territories such as Weigel's Saxony. In order to terminate such disputes and consolidate the religious integrity of his territory, the Saxon elector prince commissioned and rendered mandatory the Formula of Concord, in essence a codification of approved doctrine to which a condemnation of unacceptable doctrines was appended. Though it is now considered a founding document of Lutheranism, the Formula (1577) or Book of Concord (1580) at the time appeared to some to violate the Lutheran principle of *sola scriptura*, or theological authority based solely upon the Bible, by instituting an official interpretation of scripture and doctrine. The Formula or Book of Concord also seemed to some critics, including the great German astronomer Johann Kepler,[2] to exacerbate religious discord and violate Christian conduct by condemning other believers.

Weigel wrote from the vantage of a man who could look back at the original elation and sense of freedom of the Reformation, at the same time recognizing its pull toward enforced conformity and anticipating the mobilization of confessionally consolidated states in preparation for religious war. Freedom and compulsion, inner religious autonomy and the subjugation of faith to priestly or princely politics, inner peace and religious strife: these are the historically conditioned tensions between which the writings reproduced in this volume came into being. We need to consider how the light and shadows on the larger historical canvas played out in the contours and nuances of Weigel's own path of life.

WEIGEL'S LIFETIME AND LITERARY AFTERLIFE

Weigel—the dissenting advocate of an invisible congregation without exclusionary barriers—lived the staid life of a Lutheran town pastor during the latter part of the sixteenth century. If the story of his life is easily told, its religious and political context is exceedingly complicated. His Saxon homeland was torn and pressured in ways that confuse us now and which indeed also confounded his generation and in so doing helped to shape his writings.

He was born sometime in 1533 in the Albertine Saxon town of Hayn or Großenhayn. There were two rival Saxonies in his day. Toward the end of the fifteenth century a dynastic division had split this important Northeast German territory between Ernestine and Albertine lines of succession. Ernestine Saxony was ruled by an elector prince. (An elector was one of seven princes empowered to elect the German king or Holy Roman emperor.) Albertine Saxony was ruled by a duke. Dynastically divided, the two Saxonies were further split by the Reformation. It was in the territory of the Ernestine elector, Friedrich the Wise, that Luther's Reformation emerged and established itself. One of its bitterest opponents in its first years was the Albertine Saxon ruler, Duke Georg. He was determined to adhere to and keep his subjects within the Catholic faith.

Since Weigel's home city was in Albertine Saxony, he was almost certainly born and christened a Roman Catholic in 1533. In 1539, when Valentin was approximately six, Duke Georg died without living sons and was succeeded by his brother Heinrich, a staunch Lutheran. Heinrich immediately set about reforming his Saxon territory in collaboration with Luther and the Wittenberg theologians. After Duke Georg's harsh suppression of religious freedom, this may have been a congenial turn of events to many or most Albertine subjects. No opinion polls were conducted. But the territorial conversion was not universally affirmed, not even in Weigel's town. Those who clung to the old faith were punished or driven into exile.[3] The liberating message of salvation by faith alone was trailed by the shadow of princely domination.

Politically, the two Saxonies continued to be rivals. Their rivalry was a discordant counterpoint set against the religious developments within Lutheranism. Just after Luther's death in 1546, in Weigel's childhood or youth, the Lutheran Albertine Duke Moritz went to war as an ally of the Catholic emperor, Charles V, against the Protestant German Schmalkaldic League. The imperial forces were victorious. Moritz took some Ernestine territory and the electoral dignity for the Albertines. Lutheranism in all of Saxony was cast into the most precarious situation. The emperor pressed for a compromise between Lutherans and Catholics. Moritz urged the Wittenberg theologian Philipp Melanchthon, the foremost colleague of the deceased Luther, to work toward this compromise. Melanchthon complied in working out a document that became known as the Leipzig *Interim*. It was thus called because it was to be temporary, pending the resolution of all differences by a general council. The Leipzig Interim attempted to conserve the central Lutheran doctrine of salvation by faith alone, at the same time making compromises in certain purportedly less consequential or "indifferent things" *(adiaphora)* of ceremony. A brilliant young Lutheran Wittenberg professor of Croatian origin named Matthias

Flacius Illyricus opposed the agreement, arguing that, in matters of faith, nothing done under compulsion is inconsequential. Led by Flacius and the older reformer Nikolaus von Amsdorf, a group known as the Gnesio-Lutherans (the *Genuine Lutherans*) opposed the compromises offered by Philipp Melanchthon or his supporters (the Philippists) and the imposition of the Interim agreement. The Gnesio-Lutherans launched a publicistic campaign and prepared the unswervingly orthodox burghers of the Free Imperial City of Magdeburg to resist Moritz.

Depending on one's point of view, their resistance is either a heroic chapter in the quest for religious freedom or a triumph of fanaticism over common sense. Living in a secular age, we may be inclined either to view Flacius's rejection of all compromise as a kind of extremist nit-picking, or, conversely, to hail the Gnesio-Lutherans as early champions of popular sovereignty and, in either case, to assign the opposing, positive or negative, valence to the Philippists. However, this would certainly oversimplify the historical quandaries confronting Weigel and, in so doing, obfuscate his grounds for attempting to transcend the terms of conflict. Since Weigel's key statements about his arrival at his understanding of faith allude to these controversies, they merit closer examination.

The long Gnesio-Lutheran controversies were many-sided, not fought over one issue but several.[4] During most of Weigel's lifetime these controversies raged on, sometimes escalating into violence and repression. In certain instances state power was brought to bear against the people. Teachers and preachers were relieved of their positions and thrust into exile as accused Philippists or Flacians. Two of Weigel's esteemed teachers were affected, one as a purported Philippist and another as an alleged Flacian. Like Montaigne's *Apology for Raymond Sebond* of the same era, Weigel's writings express dismay at the endless quarrels and recriminations hurled back and forth by the professional theologians. The impasse led, by his own account, to the seminal recognition out of which his root convictions grew. At the implicit center of Weigel's reformulation of Lutheran theology stands the lay believer, whose

14

self-assertion against the professional clergy coincides with the mysticism in Weigel's writings.

Though the Lutheran theologians quarreled on in controversy after controversy, the discordant counterpoint of power and faith came full circle when the combative Elector Moritz, the erstwhile traducer of the Lutheran cause, suddenly became its armed savior. In 1552, when Weigel was approximately nineteen, Moritz switched sides, attacking and defeating the Catholic emperor. He thereby laid the ground for the Peace of Augsburg in 1555. The fortunes of the Lutheran faith and of the religious peace were lifted out of their low ebb by this victory of worldly power. The disputes of the theologians, however, continued until Elector August, the successor of Moritz, forced an end to them by disciplining first one doctrinal group and then another and, ultimately, by enacting the Formula of Concord in 1577.

Weigel studied at the University of Leipzig and subsequently at the University of Wittenberg, where he may have briefly taught as well. By now, Luther's famous university was in full decline. The lingering radiance of theology was being eclipsed by the doctrinal controversies. This state of affairs is evoked in Weigel's reminiscence of his seminal spiritual experience, as recounted in *Der güldene Griff* of 1578, but presumably drawn from his youth or student days. He recalls a melancholy condition of mind prior to his discovery of what he refers to now as "the true faith":

> Before I came to the beginning of the true faith, and also [when] I believed along with the others so as to please the crowd, I was often very worried about this or that article [of faith] and would have liked to know on what I should have built [my belief]. I took up the books of many authors [and] read through them. But no satisfaction came to me. My heart was more and more uncertain. I could find neither ground nor truth. I regarded and considered our miserable darkness, the skirmishing, groping, and going astray. I found so many beliefs and sects now, even among those who wanted to be certain of their belief and ground, and [who] wanted to secure their protection from Holy Scripture. I beheld what a confused Babel was among us. Where the one spoke of faith, the other wanted

to have works, where the one spoke of fruits, the other would recognize nothing but a spurious faith. The third said that the sacraments were necessary for faith or for salvation. The fourth asserted that one must first take faith from the sacraments. The fifth considered that faith had to precede the sacraments. Otherwise they would not be effective or useful. The sixth said that the true faith in Jesus Christ alone makes just and saves, nothing else, no matter what. For that, he was called an Enthusiast and Sacramentarian. I saw thus how one denounced the other to the worldly authority, imprisoning, exiling, and the like on account of original sin, free will, the person of Christ, and so on; and there was such a going astray and skirmishing for the sake of heaven, into which no one wanted to enter, even as [such things still] are going on in this present year 1578, and no end. And as I was so uncertain and sorely worried, with inner sighing to God and praying: Oh, God and truth, be told how we walk in darkness; it's as if the blind had been aroused against one another to do battle in darkness, where one as readily strikes his best friend and strikes at his throat as if [he were] an enemy. Let your light shine to me, Lord! Thereupon I, [along] with others, was saved from this wilderness of darkness. As I thus called and prayed to the Lord, grace was visited upon me from above. For a book was shown to me that delighted me and illuminated my heart, so that I could judge and know all things [and I] could see more clearly than if all teachers in the entire world had instructed me with their books. For from it all books had been written from the beginning of the world, and this book is in me and in all human beings, in the great and the small, in young and in old, in the learned and the unlearned. But few indeed could read it. Indeed worse still, many of the worldly wise rejected and denied it [and instead] adhered to the dead letter which is outside them and neglect the book of life which is within them. (PW 8:89–91)[5]

This is Weigel's recollection of the cacophony of doctrinal arguments. There are echoes here of the Majoristic controversy over good works, as well as of disputes involving the efficacy of the sacraments. A passage in his earliest recorded work *(Two Useful*

Treatises, the First on the Conversion of the Human Being, the Other on Poverty of the Spirit or True Abandonment, 1570) documents Weigel's concern with the synergistic controversy over the question whether the human nature in the believer cooperates toward effecting its salvation, or whether human nature is wholly corrupt and degenerate after the fall from grace:

> There is a dispute among the false theologians concerning works or cooperation, concerning wanting or not wanting, [concerning] whether the human being through free will can cooperate in achieving the new birth or salvation. (ZW 3:16)[6]

These passages indicate that Weigel's seminal experience lay in a revulsion at the interminable controversies and their spirit of denunciation and recrimination. We cannot ascertain precisely when his reaction and change of heart took place; but since his earliest writings are dated only three years after his accepting the office of pastor in Zschopau, and since his first three years must have been filled with the labors of initiation, when he was preoccupied with establishing the foundations of his family and professional existence, it is likely that the melancholy refers back to his time at the university, where the controversies would have been experienced with greater intensity than in his isolated parish.

In November 1567 Weigel became the Lutheran town pastor of Zschopau. He had married two years earlier. In the first years of his pastoral tenure, he and his wife, Katharina, became parents to three children. Lutheran pastors were not wealthy, but Weigel enjoyed a secure and advantageous position and apparently also the esteem of his congregation and Lutheran superiors. In 1572 a denunciation by the pastor of another town implied that Pastor Weigel had cast aspersions upon Luther's doctrinal purity. This accusation called for a response. It was duly addressed to the Lutheran superintendent. Weigel's official response, entitled *A Small Book on the True and Saving Grace* (ZW 5), has been preserved. Though the apology is a sincere and compelling defense of the author's Lutheranism, it is bold in utilizing his characteristic terminologies. With this defense and the support of his parishioners,

Weigel carried the day; he seems to have been unthreatened subsequently. The many treatises and sermons he penned were in any event only circulated in manuscript form, so their sense of bitter opposition and frustration was not broadcast in print during his lifetime.

Weigel's divided sense of Lutheran faith and covert dissent is reflected in his late work, *Dialogus de Christianismo (Dialogue on Christianity)*, in a passage that alludes to the compulsory signing of the Formula of Concord in 1577 by the Saxon teachers and preachers. The Formula of Concord had been worked out under the auspices of the Southwest German Lutheran Jakob Andreae and then imposed under threat of dismissal upon the Saxon clergy and teachers by Elector Prince August.

To present-day Lutherans the Book of Concord is a founding document that saved Lutheranism and codified it for all time. To Weigel and some of his fellow Lutherans it was an unforgivable intrusion of worldly power in the realm of the spirit. Whether out of weakness, uncertainty, or futility, Weigel signed but never accepted the formula of faith, with its condemnations of false teachings. In his *Dialogue on Christianity* (1584), the voice of the Auditor (that is, the lay believer who defends his faith vis-à-vis the orthodox Lutheran Preacher) describes both the pressure to sign and the failure to find clear grounds to resist:

> I did not subscribe to their teaching or human books, but rather since their intention was aimed at the apostolic scripture and the same is to be preferred to all human books, as it should be, I could suffer it. But had they placed one single other book above the scriptures of the prophets and apostles, I would not have agreed to it. Besides, it all [happened in] a rush or an over-hastening, so that one wasn't permitted to think it over for several days or weeks. Instead, in a single hour they read off the entire convolute and demanded a signature right away. Third, I poor Auditor didn't see fit to prepare and serve a feast for the devil, [knowing] that the whole lot would have cried out: "There, there, we knew it all along: he is not in conformity with our doctrine!" (ZW 4:59–60)

INTRODUCTION

Like the Auditor, Weigel remained convinced of the truth of his own position but bowed to pressure.

If the above passage appears to bespeak the despair of an isolated dissenter without friends or following, we know a bit about Weigel's circles and a good deal more about his posthumous impact. During his pastorate he exchanged ideas with and even lent his manuscripts to pastoral colleagues or like-minded lay correspondents. He was joined early in his Zschopau pastorate by a deacon or pastoral assistant by the name of Benedikt Biedermann and, somewhat later, by a cantor, Christoph Weickhart. Both men sympathized with his opinions. In fact, Biedermann and Weickhart are thought to have helped write the corpus of works that became famous under Weigel's name. Since nothing by Weigel (except an unremarkable funeral eulogy) appeared in print in his lifetime, the endeavors of the three probably became conflated by the time the copies, and copies of copies, began to surface in print. It is only now that the welter of manuscripts and books conflating the authentic with the spurious is being sorted out and published in a comprehensive edition by the German publishing house Frommann-Holzboog. The editor who is attempting to resolve the centuries-old conundrum is Dr. Horst Pfefferl of Marburg. It will not be possible for this new edition published by Frommann-Holzboog to resolve every puzzle in the Weigelian corpus. However, within the confines of the possible, important information bearing on Weigel and his relation to Lutheranism and dissent are coming to light with each new volume. Some of the important discoveries (such as the autograph of *The Golden Grasp* found by Carlos Gilly in Leyden and published with related correspondence in volume eight) were made in connection with the works reproduced here.

The prehistory of the printed edition of Weigel's works goes back to the beginning of the seventeenth century. The first book of Weigel's clandestine opus to appear in print was *De Vita Beata* in 1609. This relatively moderate work written in Latin seems to have favorably impressed and perhaps influenced orthodox Lutheran theologians. But more radical works soon followed. *Der güldene Griff*, reproduced here as *The Golden Grasp*, came out

19

between 1613 and 1618 in four editions; the *Dialogus de Christian-ismo* between 1614 and 1618 in three. These publications were far more openly radical, anticlerical, and anti-authoritarian in tone and content. Scholars have judged them to be authentic. Others works, in part authentic and in part imitative, followed in print. The wave of publications peaked at eighteen editions in 1618, the first year of the Thirty Years' War. The long-deceased author, who was only now making his debut as events escalated toward war, emerged as a prophet in such passages as this in *On the Life of Christ* (1578):

> Just look what the supposed Evangelicals wanted to do a year or seven years ago: with violence, they wanted to fight for the faith. If they had had an army, the would have done it. The pope chases away the Lutherans; the Lutherans expel the Papists; the Calvinists drive out the Flacians; and the Flacians again the Calvinists and Synergists; and there is no end. Oh, if only we would all fall to our knees under God and confess to one another our sin, our own blindness, that we had entirely departed from faith, from the life of Christ, then we would be helped.[7]

As the Thirty Years' War came into full swing, the wave of publications subsided. However, a specter soon began to haunt hate-ridden Germany in its three decades of religious war. Real or imagined "Weigelians" came to be seen as a cabal of heretics, neutralists, rebels, and nay-sayers. They were the oppositional phantom, the Freemasons or Red Threat, of their period.

The phantom may have been a projection of the bad conscience of those who preached religious war. There is some evidence that antiwar sentiments motivated the publication of the Weigelian or pseudo-Weigelian works; however, it would be a gross exaggeration to present the so-called *Weigelianer* as a cohesive movement set in motion by its eponymous founder. In a time of religiously motivated hatred and destruction, various voices of anticlerical and mystical opposition were in the air. Jacob Boehme (1575–1624) inherited and re-created Weigelian themes in works appearing after 1612.[8] The Rosicrucian publications were also oppositional in spirit. All dissenters and opponents of violence were seen by the orthodox as a dark league of heretics. A courageous female protest poet of the later Thirty Years' War, Anna Ovena Hoyers (1584–1655), summed up matters as follows: "Whoever comes along and speaks of the spirit/ Is sent off very harshly/ Accused as a heretic, imprisoned or driven into exile/ Labeled a Schwenckfelder or Phantast/ Rosicrucian or Enthusiast/ Chiliast or Weigelian/ Davidian or Neutralist."[9]

LUTHERAN CRISIS OF CONSCIENCE AND INNER RETRENCHMENT

The Age of Faith in which Weigel lived knew heroic sacrifice for the sake of faith as well as terrible violence committed by the faithful against those professing other doctrines. It knew both the exaltation of love and fellowship and the unleashing of inhuman persecution and religious war. At root, Weigel's thought is invested in an attempt to purify faith of these contradictions of violence and intolerance by cleansing it of its *worldliness*. The *world* in this sense encompasses individual human self-seeking and willfulness, institutional imposition of doctrine by state power, and finally nature itself as the spiritually corrupting, unfree sphere in which force and necessity prevail. It is not easy to recapture the deeply felt coherence of such associations. How, we might ask, could Weigel reject Lutheran doctrines yet defend himself as a Lutheran? Wasn't his rejection of doctrine in itself doctrinal? How could he condemn clerical intolerance without being intolerant? And isn't the theological neutrality of nature and secular society actually the proven guarantor of religious and intellectual freedom?

Without denying these difficulties, we need to reconstruct the archeology of his convictions from the ground up and with an eye especially trained on how the seemingly disparate Lutheran, mystical, and Paracelsian elements cohere in his writings. Our objective is to show how, within their given historical context, these very disparate elements could seem to constitute a coherent whole. Weigel's understanding of world and spirit, of outer and inner, stands in a centuries-old tradition. Concerning this tradition

Bernard McGinn has written: "Early medieval mysticism was dominated by the motif of withdrawal from the world in order to join a spiritual elite." However, in subsequent centuries, the withdrawal into a separate monastic elite was redirected. McGinn continues:

> This emphasis begins to change in the early thirteenth century as we witness the first stirrings of a process of democratization and secularization that was to grow over the next five centuries. By democratization, I mean a conviction that it was practically and not just theoretically possible for all Christians, not just the *religiosi*, to enjoy immediate consciousness of God's presence. By secularization, I mean that flight from the world was not considered a necessary precondition for attaining such divine grace—God could be found in the secular realm and in the midst of everyday experience.[10]

What McGinn characterizes here as the gradual shift from an elite withdrawal from the world to a democratization and secularization informs Weigel's assertion of the authority of the "inner word" and the lay believer. As we shall see, Paracelsism complements this inward turn by rendering relevant to the spirit the natural and secular sphere into which faith was thrust by the gradual shift delineated by McGinn. Paracelsism makes nature or world into the appropriate opposite and correlative to spirit. For Weigel, Paracelsism effected a theoretical semi-spiritualization of the world and nature by means of such concepts as microcosm and macrocosm; the Tria Prima of sulphur, mercury, and salt; or the animate elemental spirits, which, according to Paracelsus, inhabit material nature. For Paracelsus or Weigel, these are not the common substances of the same name, but rather aspects of nature understood as process, whereby the natural process coincides at its extremes with the eschatological condition of having been made by God out of nothing and of being destined for destruction and transformation into nothing at the very end of time. Paracelsus sometimes characterized his "first three things" or substances as comparable to fuel, flame, and smoke.

An important watershed in the shift toward democratization and secularization summarized by McGinn arrived with the

Lutheran Reformation. Luther, as man and idea, was the exemplary founding figure of Weigel's confession. Just as the American Revolution lives in the popular awareness in certain ringing phrases, the Reformation has its winged words and mythic images: the *Ninety-Five Theses*, which Luther is pictured nailing to the door of the Castle Church in Wittenberg on October 31, 1517; or his legendary defiant words spoken before worldly power at the Imperial Diet of Worms—"Here I stand, I cannot do otherwise"—establishing that the free believer is God's servant, loyal unto death. The Reformation disbanded religious orders and abolished the distinct, elite legal status of the spiritual estate. The early Luther between 1520 and 1523 recognized the universal priesthood of the baptized laity. What is referred to by modern scholars as the "doctrine of the two kingdoms" bore various implications for Lutherans, ranging from the requirement of political submission to secular rulers, to the assertion of the autonomy of the spirit against worldly power. Inevitably, the separate and autonomous status of faith came into conflict with new religious institutions that sought to codify and enforce standards. Out of this variety of Lutheran impulses there arose a tension between religious autonomy on the one hand and a new institutional authority on the other.

Though Luther's personal authority among Lutherans had become so great in the second half of the sixteenth century[11] that we find Weigel ridiculing the mindlessness of his devotees (to them, Luther is a "Pythagoras" worshiped by slavish acolytes who believe even his limitations are to be imitated), to Weigel the core of Lutheran doctrine remained a unity that transcended personal authority. The three "onlys" of the new creed—"*only* by scripture," "*only* by divine grace," and "*only* by faith"—were pillars of a single Truth and Word. Weigel adhered to Luther's sense of an either/or centered in the doctrine of salvation by faith alone. The choice for the critical-minded Lutheran Weigel continued to be between truth and falsehood, as if between light and darkness, freedom and tyranny, God and devil, or spirit and world. This must be stressed at the outset, since otherwise the shift of authority from "the outer" or "the world" to the "inner word" can appear from our vantage as a shift toward subjectivism.

The turn to mysticism was by no means an abandonment of the authority of scripture. As cited by Weigel, the Lutheran Bible offers key testimony to the inner testimony of the Holy Spirit. No passage occurs more often or more emphatically than Jesus' reply to the Pharisees when asked when the kingdom of God would come: "The kingdom of God does not come visibly, nor will people say, 'Here it is,' or 'There it is,' because the kingdom of God is within you" (Luke 17:20–21). Luther had cited this passage in rebuking Karlstadt's understanding of the communion, similarly concluding against Karlstadt's purported localization of Christ, that "the kingdom of God is within you."[12] To Luther, Christ is not restricted to the Father's right hand in heaven but is instead omnipresent. In asserting this, Luther equates spatial determinacy with the substitution of law (as the binding of the free conscience) for faith or gospel freedom and truth. Much as Luther and Weigel might differ in certain respects, those who say "Here it is" betoken to both men the guardians and gatekeepers of a legalistic church with its ceremonies that serve to restrict access to heaven. For Weigel, Jesus' same words in extolling spiritual rebirth to Nicodemus dichotomize the realms of flesh and spirit ("Spirit gives birth to spirit"—John 3:6). Jesus' words also confirm that the church of the spirit cannot be bound by laws or ceremonies. "The wind blows wherever it pleases. You hear its sound, but you cannot tell where it comes from or where it is going. So it is with everyone born of the Spirit" (John 3:8).

Significantly, precisely this passage is quoted in Weigel's earliest known work, the first of his *Two Useful Treatises, On the Conversion of the Human Being* of 1570. In condemning the quarrels of the theologians and pastors, this treatise explicitly alludes to John 3:8 (see ZW 3:24–25) to counter the claim that the ceremony of baptism is essential for the baptism of the Spirit:

> The new birth is not in powers, nor in authority *(nicht inn Krefften noch inn Gewaldt)* or power of the priest or of the water, but rather in the power of God, who lets his Spirit spirit as he will. And a reborn human being experiences and feels the

spiriting, the blowing, the good motion toward all virtues, but "the human being can neither give such things to it nor take them away." (ZW 3:24–25)

Weigel's theological opponents, who are translated here as "Pharisees," are called in German "Schriftgelehrten," which means "scholars of scripture." Against their authoritarian use of the *Historia* of Jesus, Weigel emphasizes the Apostle Paul's words in Second Corinthians 3:6: "The letter kills but the spirit gives life." Weigel states the matter in full: "It is proper for the Christian to observe the sense and meaning of scripture rather than the letter. The letter kills, the spirit gives life" (PW 3:104). We would oversimplify the meaning of this by equating "letter" to literal meaning and "spirit" to allegorical sense, as is sometimes thought. The *spirit* is freedom and the true faith. Spirit is whatever accords with the underlying cohesive message, as understood by Weigel, of Christ and the gospels, and of their resonances in nature, philosophy, and the entirety of the Bible. All that engenders tyranny, exclusion, and divisiveness pertains to the "letter"; all that reconciles through love pertains to the "spirit." The pouring out of the Holy Spirit on Gentiles as well as Jews in Acts 10:44–48 betokens to the Spiritualist Weigel the nonexclusionary nature of the church of the reborn:

> Read the Acts of the Apostles, and you will find that even the heathens received the Holy Spirit without any water baptism, and, conversely, that even those baptized in the name of Christ did not receive the Holy Spirit. When Peter preached the word, the Holy Spirit fell upon all who heard the word. And the faithful from circumcision who had come with Peter were shocked *(entsatzten sich)* that the gift of the Holy Spirit had been poured out even onto the heathens; for they heard how they [the apostles] spoke with tongues and praised God highly. Thereupon, Peter replied: Might anyone refuse the water so that they would not be baptized who have received the Holy Spirit just as we have? And [he] commanded that they be baptized in the name of the Lord. (ZW 3:28)

Weigel centered his interpretation of the Bible in passages such as these because they sustained his need for inclusion. He disregarded the historical or institutional contexts of salvation and, with these contexts, whatever appeared as law, commandment, or as a salvational quid pro quo. In his judgment the Lutheran doctrine of "imputed justification" allowed for false faith as a kind of indulgence paid by Christ's redemption: "We drink at his expense; *imputativa justitia* is enough for us" (ZW 4:10). The "indwelling presence" of Christ is not conceived as a form of works righteousness but rather as the true sense of the Lutheran theology of the cross itself.

This immediacy of faith also sets aside every criterion for admission to the visible or exclusive church. To be sure, as a pastor, Weigel did not disdain the "external sign" of baptism. He merely denied its power to effect spiritual rebirth. Unlike baptism with water, true spiritual rebirth could not be publicly performed and therefore could not be turned into a gate barring anyone from the spiritual church: "Whoever has this new birth within, whether woman or man, young or old, Jew or heathen, Christian or Turk, will be blessed [*seelig*], and even if he has not already been baptized with water" (ZW 3:31). To deny the power of the ceremony of baptism was to affirm a nonexclusionary tolerance. Perhaps mindful of his recently born children, Weigel defended the unbaptized children of the "Jews, heathens, and all peoples," to whom no one had a right to deny salvation: "Whoever believes and is baptized is saved, etc. Such baptism or new birth is not only in the children of the Christians, but also in the children of Jews, heathens, and all peoples" (ZW 3:32–33).

In order to find grounds for asserting that even the children of nonbelievers in some sense believe, he posited a Pauline anthropological trichotomy of body, soul, and spirit, and wrote of the latter that "through the light of this spirit [the infant] believes in Christ" (ZW 3:32).[13] Without this spiritual faith the ceremony of baptism could effect no salvation in the infant.

For his project of reconciling Lutheranism with mysticism, Weigel discovered precedents not only in the Bible, including Luke 17:21, as emphasized similarly by Luther, but also in the mystical treatise that had been so highly esteemed by Luther at the outset of the Reformation and that had been designated by him the *Theologia Germanica*. Weigel's earliest effort to revive the mystical tradition in order to offset the theological malaise of his time is manifested in an early work of recapitulation and commentary, *A Short Report and Introduction to the "Theologia Germanica."* This work was signed in Zschopau in March 1571 and dedicated to a Lutheran pastoral colleague, Christopher Corner of Rückerswald. Weigel's *Report* was only the latest in a series of Lutheran dissenting voices that sought to lead the Reformation back to pristine origins. After being edited by Luther at the outset of the Reformation, the work by an anonymous fourteenth-century "Frankfurter" had had an extraordinarily influential career. The small treatise shunned systematic exposition and contextual exegesis in order to focus Christian faith instead in such simple and immediate contrasts as self and God or world and spirit. The human being is created by God free but must freely renounce self-will in order to live in accordance with the divine will and thereby become deified in selflessness.

Following the example of Luther's preface to the *Theologia Germanica* of 1518, Weigel's *Short Report* introduces it and the Bible conjointly. Both are said to require special application. Moreover, anticipating a lifelong project, Weigel observes that the first three chapters of Genesis (creation, Adam and Eve, and their fall and expulsion from Paradise) in some sense articulate the same content as "this beautiful little book," the *Theologia*. The *Theologia* and the first three chapters of Genesis either condense or anticipate the entirety of scripture, since the Bible actually teaches nothing else but "that Adam should die in us and Christ be resurrected and live in us" (ZW 3:94). In making this claim Weigel turns the historical content of the Bible into a conceptual essence, a reduction characteristic of his thought. Repeatedly in the course of his writing career, he calls for a mystical and speculative interpretation of Genesis. God's having created man from a clump of earth is understood to mean that the human being, in essence, did, and still does, encompass the whole of nature, which is thereby bequeathed to human nature. The human being is thus a microcosm. Like Paracelsus, Weigel believes that Genesis alludes in nucleus to an analysis of the macrocosm of nature and the microcosm of the human being. These two worlds sum up the biblical fall and redemption. In his final decade Weigel even undertook to combine these themes in his *Fourfold Interpretation of the Creation*. A perennial objective, the interpretation of Genesis underlay his efforts to combine a biblical understanding of nature with the findings of astronomy in *On the Place of the World* and with a spiritualized epistemology in *The Golden Grasp*.

Despite the intricacies of his exegesis, his interpretation remained subordinate to a simple pragmatic outlook. The aura of significance cast for Weigel by the *Theologia* and other related sources clearly lay in their condensation of doctrine to a simple bipolar alternative or set of equivalent alternatives. Good and evil contrast with each other as the fullness of divine being with the illusory nothingness of the creature and of sin:

> Now each creature of necessity has two things in it, the good and the evil, the good from God as being, life, light, spirit, and so on. The evil from itself, that is, [from] its own nothingness. For creature is nothing in itself; but what it is and has, it has entirely from God. Tauler says, drawing upon Eckhart: What has been made is not true being, but rather like an image or shadow or accident, and so, too, the *Theologia* speaks in its first chapter: that God alone is true being, for he is of himself, and is his own being, and cannot deny himself: He cannot be nothing, he is necessary being. But creature, as angel or human being, is not true being, for it is not of itself, and creature has nothing of its own of which it could boast: It is all from God, "for God is the being of all beings, the life of all living things, and the wisdom of all wise beings." (ZW 3:108–9)

Such passages distill a complex tradition into a simple moral-religious outlook. One might object that the equation of God to being or of creature to nothing is Neoplatonic and hence alien both to the Bible and to the true intentions of Luther. Although Weigel drew on philosophical and mystical sources that were alien to Luther, a similar dichotomy to that between being and nothingness could have been drawn as a corollary of Luther's doctrine of divine omnipresence and omnipotence, which was surely well known to Weigel. Implicitly, Luther's account of the divine omnipotence in *On the Bound Will* (1525) renders everything except the divine power ephemeral. The devil himself is an instrument of the divine will. Understood in its radical implications, the contemplation of divine omnipotence turns creatures into puppets, just as the notion of divine omnipresence turns them into masks. Similarly, Luther's understanding of a continuous creation in which all of nature is perpetually renewed and preserved by God casts all creatures in a dual light. Though what is created is not God, its persistence is nonetheless an immediate divine work. The perpetual emergence of all things or beings out of a state of preexistent invisibility into the state of visible presence is a miracle that testifies to the supreme power of an invisible God, known to faith. According to Luther:

> If God were to withdraw His hand, this building and everything in it would collapse. The power and wisdom of all angels and men would not be able to preserve them for a single moment. The sun would not long retain its position and shine in the heavens; no child would be born; no kernel, no blade of grass, nothing at all would grow on the earth or reproduce itself if God did not work forever and ever.[14]

> Christ is the man who brings forth something visible from that which is still invisible. Thus through Him heaven and earth were produced from that which was invisible and nothing and were rendered visible. And it is Christ the Lord, who was present at the time of the creation of all things not as a mere spectator but as a coequal Creator and Worker, who still governs and preserves all and will continue to govern and preserve all until the end of the world. For He is the beginning, the middle, and the end of all creatures.[15]

For Luther, then, no less than for Weigel, the world bears a contrasting aspect. The degrees of authority Luther and Weigel were willing to accord to nonscriptural sources differed, yet for Luther, nature was no less dichotomous. Nature is not God, but its entire being is at every moment dependent upon and, in this sense, passively infused with divine power. To say this is not to maintain that Weigel's thought is an adequate interpretation of Luther's intentions—it surely is not—but only that it *is* a possible interpretation of certain of Luther's statements about God and therefore need not be rationalized away as Gnosticism or non-Christian philosophy.

The problem for Weigel was to understand the creature as being both like and unlike God in accordance with the human will. This understanding was effected by means of the concept of the image, which was found in Eckhart and in the *Theologia,* as well as in Paracelsus (about whose notion of image more will be said subsequently). *Gnothi seauton* (1571) was Weigel's initial effort at a larger theoretical argument employing binary antitheses. These clarify into simple correlatives the many doctrinal terms that had become ensnared in contradictions. According to Weigel, this list of alternatives is to be borne in mind in reading the scriptures:

Adam	Christ
Disobedience	Obedience
the Natural Man	the Supernatural
the Letter	the Spirit
Death	Life
Darkness	Light
Blindness	True Knowledge
Law	Gospel
Ungrace	Grace
Transgression of the Law	its Fulfillment
Injustice	Justice
the Old Birth	the New Birth
Self Will	Divine Will
Bound and imprisoned for Death	Free and loose for Life

The author points out that these oppositions are found in the Bible, especially in Paul.[16] They represent a crossroads in theology between literal or spiritual biblical exegesis, as well as between worldly or spiritual experience. In their simplicity they are intended to serve as an uncomplicated response to the intricacies of theological controversy and recrimination. They are to remind the reader that all choices are at root one choice: between God and self.

INTRODUCTION

When Weigel was compelled to defend his Lutheran orthodoxy in 1572, he highlighted precisely these antitheses, knowing that they characterized Luther's own writing. Luther's work of 1520, *On Christian Freedom*, began with a paradoxical antithesis: *The Christian is a lord over all things and subject to none. The Christian is a bound servant in all things and subject to all.* This antithesis of freedom and bondage is conceptually akin to the duality of the kingdom of God and the kingdoms of this world. It is as mysterious as the paradox of divine being and creaturely nothingness, and as incisive as the dichotomization of light and darkness. The human creature exists in accordance with the two aspects of Christ and the world, grace and nature. The paradox of freedom and bondage expresses Luther's dualistic view of the Christian as a creature of spirit and flesh; it corresponds to the reformer's own demand for a strict separation of the realms of faith and world. As he put it:

> There is a vast difference between the kingdom of Christ and the secular government, the domain of the princes and lords. And let the preacher keep his hands off the secular government, lest he create disorder and confusion! It is our duty to direct the church with the Word, the oral sword. The secular government, on the other hand, wields a different sword, a fisted sword, and a rod of wood to inflict physical punishment. The preacher's rod smites only the consciences, which feel the impact of the Word. Therefore these two rods and swords must be kept apart and separate, so that the one does not infringe on the province of the other.[17]

In conformity with the words of the apostle Paul (Rom 13:1–7), the Christian, according to Luther, though free in faith, must obey the worldly authority of government. Since salvation lies within, it is affected neither by human works nor by obedience to the laws that govern the outer human being. The realm of inner freedom or spirit is accordingly extraterritorial to the prince. Spiritual freedom lies outside the world, in the final reckoning infinitely outweighing and overshadowing it.

MEISTER ECKHART, PARACELSUS, BOËTHIUS, CUSANUS

Though, as we have seen, Weigel proceeds from scripture and continues to see himself as a Lutheran, his critical reaction to the quandary of Lutheranism in his time compelled him to embrace medieval mysticism and entertain striking theories of nature and the human being. This development is evident in his earliest works, in which he announces an intention to find new "theological terms" that should be more akin to Christ than to the terms of controversy. Explicitly critical of the contentiousness of the theologians and pastors, Weigel's *Two Useful Treatises* of 1570 bear out his recollection that doctrinal discord had depressed him and stimulated his critical realization that the truth lies within. His *Short Report and Introduction to the "Theologia Germanica"* (1571) is even more decisive in rejecting rancorous debates over "the controversial articles" *(den streitigen Articuln*—ZW 3:113), such as those of free will or good works, vowing instead to redirect "the terms of theology" *(die terminos Theologiae*—ZW 3:114) away from the human beings to Christ: "For Christ does not make sects nor heretics nor controversialists in theology [*Zancker in der Theologey*], but rather leads [us] into the pure truth" (ZW 3:114). As we have seen, these earliest theoretical writings establish the primacy of Weigel's reaction to doctrinal controversy; they also indicate that his response to it entailed a renewal of the mystical tradition of Eckhart, Tauler, and of the *Theologia Germanica*.

The mysticism of Meister Eckhart oriented Weigel toward a minimalist theology that had originated in part from an effort to address untutored nuns or lay folk and supplant the polyvocal authority of the learned theologians. Eckhart, as well as the Renaissance mystic and philosopher Cusanus, offered approaches to transcending conflicts. The spirit of tolerance seemed palpable in Eckhart's citations of many masters who echo the same truth or in his acceptance of the authority of the Jew Maimonides or the pagan Plato. We do not know which works of Cusanus were known to Weigel, but a theoretical or practical tolerance spoke from his speculative treatise on the coincidence of opposites *(De Docta Ignorantia)* or his colloquy between diverse believers *(De Pace Fidei)*. Like Weigel, this brilliant German scholar and churchman inclined toward a Christian philosophy with strong mystical and Platonic elements in accordance with his pursuit of a conceptual reconciliation of differences of belief. According to Cusanus's earliest sermon (on the text "In the beginning was the Word"— John 1:1), various peoples had given various names to the same God who is "one, supreme, infinite, ineffable, and unknown."[18]

Weigel's access to Eckhart and Tauler was a volume printed in Basel in 1521 and 1522. Though commonly referred to as the Basel Tauler *(Basler Tauler-Druck)*,[19] Weigel was explicitly aware of Eckhart as a distinct author. The second of the *Two Useful Treatises, On True Poverty of Spirit*, is for the most part a compilation of direct citations from Eckhart, Tauler, and the *Theologia* on the theme, "True poverty of the spirit is when the human being 'wants, knows, and has nothing'" (ZW 3:62).

> The masters say that God is a being and a rational being and knows all things, etc. But I say: God is neither being nor reason, nor knows anything, this or that. For this reason God is free of all things and for this reason He is all things. (ZW 3:64; cf. Eckhart, *Deutsche Werke* 2:497)[20]

Speaking verbatim through Weigel's treatise is the voice of Meister Eckhart addressing nuns or laypeople who were bewildered by the volleys of scholastic doctrine sallying overhead in what was both a great age of theology and a dark age of persecution of theological deviance. In quoting from Eckhart's sermon 52 *(Beati pauperes spiritu)*, Weigel closes his chapter with the Master's whimsical conclusion: "Whoever wants to understand this chapter must become like its truth; otherwise, it will not be understood" (ZW 3:68). This implies that, beyond all the differentiating entanglements of a discursive theology, there may be a simpler understanding *qua* being that can bridge the gulf between the human and divine and, since this gap gives rise to theological differences, thereby also heal the rifts between the conflicted believers themselves. In citing extensively from such sources, the author appears in the first flush of enthusiasm for his newly discovered alternative to the theological quarrels bemoaned in his treatise. A programmatic ring heralds Weigel's reiteration of Eckhart's summons to carry "the teaching of the image" out of the school and onto the pulpit for the benefit of the full congregation.[21] The "teaching of the image" likens the creature to a mirror image or shadow of the Creator. As image or shadow, the creature is nothing in itself. For the creature exists only insofar as it embodies its source; ultimately, only insofar as it accords with the example of its Creator, the Christ who negated his own will before the cross, so that the will of the Father might be done:

> This teaching of the image [*Lehre von dem Bildnus*] belongs not only in the school, but also onto the pulpit for the people; for from such consideration we learn what the will of God is toward us in time and in eternity, namely, that we are instructed to know Christ, how we should comport ourselves toward God here in time and afterward in eternity. (ZW 3:107)

The concept of *image* is central to Weigel's synthesis. It links his thinking both to Eckhart's tradition and to the nature speculation of the sixteenth-century philosopher and medical theorist Paracelsus (1493–1541). In a sense, Eckhart, who so emphasized inner being, and Paracelsus, the theorist of nature and medicine, were opposites. But though they appear otherwise diametrically opposed, they were similar in their understanding of the created being as an image of its Creator. Where Eckhart applies this to the inner human being and to being itself as a manifestation of the absolute being of God, Paracelsus in a somewhat different sense understands nature as an image of the divine being. When Eckhart speaks of created things as images of God, he seems to occupy a plane of high abstraction: All things were in God before creation; God remains in them after creation. Insofar as being and goodness are divine essences, all that is *is* good and divine. Following this path of reasoning, Weigel even goes so far as to proclaim in *On the Place of the World* that the devil, insofar as he has being, is good.[22] For wickedness is a turning away from God toward creature, tantamount to nothingness. In this sense, all creation, insofar as it has being, is an image of the Creator in the tradition of Eckhart.

Compared to Eckhart, Paracelsus is relatively concrete in his representation of created things as images of their Creator. Since God is triune, all things in nature exist by virtue of a threefold substance, designated as sulphur, mercury, and salt. In one of Paracelsus's theological works, these three are even equated to the persons of the Trinity; and they correspond also to the anthropological trichotomy of soul, spirit, and body (the human being having been created even more explicitly as the image of God).[23] Where Eckhart typically thinks by means of contrasts and paradoxes that present things in the dual light of creature and Creator, of being and nothing, Paracelsus, though not without recourse to dichotomy, tends to favor trichotomies that ascribe a more complex and vivid materiality to nature. Thus, his three principles of sulphur, mercury, and salt are conceived as flame, smoke, and ashes within the process of combustion. Where Eckhart had written that every creature is full of God and thus like a book,[24] Paracelsus recognizes the signatures of creation: Plants bear the visible marks or signatures inscribed either by God or by a nature in which divine forces are in operation. Eckhart had credited matter with a lower reality than spirit. Paracelsus is more vivid in imposing spirit on matter. He recognizes invisible "elemental spirits," which inhabit the elements. Like Eckhart, Weigel holds that everything creatural is in itself nothing, but like Paracelsus, he accepts the view that the evanescent created sphere is teeming with invisible spirits that are alive but lack a soul. Scholars who prefer to see in Weigel only the modern or relatively orthodox thinker have ignored or underestimated his interest in invisible spirits in nature.

A characteristic citation by Weigel is the Paracelsian *De vita longa*. This was a treatise of alchemical medicine that sought to explain the long lives of Adam and Methusala. To all who see Paracelsus only as a figure of medical history, Weigel's citation of this work in connection with the Eckhartian "powers" (*kreft*) in the soul must seem incongruous: "And that in the art *de longa vita*, a human being collects all forces into the inner being and remains entirely still, with a forgetting of his self and of all the world" (ZW 3:81). But in fact, Eckhart had recognized a power in the soul that, if perpetually united with God, would prevent the human being from aging: "If the spirit was always united with God in this force, then the human being would not age."[25] Weigel's linking of Eckhart and Paracelsus in the same treatise and in association with their shared terminologies characterizes his project of harmonizing a negative theology or introvertive mysticism, which tends to disregard the substances and processes of nature, with concepts drawn from a philosophy of nature that acknowledges the body and the physical world.

Winfried Zeller's edition of Weigel's early writings also documents indirect citations from Sebastian Franck and Boëthius. Franck was himself a great compiler and synthesizer of sources. To Franck, the idea of *paradox* entailed opting for truth in open defiance of an unbelieving world. Antithesis was therefore not only a matter of logic and disputation; it was also an essential and defiant act of faith and resistance: "Paradox, dear friends and brothers, means to the Greeks a statement that, though it is certain and true, is regarded as nothing less than true by the entire world and by everyone who lives in accordance with the human being."[26] As a great compilation of sources, chosen so as to reveal that the truly faithful nonconformist had always believed in defiance of common opinion of the world, Franck's *Paradoxes* of 1534 preceded Weigel and opened the way for him.

A second, equally important source is of far more ancient origin: the work of Anicius Manlius Severinus Boëthius (c.480–524). Boëthius's *Consolation of Philosophy* directed the mind both inward toward self-knowledge and outward toward speculation concerning nature. For the dissenter Weigel, beset by the ups and downs of doctrinal and political warfare, Boëthius bestowed other blessings as well. He offered a cherished model of defense against all the depradations of the "goddess Fortuna," a tranquil contemplation of the *Summum Bonum* that is accessible within, and a venerable precedent for Weigel's own "Sophia Christiana." A classic work of Christian philosophy, Boëthius's *Consolation of Philosophy* appreciated nature but understood the world as offset by an inner realm of soul or spirit.

Another venerable source, the twelfth-century Scholastic author Hugh of St. Victor, helped Weigel to formulate his theory of self-awareness and the three successive stages of knowledge, that is, the sensory, the rational, and the mystical or contemplative. Hugh is cited by name but not by the title of any work.

Weigel's early *Short Report* also seems to draw terminology from the work of Nicholas Cusanus,[27] though the name itself never occurs.

> In the nut is concealed a root, trunk, branches, twigs, leaves, and several thousand nuts, and the single nut is a being [or essence] of all these things and is all itself, *sc. implicite*, and yet the nut is not the root, nor the trunk, nor the tree as a whole, *sc. explicite*. Thus God is "the being of all beings and the life of all living things" *complicative*, and yet God is not creature, *sc. explicative*. Another example: The ABC has twenty-three letters, and is a being [or essence] of all syllables, of all words, and all speech, and none can exist without the ABC, etc. Thus is God of all creatures being, life, light, and spirit, for in God stand and go all creatures much more than [they do] in themselves, and yet God is not [a] creature, much less is the creature God. It is but a shadow or image of the true being, and cannot exist a single moment without God. (ZW 3:118)

The nut or the ABCs are analogous to God as the being or essence of all that arises from God as his creatures. To state that they are concealed *within* God is to elevate the inner over the outer in another sense, the sense of creation, in addition to that of spirit or knowledge. Cusanus's thought was itself a synthesis of many sources. The distinction according to which God is present in all things, either implicitly or explicitly, that is, either enfolded or unfolded, made it possible to present all things as reflections of the divine being without resorting to pantheism.

The binary turn of thought that Weigel took from Luther and from introvertive mysticism was limiting insofar as it ignored the world of nature and natural human society in which every lay believer was perpetually immersed. The *Theologia Germanica* may have reflected the experience of a religious order in which all life revolved around prayer and contemplation. Accordingly, the work spoke disparagingly of "the light of nature." By contrast, Weigel's *Short Report and Introduction* recognized in the manner of Paracelsus two "lights," that of spirit and that of nature. Weigel even implied that he had drawn from the natural realm insights of value for the understanding of the spiritual being (ZW 3:96–97). In rendering self-knowledge central to spiritual experience, *Gnothi seauton* posited dual and triadic perspectives: The human being as soul is the image of God. The trichotomous human microcosm that consists of body, soul, and sidereal spirit contains the entire world in a nutshell. The *spiraculum vitae* is the divine, life-giving force of the soul that was imparted to Adam and the human race by the Creator. Self-knowledge, when it is deepened, leads to knowledge of both nature and God.

In turning to nature, Weigel appears to depart from Eckhart, the *Theologia*, and Luther. It might seem especially un-Lutheran to scholars that Weigel should have correlated biblical theology with discussions of microcosm and macrocosm, claiming that these are in conformity with Genesis. Paracelsus was in fact alien to Luther (if known to him at all), and it is true that mainstream Protestantism soon characterized him a heretic. However, there were also Lutherans who regarded Paracelsian philosophy as the natural complement to Lutheran theology. Their number included not only such notorious dissenters as Boehme, Weigel, and the eighteenth-century Pietist Friedrich Christoph Oetinger, but also the professing Lutheran pastor Johann Arndt and the unimpeachably orthodox Philipp Nicolai. Indeed, Luther's own commentary on Genesis read the biblical account of creation as a text bearing on questions of nature and the human capacity for knowledge. He even accepted the concept of the *microcosm* as unobjectionable, though it was of no particular interest to him.[28] In Luther's stated view, prelapsarian Adam had enjoyed an oceanically immense knowledge of nature, a faculty corrupted by the fall from grace. Even after the fall, the human ability to measure the distance to the stars provided evidence of the soul's nobility and potential worthiness of eternal life.[29] Though the term itself was alien to Luther's usage, the Paracelsian concept of *sidereal spirit*—the starry, intellectual faculty in the human being—represents virtually the same thing.

Weigel certainly took issue with the low estimation of the postlapsarian human being. He disagreed with the Flacian opinion that the fall had utterly corrupted human nature. He went beyond both Flacius and Luther in arguing that human self-knowledge and indeed knowledge of nature could lead the soul toward a knowledge of God. His humanistically or mystically conditioned departure from Luther is signalled by his citation of a threefold faculty of knowledge that progresses from the knowledge actively acquired by the senses and the reason to the mental contemplation in which the human spirit passively receives directly from God an understanding of divine or celestial things.

Instead of progressing upward, by way of the professional expertise of the astronomer or theologian, from the sublunary world to the celestial and divine worlds, for Weigel the path to God instead leads deeper into the inner being of the believer, from the world to spirit. This interiorization of hierarchical levels is possible because, like Paracelsus, Weigel regards the human creature as a microcosm of the natural and supernatural worlds, containing even the *spiraculum vitae*, the divine breath or human soul. Heaven is no longer above but rather within for the individual believer, who is no longer subject to a hierarchical authority. *Gnothi seauton* and Weigel's early Latin humanistic treatise *De Vita Beata* (1572) combine nature theory with theology by arguing that, since there is only one world, the kingdom of God is to be entered inwardly.[30]

The shift entails a transition in devotional orientation as well. Weigel wrote his *Prayer Book (Gebetbuch* or *Büchlein vom Gebet*, 1612) in a period of pastorally oriented writings between his *Defense* of 1572 and his resumption of speculative writing in mid-decade. The Preface to the *Prayer Book* incorporates extended paraphrases of Luther's discourse on the Lord's Prayer, including the admonition against verbose prayer and for meditative silence: "For then the Holy Spirit preaches and one word of that sermon is better than a thousand of our prayers" (PW 4:4, see footnote 7). Luther's understanding of divine omnipresence seems to sustain the Spiritualist inner access to God as a prerequisite of prayer:

> For you, Lord, are everywhere and fill heaven and earth (Jer 10[:11–12]). You are nearer to all creatures than they are to themselves. *Intimior es omni Creaturae quam quæ sibi ipsi sit.* [Pfefferl's edition observes that this Latin quotation recalls Eckhart, who was in turn quoting Saint Augustine.[31]] You are outside of all, in all, and through all. One may not seek you externally in a certain spot or place, but rather in the inner ground, in the spirit. All places are in your eyes a single place, just as all times are before you but a single time. (PW 4:51–52)

In the same way that the human mind does not progress upward by means of the expert knowledge of the professional astronomer, mathematician, or theologian, but rather inward, by means of the self-knowledge that is microcosmic of the entire world, so also the devoted soul approaches God, not by way of ceremonies, works, or loud prayers, but by means of silent absorption.

Of the same period as Weigel's *Prayer Book*, the so-called *Manuscript Collection of Sermons* (composed between November 1573 and March 1574) is directed to the spiritual needs of the laity. Theoretical speculation on nature as macrocosm and microcosm and the use of antithesis and paradox are therefore marginal, though not altogether absent in its sermons. Human and divine knowledge are differentiated when Weigel preaches on John 1:1 ("On the Day of John the Evangelist. *In principio erat verbum*"—ZW 6:114). The divine birth is known only by faith. But since the divine Word is the light and life of all human beings, "It [the Word] illuminates all human beings and the human being has been made through it" (ZW 6:114). Weigel writes that "the external seeing and hearing or knowing in accordance with the flesh makes no one blessed, but rather the inner hearing and seeing in faith: that is the true to which Christ speaks and to which all of scripture urges us" (*Am Sontag Judica. Joh. 8*—ZW 7:410).

In another sermon of this collection, the teaching of the threefold world or three heavens is mentioned as correlative of the three challenges or assaults from evil; however, their full exposition is deferred to another book (*"Alia dispositio huius Euangelii Inuocauit"*) (in Sermon on Matthew 4 [ZW 7:348]). Predominant in the sermons is the duality of inner and outer. The preacher reminds his flock that the outer "history" and "letter" of Christ is no help because the kingdom of God is within (ZW 7:428, 430).

Another recurrent theme is the defense of those accused of heresy. The sermons allude to recent defamations of heretics: "This one is a new heretic, an Enthusiast, a Schwenckfelder, a seducer, a Samaritan. He has the devil, makes the people errant in their faith, away with him! He doesn't let things remain as with our forefathers, he introduces new things. Just so Christ was always persecuted" (ZW 7:413). One of Weigel's most terse and effective sermons on the theme of tolerance (the sermon on Matthew 13:24–30, the parable of the good seed and the weeds, ZW 6:243–56) is translated and reproduced in this volume.

As Zeller observes, the *Manuscript Collection of Sermons* was discontinued after the sermon for March 28, 1574. On April 1 of that year Weigel's Saxony was overtaken by the suppression of the Philippists or Crypto-Calvinists, who had, until then, been the prevailing doctrinal party under the aegis of Elector Prince August. The reasons for this sudden reversal had much to do with politics. The St. Bartholomew's Day Massacre (1572) of Huguenots in Paris had stirred some militant sympathy for Calvinism, which in August's Lutheran territory could have engendered a movement favoring the anti-imperial policy of the rival German Protestant territory of the Palatinate. The court official Cracow and the Wittenberg professor Caspar Peucer, Melanchthon's son-in-law, were imprisoned or tortured, and alleged Crypto-Calvinists driven into exile. The same trauma of a doctrinal shift following on a dynastic change was repeated in Saxony and other lands, causing much hardship, hatred, and bitterness. Following the Peace of Augsburg, the religion of the ruler was supposed to determine that of the subjects (a rule that later acquired the designation *cuius regio eius religio*). From the vantage of those like Weigel who adhered to the Lutheran notion of an inner freedom of faith and refused to be drawn into the spirit of interconfessional hatred, the compulsory Formula of Concord of 1577 was yet another of the world's sieges conducted against the inner citadel of spirit.

ON THE PLACE OF THE WORLD AND THE GOLDEN GRASP

The two longer theoretical treatises reproduced here are of this period. In effect, they theoretically bolster the autonomy of spirit. In *On the Place of the World* this entails looking at the world as known to the senses and realizing that it is unfathomable in its finitude; the reader should be led to an understanding of the spirit within and of the God in whom all paradoxes of the finite and the infinite are resolved. *The Golden Grasp* proceeds, so to speak, from the inner presence of the Creator Spirit outward into creation. Just as creation proceeds from the inner being of God, knowledge proceeds from within outward, thereby legitimating the autonomy of spirit against the encroachments of an authoritarian clergy bolstered by the worldly power of the prince.

Both treatises begin with what is offered as the irrefutable evidence of the senses. By rationally reflecting on this, they move from the factual to the transcendent and thereby from the outer to the inner. In *On the Place of the World*, the factual point of departure is earthly or navigational measurement (which the author, though not himself a traveler, admires as useful and pleasing). He admires the detailed account of the calculation of the longitude and latitude of position. His point is that every place in the world can be scientifically localized relative to the world as a whole. The problem of the title, *On the Place of the World*, is therefore thrust into the foreground by a rational reflection on the evidence of the senses: What is the place of the world itself? Since it is self-evident to Weigel that the visible world is finite and geocentric, the reader is brought before the vision of a world hovering within an infinite abyss. This is an outer image of the inner being of all things, which is autonomous spirit. Both the outer world and the inner spirit are in turn images of the free self-sufficiency of the deity.

INTRODUCTION

The work is divided into twenty-nine chapters. Like *The Golden Grasp*, it is a relatively short book. Approximately the first third of its chapters read deceptively like a practical manual of navigation or cosmography. The work gradually reveals all the elements of Weigel's synthesis: the Spiritualist's Bible; Boëthius; Hugh of St. Victor; Eckhart; the *Theologia Germanica*; Cusanus, who is quoted but left unnamed; Franck; and Paracelsus. More than the early works or sermons, this treatise deliberately ascends from world to spirit, from creature to God. References to the threat of exile accompany the discussion of place and lend the exposition an atmosphere of historical crisis. Repetition in this treatise exceeds that found in the sermons. This could of course reflect the author's concern that the reader be led step by step along an unaccustomed and prescribed route, but it seems more likely that repetition is consciously intended to maintain the object of contemplation in its entirety before the reader's contemplative mind. This is necessary because the premises and conclusions depend on analogy to a degree never conceded by and perhaps not conscious to Weigel. The inner is analogous to the invisible and the invisible to the eternal or spiritual, which is known only to the mental eye of faith. The reliance on analogy connects the scientific or philosophical content of the treatise with its intended theological significance. *On the Place of the World* is dated by an internal reference to the year 1576.

The Golden Grasp contains in its text its dating to the year 1578, the year after the Saxon teachers and clergy, and with them Weigel, were required to sign the Formula of Concord. Here the thrust of the work is not exile and withdrawal inward. Instead, speculation proceeds from within outward, in accordance with the direction of creation and the trajectory of active knowledge. As usual, certain premises and analogies are givens. The creation of the world proceeded *ex nihilo* from God. Since material nature is always understood as the outer, the creation can only proceed from within. The implication that creation was carried out by God *ex se*, or out of his own being, is inescapable and resonant with Weigel's conclusions, but it is not enunciated explicitly. Instead, the author shifts from the centripetal speculation on creation to the centrifugal trajectory of the process of knowing. Here as elsewhere, Weigel asserts, as a matter of common sense, that all seeing comes from the eye and all knowing from the knower and not from the thing known. The reader is led to this assertion not by way of epistemological analysis but by the fact that conflicting doctrinal positions are held by the theologians who invariably appeal to the common authority of Holy Scripture. If knowledge came from the external object, in this key instance the Bible, there could be no such thing as multiple doctrines and disagreements.

This epistemology captures the aporia of the Age of Faith and its inability to approach peace and unity by way of biblical doctrine. According to Weigel, unity cannot be achieved through an active seeing and knowing, which claims to draw its authority from the Bible yet in reality only projects our human willfulness as creatures of nature. Unity is, and always has been, achieved, according to the author, by an understanding mind that renders itself passive in order to be informed by a divine knowledge in which God's self-recognition comes in the passively receptive human image. Weigel's claim that all who truly believed have arrived at a "concordance" reflects his assumption that the mysticism of Eckhart, Tauler, *Theologia Germanica*, Paracelsus, or Franck was invariant. In effect, he counters his contemporary theological Babel by resurrecting a tradition that seems to echo through the ages and across confessional boundaries. Even his view that the truly faithful ones believe in accordance with the Bible can be validated to the extent that he, like they, focuses on certain key scriptural passages, such as the creation account in Genesis and the Prologue of the Fourth Gospel. Such passages shifted attention away from an existence in time and place toward the contemplation of an infinitude or eternity—perceived by the human mind through the dark glass of paradox. The focal point of truth was thereby shifted away from the realm of division and political conflict to the latently omnipresent inner world of the divine and eternal, a realm that transcended and obviated all conflicting differences.

Where *On the Place of the World* is consolatory, *The Golden Grasp* is polemical. The unending disputes have induced weariness and anger in the author. The pastor's opponents are none other than the Antichrist. Nevertheless, this work also employs repetition and a gradual progress from premise to conclusion to maintain its entire object, encompassing God and the world, perpetually before the eye of the mind. As in the preceding theoretical tract, *The Golden Grasp* has a repetitive rhythm in which the slow ascent of argumentation is punctuated by the back and forth of antithesis and the clash of paradox. The meditative, almost incantatory, character of the exposition is sustained by the brevity of its chapters. Most of these in either treatise conclude with the devout prayer that the insights thus adumbrated might be imbued in him and his readers.

The speculative and at the same time meditative or prayerful nature of the sermonlike exposition is relevant to the opposing issues of Weigel scholarship. One school, represented by the eminent historian of early German philosophy Siegfried Wollgast, has tended to cast Weigel in the role of a philosophical critic of religion per se. Another school, represented preeminently by Weigel's editors Zeller and Pfefferl, reclaims the hereticized author for the Lutheran fold. The oldest tendency of Lutheran reception had banished Weigel from this fold, condemning him as a heretic. There is irony in the fact that Wollgast's secularist presentation draws on those older condemnations of Weigel as an arch-heretic. The recent presentation by church historian Martin Brecht puts him in the early history of German Pietism.[32] This is no doubt accurate as far as it goes, but it does not do full justice to the speculative elements in his work, which were alien to much of later Pietism. Further research is needed on Weigel's debt to Paracelsus, the radical reformers, especially Schwenckfeld and Osiander.

The answer scholars will give to the question of Weigel's relationship to the Protestant mainstream will undoubtedly depend on assumptions about the relations of mysticism and Neoplatonism to revealed religion. Did the history of mysticism contaminate scriptural purity with pagan philosophy? Or was it rather the case that Christian thinkers, from Eckhart to Weigel, could not accept what amounted to a dual theory of truth, dividing truth between rival doctrines or between revelation and philosophy or revelation and science? Theologians and historians will continue to debate whether philosophical, Neoplatonic, or mystical and Eckhartian ideas can be reconciled with Lutheranism.

I would suggest that this way of approaching the question risks missing a significant distinction. Weigel's use of analogy and paradox or his uses of the philosophical views of Boëthius, Paracelsus, and Cusanus were not elaborated in order to state a distinct new doctrine. Instead, he intended to obviate doctrinal controversy by revealing that religion could be something simpler than a set of controversialist propositions. This was only one of many comparable attempts at redirecting the focus of religious experience away from divisive doctrine and toward the inner life. (Later endeavors include Schleiermacher's theory of religion and the modern study of spirituality.) With regard to the difference between art and science, or between literature and logic, our own secular understanding of language allows for differences between the unequivocal propositional language of doctrine and a symbolic usage. In the latter, terms may mean many things because meaning has sources that are independent of our definitions. We should recall the immense and heterogeneous inspirational fecundity of the *Theologia Germanica*. As with its many-sided influence, the elements of contemplation and mysticism in Weigel reflect the difference between the sort of devotional writing that inspires contemplation of symbolic objects and a systematic writing that instead aims at a logically unequivocal exposition. (Of course, Weigel's objects of contemplation include the world as a finite whole and the knowing faculty itself.)

The distinction is analogous to that between text and melody in song. Melody and text must fit together, for both are bearers of meaning. But they are hardly the same thing. In our analogy *text* consists of doctrinal propositions that refer unequivocally. Antithesis and paradox in the *Theologia* or in Weigel are a style or movement, as well as a content, of thought. As the former, they are more like rhythm or melody in song than like doctrine, more akin to spirit than world. Just as the same *Theologia* could be adapted to various theological arguments, the same melody can be fitted with various texts. Melody and text become one in song when sung in a particular spirit (a different spirit for those on the march or those alone and attempting to surmount fear). Analogous to the equivocal yet significant melody, the paradoxes of the *Theologia Germanica* or the abstractions of Neoplatonic tradition embody exaltations and binary rhythms, of the self and God, the imperfect and perfect, image and source, many and one. The pairs attain resolution in the flowing course of the tract, as freedom renounces selfhood and the image acquires a true self-knowledge, thereby recognizing that it is as if nothing without its divine source. By way of a self-knowledge attained through renunciation of self-will, the creature strives to render itself an extension of God's will; it only understands because of its identification with its object. In operation, the inspiring symbolic language of the *Theologia* must have affected readers in a way not unlike the chords and primal images of Luther's famous song "A Mighty Fortress," a hymn that arouses the heart and gives voice to the spirit when sung in churches of many different denominations. In this sense the hymn is analogous to the contemplative movement from self to God, from nothing to all, from image to source, from the partial to the complete—analogous to the oppositions in the *Theologia* that inspired reformers as diverse as Luther, Müntzer, Franck, and Weigel.

The Shakers, who were arguably American Spiritualists, are said to have avoided writing down their theology, incorporating it instead into their songs, and, in the event of disagreements, singing until their differences were resolved. If the analogy between music and mystical-spiritualist writing is useful, there is another reason as well why singing may be relevant to Weigel's invocation of the *Theologia Germanica* or the mystical tradition. Weigel often cites Lutheran church hymns in order to validate his arguments. These were the common property of the clergy and the laity, expressing a shared spirit and commonly understood sense of its worship.

WEIGEL'S PLACE IN TRADITION

The long tradition of German mystical literature appears at first glance to have many subdivisions. The German mystics can be divided between medieval and postmedieval authors or between

Catholics and Protestants. There are the highly learned authors such as Meister Eckhart or Nicholas of Cusa, and there are the lay or purportedly unlearned authors such as the shoemaker-mystic Jacob Boehme or the *mulier ignota* Hildegard of Bingen. There is also the apparent contrast between two seemingly opposite orientations: on the one hand, toward inner experience (following the example of Eckhart), and on the other, toward an outer nature that is contemplated as a testimony and embodiment of the divine presence (a tendency anticipated by Cusanus and Paracelsus but exemplified most completely by Boehme). As we have seen, Weigel in many ways transcends the apparent divisions and, in so doing, intimates that these contrasts are aspects of an evolving unity. He draws on medieval Catholic sources and unites their impulses with a Protestant outlook. Anticipating Boehme, he combines an Eckhartian inwardness with a Cusan or Paracelsian contemplation of nature. Like Cusanus, Franck, and Boehme, Weigel seeks terms of reconciliation in order to obviate the doctrinal conflicts of his period. His work vindicates the authority of the common man or woman who is concerned with the applications of doctrine in immediate experience—the living spirit rather than the letter of doctrine or scriptural exegesis. Chapter 24 of *The Golden Grasp* suggests how a despair brought on by historical conflicts could serve as the catalyst for mystical inspiration. Weigel's writing, therefore, shows how specific historical conditions elicited and defined the mystical quest for the eternal, as the darkness might adumbrate and define a source of light.

This context is important because Weigel's historical and cultural experience was in many respects comparable to our own. His age was a time of rapid transformations. The order of the medieval empire under a single church had been shattered. The Aristotelian understanding of the natural world was being altered by innovations in astronomy and alchemy (a precursor of chemistry) and by a cosmography driven by new explorations. No new consensus or order in nature, religion, or politics was yet in sight. Startling innovations in theology and Bible studies had an impact that was magnified by a new information technology embodied in the printing press. Quickened by this information revolution, the Reformation confronted contemporaries with the pressing choice of either adhering to old doctrine or embracing the new. When the first surge of reforming zeal was followed by the fragmentation of the movement, the religious quarrels were embittered by internecine recriminations and then sharpened to serve as a rationale for war. The early elation gave way to a crisis of conscience in some of its more thoughtful adherents whose writings have been passed down to us. Of these, few are more far-sighted and theoretically innovative than the writings reproduced in this volume. Even if we cannot embrace Weigel's solutions, his ingenuity and subtlety can remind us that we share his dilemma in attempting to adhere to truth while respecting beliefs that differ from ours.

NOTE ON TRANSLATION

In translating Weigel's writings I adopted the following procedures for clarification. Footnotes are used for those few commentaries that were inserted into the printed pages of *Vom Ort der Welt.* (Since no manuscript survives, the printed edition of 1613 was the source for the 1962 edition of Frommann-Holzboog. I made use of both editions in translating.) My more extensive comments are relegated to the endnotes. Square brackets are used in order to mark off brief glosses, of which the most common are the completions of Weigel's references to the Bible, the glosses for his Latin terms, and the amendations of his German phrasing. The latter are intended to enhance the flow and intelligibility of the translation without compromising its faithfulness. Since the elucidation of Weigel's Paracelsian terminologies requires a more extended context, the reader should consult the Introduction where necessary.

As translator, I have attempted to be as faithful to the original as possible. The reader is reminded that Weigel was writing hundreds of years before present sensitivities to inclusive language were established.

I

VALENTIN WEIGEL

*S*ermon on the Good Seed and the Weeds

(ca. 1574)

✳

✦ • ✦

[Sermon for the] Fifth Sunday after Epiphany.
Gospel According to Matthew 13[:24–30],
De bono semine et zizania.[33]

The parable of the good seed and the weeds is interpreted by the Lord himself, [for he] says that the good seed is the word of God, [and] the field the world; [and] indeed [that] the good seed are the children of the kingdom and the weeds alongside the wheat are the children of wickedness. The enemy who sows the weeds is [accordingly] the devil; the harvest is the end of the world; and the harvesters are the angels. We are taught above all from this that the good comes wholly from the good God. It is only he who sows the good wheat into the field of the world. He creates all things good and nothing evil. But by free will, the evil person sets himself apart; it is from neglect by the human beings that the weeds arise. Thus, the good field with the good wheat must be as a cause or occasion of the weeds, not because the good seed causes the weeds, but rather because the weeds of themselves spring up alongside the wheat. For if there were no good seed and field, neither would there be any weeds; and if there were no light, neither would there be darkness. If there were no good, then neither would there be any evil. Thus, too, after the fall, good and evil have arisen in the human being; and so it is in the world as well that good and evil human beings exist alongside one another. No human being is commanded to weed them out. Rather, it is reserved for the angels alone and for the end of the world. For human beings do not know which is wheat and which are weeds. They might root out the wheat in place of the weeds. From that, it is to be learned that one should not kill heretics. Rather, one should let them remain alongside the just until the time of the harvest. After the fall, the human being can either adhere to the good and live in accordance with the wheat, that is, in accordance with the word of God by divine realization, or he can adhere to evil by his own will. If he adheres to the good, then he is born out of God, a child of the kingdom of heaven, and will be gathered into eternal life. If he adheres to evil, then he is a child of evil and faithlessness and will be gathered into the eternal fire at the end of the world. For nothing burns in hell but self-will,[34] and all those who have adhered to it.

"The kingdom of heaven is like a human being who sows good seed" etc., *legitur totum Evangelium* [the whole gospel is read]. Let us reflect together a bit what is the sower and what is the seed on the good field, and whence arise the weeds, both in the human being, alongside the wheat, and outside the human being, in the world, where there are pious and evil people, just and unjust people. God, the eternal Creator, is the true plowman and the human being is God's field (1 Cor 3:9). God is the sower. The seed is his word. God is good and sows only good seed and not evil. God created all things well and good, as we read in Genesis 1[:31]: "Behold, that everything was very good." After all the works of God, the human being was created from the clump of earth in accordance with his visible, external body. Out of clay the human being was formed, and into this clay God breathed the living soul [Gen 2:7]. Thus, the human being became an image of God [Gen 1:27]. God gave unto [the human being] God's almighty spirit; he spoke his spirit into a piece of clay. He sowed the wheat seed into the field and put him into paradise, so that the human being would not remain its own [will], but rather God's; so that he would not live according to his own, but according to the will of God. Thus, the human being was good, a good seed sown and planted by God himself for a good tree. But he was not compelled to be good; rather, he had the choice, to be and to become good or evil. Behold, thus, that God himself was the word or seed in the human being, and the human being was a good wheat or seed in, with, or by God. No evil seed had been sown; there were no weeds. What happens? As soon as the human being got into a [state of] security and disregarded the commandment of God, the weeds were sown alongside the good seed, as the text says: "As soon as the people were asleep, the enemy came and sowed weeds among the good seed" [Matt 13:25]. And when the wheat and the weeds grew up with each other, freely, without any compulsion, the human being turned away from God and knew good and evil. Thus, both were planted in the human being, the evil alongside the good. There remained two seeds in the human being and in the world, the seed of the woman and the seed of the serpent [Gen 3:15]; they cannot be separated from one another until the time of the harvest. At the end of life the one must separate from the other.

There remain these two seeds in the human being as a test, and also in the world as a test, so that the pious will be tested by the evil ones, and [so that] no human being should presume to kill and root out heretics; one might in so doing seize the wheat instead of the weeds, as indeed has happened with the hotheaded inquisitors, [who] have condemned and deprived of livelihood the pious teachers as [well as the] false ones. Only the angels and not the human beings are commanded to root out heretics, and to do so only at the end of the world. God wants to let the weeds stand alongside the wheat. For that reason, the text says to those servants who want to go and tear out the weeds: "No, you should not do this lest you tear out the wheat along with the weeds! Let both grow together until the harvest; and at the time of harvest, I will say to the reapers: First, collect the weeds and bind them into bundles to be burned; but collect the wheat into my bins!" [Matt 13:29–30].

How should human beings judge heretics? They are often themselves the worst heretics. And, truly, the very ones who presume to judge and to condemn others as heretics are often the weeds that belong in the infernal fire. They interfere in God's judgment by themselves judging, though they know that not human beings but the angels alone are commanded to do this, and that God indeed [wants] to let both [wheat and weeds] grow together until the harvest, until the end of the world. Oh, how many pious, God-taught men have already been named heretics by the unworthy, false lot, as is apparent to all eyes from Sebastian Franck's "Chronicle of Heretics"[35] and from all of scripture.

Now, when we regard the small world, the human being, we find in the human being two seeds, weeds alongside wheat. When we also regard the great world, we likewise find weeds alongside the wheat, evil alongside good, and the one is always against the other, and they may and should not be parted from one another, for one might then tear out the good along with the evil. But at the end of the world the angels will do so. Evil will [then] be resisted. For it will be collected into the eternal fire and the good seed [taken] to God in heaven.

Do not be led astray that I say to you: God is the sower and his word is the good wheat or seed; and that here in the text it says as well the human being is the good seed [Matt 13:37–38]. God himself is the word and the seed. He is himself the good wheat in the human being. He makes the good field and sows in it the good seed. This good seed and field is the human being sown from God and born to be a child of his kingdom. Thus, the human being is in God and with God a good seed* in the human being and with the human being, and not without the human being.

Both of these [are] with one another, neither without the other. If the human being remains abandoned to God in obedience, he is a good seed, a good field. In it, there are no weeds or bad seed. So whence come the weeds, if you, Lord, created all things good? *Responsio textus* [the response of the text, cf. Matt 13:28]: "The enemy did that." For, when the people were asleep, he came and sowed the weeds among the wheat. So now both are together, and it would be dangerous to root out the weeds. The enemy is the cunning snake that advised the human being to eat from the forbidden tree. From this eating, the weeds have been sown among the wheat; [they] will remain together with each other in each and every human being until the physical death [of the human being], and in the world until the Day of Judgment.

If there were no wheat on the field, neither would there be any weeds alongside it. The wheat is often hindered by [wild] poppies, cornflowers, and [wild] peas, and the world takes more delight in [these] weeds than in the good wheat itself. The reason is that the world does not properly understand what good and evil, just and unjust, are. Therefore, it is forbidden to all servants and teachers to root out the weeds. They might seize upon the wheat instead of the

---

*Zeller suggests that at this point the words may have been omitted "and God a good seed," which completed the thought of the sentence in an uncorrupted version of the text (ZW 6:249 n. 20).

poppies, cornflowers, and wild peas; just as it has always happened that one has condemned the pious prophets and deprived them of their living in place of the false [prophets]; and [one] has always thought that, in so doing, one performed a great service and favor to God. If you care to recognize whether someone is a true teacher of God of the wheat, or a poppy preacher of the weeds, then observe [this]: If someone presumes to condemn and damn others as heretics, or works to bring it about through governmental authority that others are killed and exiled, then he is certainly one of the evil seeds, of the devil and not of God, [and] the greatest heretic and seducer [of all]. For his God will certainly teach him that no human being is enjoined to root out weeds; God wants it [all] to remain together for many reasons.

The true teachers are not heretic hunters. They endure their enemies with patience and allow them to remain alongside the wheat until that time, as Moses did with Jambres [2 Tim 3:8], Paul with Elymas [Acts 13:8ff.], Christ with the Pharisees [Matt 23:1–33], [and] Peter with Simon Magus [Acts 8:9–24]. They [the true teachers] do not interfere in God's judgment. For they know that the heretics are more useful for exercising the pious than they are harmful. They [the true teachers] indeed know that Christ comes in order to bring dissension [Matt 10:34].[36] Just as soon as a pious one rises up and begins preaching about the good wheat, the false crowd rushes hither and cries [that this] is heresy, Enthusiasm, Sacramentarianism, and [evil] seduction; and the world could not endure Christ. It prefers to be fed on poppies, cornflowers, and wild peas instead of pure undiluted wheat. Many have the obtuse concern that the simple folk might be seduced by the heretics. For this reason they appeal to governmental authority in order that those whom they consider heretics and seducers are deprived of their livelihood, exiled, or even killed. But there would be no need of such a concern if they considered and knew that the New Testament is faith, life, and spirit, and that the faithful chosen ones indeed recognized the voice of Christ [cf. John 10:27].

The church has never been better off than when it was among its enemies, sects, and wolves. For Christ did not come in order to give and bring about for his church an external, worldly peace, but rather his peace, namely, that of the conscience, [in order] that, directly under the cross and surrounded by our enemies, we should have peace. Indeed, he came to destroy the external peace that we had with the world, so we would have nothing in common with the world. For this reason, he says that he came to bring fire and sword and separation, and not peace [Matt 30:34], as [it is] in the papacy and with the Antichrist. That is why, in our times, many are so foolishly zealous about the house of God, those who would set up a great church and a gospel codified as if by Moses, that we might all be Christians and of one accord in faith. All of which would be a good thing, if only faith were white bread for everyone, and if [only] the devil did not also have his church. They behave as if we were supposed to convince the very devil of the truth, to make him pious and bring him around with learned words. But I am afraid that they will wish more than obtain it. The church must be tested and exercised among its enemies, the grain remain with the chaff and the wheat among the weeds, until the harvest; and things have never been worse than in [the times of] peace, [for it is] as [Saint] Bernard complained about the false peace to Pope Eugene III: "'It is a peace and no peace' as the prophet says: 'Behold, bitter woe is upon me in peace.'"[37] And indeed we should have seen in the papacy what sort of peace this is, [and] what [sort of] good it brings, when the devil alone holds court and all things are at peace with the world. For the world is indeed quiet and peaceful, if one only sings its tune, if [only] the lie reigns, and the devil is god and abbot. But just as soon as Christ stirs, a fire gets started and soon it's burning everywhere [Luke 12:49]. For that reason, we should let all heresies and sects have their way and do as they might. The truth must be tested and purged and encounter the lies upon the same field. Compared with the lies, [truth] shines all the more brightly, as white against black and day against night. Hence the lies only abet the truth. Pressed down like a palm tree, [the truth] grows up all the more firmly. Therefore, there is no reason for the weak-spirited worries with which some people labor and torment themselves. They do not need to worry about heresy multiplying itself and seducing and traducing a great many, just because they [the guardians of the true faith] do not deprive them [the heretics] of their livelihood, but instead give their teaching free rein. In such a situation wisdom must be taught and justified by [the example of] the [faith of] children. If that [which the persecutors say] were true, Christ would certainly have known it as well. Yet he commands that the weeds be allowed to stand alongside the wheat, and forbids only [the persecutors, to have their way] (those very ones who are known to the church and publicly acclaimed). But now they are constantly concerned that the sky is falling down, if only we allow those [others] to live. We imagine an unbelievably feeble Christ, who might be blown over by every breath of wind. We fear constantly that we will lose it all and that both our church and our faith will be sunk. We do not consider that Christians are referred to as, and [indeed] are, rocks [of faith], erected upon the rock of Christ against all the gates of hell, storm, and deluge (Matt 7:16).[38] Whoever is blown over or moved by every wind has the sure sign of not being a sheep from the stall of Christ, [not one of those] who would hark only to the voice of their shepherd and would not heed any other voice (John 10[:27]); accordingly, they are not the rock of Peter and not Christians [cf. Matt 16:18; John 1:42]. Therefore, let that be which is not to remain, for the chaff is meant to be separated from the grain.

I say this because not only does the existence of many sects not harm Christians, [the sects even] serve as an advancement and challenge to their readiness to fight the good fight and attain the victory of eternal life:[39] *In summa:* [in sum, we receive] *salutem ex inimicis nostris* [well-being from our enemies], not *damnum* [harm] or *desolationem* [desolation], [contrary to] what we are so often told to imagine and fear, [namely], that the church should be without distinction. Moreover, Christ says it is not possible for the elect to be led astray (Matt 24[:24]). Whoever has once tasted the truth will nevermore abandon it, unless it is the case that he was not of the truth [in the first place]. The latter sort are always let go. For in such a way Christ must sweep the threshing floor, testing his own and separating the chaff from the grain (Matt 3[:12], 1 Cor 3[:12–15]). But the sheep of Christ who are of God hear only the voice of their shepherd and cannot hear the voices of the others (John 10[:27]). For that reason there are many who nurture the foolish worry and zeal concerning the house of God. For indeed, with their doings they will neither sustain nor increase [it]. It has already been decided who will stand or fall. However, when God condemns false prophets for having led the people astray, God is speaking of how things stand with them [the persecutors]. For it is they who have done this, insofar as it was possible for them to do so. Though God indeed provided and did not permit it with his own, nevertheless they [the persecutors] will properly give testimony to their [guilt], for they have not lacked the will to do so. Insofar as God judges the will and the heart, they will rightly be judged as thieves and murderers and seducers.

Behold, too, our wretched, pitiful darkness in [this] life, that should rather be called a death and a shadow of death (Rev 3[:1–2]). So many beliefs and sects are among those alone who imagine that they take their foundation and protection from Holy Scripture, disparaging all other beliefs. Behold all the Latin works-righteous people, how discordantly they build in the Latin church and Tower of Babel, how each brings something different: this one works, when faith is required; that one faith, whereupon one asks for [its] fruits. And there is such a groping, abortive seeking and skirmishing in the holy faith [in quest] of God that the occupants of this darkness are [rightly] called enemies of God: blind, deaf, dumb, godless, hypocrites, bunglers. And it is just as if one had set the blind off against one another, to struggle in darkness, whereby one just as readily strikes at friend as at foe. May God deliver us from this wasteland into his light. Amen.

Further, this God-instructed [author][40] whose words I have cited says the following about the heretics: "We would be in need of many an [Emperor] Constantine, who writes to Pope Agathon in the opening session of the Council of Constantinople:[41] 'May God be my witness: there is no preference of person with me. Instead, we should remain unpartisan toward both sides. We should therefore exert compulsion against no one. Let each believe or think as he would. Instead, we should consider all to be worthy of honor, as well as of our honest favor and treatment. And if we should agree with both parties, then, behold, God should be praised [for this]. But should they be unable to come to an agreement at all, then we should deliver them back to you with all civility, and it should be enough for us to have applied ourselves industriously to maintain the unity of the faith, and we should [thus] hope to have acquitted ourselves before Christ's seat of judgment. For it is our duty to encourage people, not to compel them; to appeal for the unity of Christians, but by no means to exercise force and compulsion.' That would truly be an exemplary course of action for a pious and reasonable emperor."

AMEN.

II

VALENTIN WEIGEL

A Useful Treatise

On the Place of the World

(1576)

∗

Contents

1. That it is useful for each human being to consider upon what sort of foundation the world stands so that it may not fall.

2. On the greatness and smallness of the globe and on the entire world and its eight visible spheres.

3. That the earth is to be divided into five zones in accordance with the circles of the astronomy of the heavens, and that ten circles are to be found on the firmament.

4. That the circumference of the earth is also divided up in accordance with the circles of the heavens.

5. On the four parts of the world, counted in accordance with the lands.

6. How the length of the earth is measured from Evening to Morning by the Equator and its parallel lines, but the breadth from Noon to Midnight by the Meridian.

7. That it is useful for a human being to regard the height of the Arctic pole, for it shows him where he is at home in the world.

8. On the form, figure, thickness, and circumference of the earth and on the four winds of the world.

9. That the earth with the sea forms a globe and stands in the middle like a point in a circle, and why it cannot fall or be displaced.

10. That this whole great world of heavens and earth stands at no place and can fall nowhere.

11. That the earth hovers in the air and the entire world is in nothing, in itself, and cannot fall down.

12. That the physical things are great and incomprehensible to the outer eye, but small and comprehensible to the inner eye.

13. How this visible world has been created without material into a material, and how it will again return to nothing in the end.

14. How it was before the creation of the world, in the world, and after the destruction of the world, and where at this time paradise or Christ is to be found, and what heaven and hell are, and where our fatherland is.

15. Where hell is now, and that this visible world is a hell of the devils that are compelled to live in the four elements.

16. That many different useful teachings follow necessarily from the above-mentioned things.

17. That nothing may be blessed or have calm unless it is at its certain and ordained place; and [concerning] that which is a definite place of the rational creature, in which it possesses calm and bliss.

18. That Lucifer has been chased and driven out of heaven and Adam out of paradise without any change of place; they remained where they were before, from which it follows that sin is not substance but accident.

19. That all the wishing, sighing, and pursuing by the creature occurs for the sake of calm, in order to possess it, and that it cannot be overtaken externally, but rather must be overtaken at ease and awaited within, through Christ.

20. That the eternal hell for the damned is their own love of themselves and their hatred of the highest good, which they desire without end but in vain.

21. How three hellish furies torment the damned and give them no rest on account of their hatred of God and their love of themselves.

22. That in that other world there will be no natural, elemental body that occupies a space or expanse and that looks this way or that

way with physical eyes, but rather a supernatural celestial body incarnated from the Holy Spirit, which is in need of no external place.

23. That in that other life there will no longer be a knowledge of languages, arts, and faculties; otherwise there would be no perfection in the eternal kingdom.

24. That in the kingdom of heaven there will be neither emperor nor pope, neither king nor bishop, neither prince nor preacher, but rather only one Lord of all lords over all, namely, God.

25. That in that other life human beings will have no more titles, names, or human offices drawing distinctions of kind among them.

26. What it means to be in heaven and in hell, and that the immutable will of God is the particular place in which all the blessed come together and dwell.

27. That for me it depends on will and not on being, whether one is in God in heaven or whether one is in the devil in hell.

28. Though the union of spirits is precisely a matter of the will, nevertheless no one can by his own will effect or give to himself rebirth [or] faith, that is, the unification with the spirit of God; rather, God himself must give it without any of our doing.

29. That heaven, the kingdom of God, the true fatherland, is much closer to us than we are to ourselves; hence, we do not need to seek for it outside of us but rather to await it in the spirit, within.

VALENTIN WEIGEL

✦ • ✦

CHAPTER ONE

That it is useful for each human being to consider upon what sort of foundation the world stands so that it may not fall

Although this visible world, composed as it is of heavens and earth, stands in accordance with its external aspect in no place, within nothing, in the infinite expanse or depths (for the world hovers within itself), nonetheless, place can be regarded here and there, as to where each country, city, or human being is situated, stands, and moves. And inasmuch as the human being has been made from the clump of earth of this world and has been placed into the middle of this world, in order to dwell within it until his appointed time, it is appropriate for him to regard and contemplate his place and fatherland, in which he has his home in such time; [that is,] in accordance with his mortal body [only], so that he might be forewarned that he has no permanent place in this world. He must soon depart and leave this world, [because] he belongs in another fatherland that is eternal and in heaven, for which he was created in the beginning. The human being was made of two parts in the beginning, [but he was made] so that he would be and remain not two but one human being, of flesh and spirit, of body and soul. In accordance with his body he needs a place or location in this time, whether on land or on the sea, and [he] must be in one place and cannot discern the [true] place of his abode; yet in accordance with the spirit, he is in need of no place, for the spirit possesses no place [and] occupies no space [and] does not admit of being enclosed or locked into any place. Whoever considers and properly understands these things strives to walk in accordance with the spirit in Christ [and] to remain in the kingdom of God, so that he may at last leave behind this narrow and pitiful wretchedness and come to his Father in heaven in the eternal expanse. For he sees clearly with what drudgery his mortal body transports itself from one place to another; how it is driven hither and yonder by men and by beasts, by hunger and thirst, by heat and cold, through day and night, summer and winter; and how it is at last entirely consumed by death and reduced to nothing. Yet, so that the location of our wretched body may be contemplated, [in order] that this should admonish us of our true fatherland in heaven, we shall begin below with the circumference of the earth and consider in which part of the world we are at home. Moreover, so that this may be facilitated, we shall have recourse to the upper spheres, the heavens with their circles, by means of which are shown, displayed, calculated, and measured the longitude and latitude and thickness of the earth together with the sea; moreover, [we shall consider] where the ascendant lies and in which part of earth lie Africa, Europe, Asia, and America. From such contemplation much that is useful [and] necessary for the mortal body is to be found. Thus shall you see, you potentates and kings on earth, how slight and weak is your regime measured against other kings, and how it is nothing at all against the eternal kingdom of Christ.

Likewise, you theologians, you who willfully serve Antichrist, shall recognize your error: [You shall see] how the kingdom of heaven may not be bound to places, persons, gestures, or external ceremonies but rather stands freely, in spirit and faith, not bound here nor there (Luke 17:[23]).[42] Moreover, it shall be clearly shown in this contemplation what paradise is and where heaven and hell are situated; how the fall of an angelic or a human creature could occur, not in accordance with place or with substance but rather in accordance with will or accident.[43] Moreover, one shall see how it had been prior to the creation of the world, and how it happens now that the world cannot fall, and how it shall again become after the destruction of the world.

Such and similar items of knowledge will show you that in that [other] world we must have invisible, spiritual, celestial, supernatural bodies that are in no need of an external place or reservation, neither of air nor light of the sun nor of anything natural, but rather it [the body] must be celestial and angelic, so that we might also dwell with God in ourselves upon the eternal expanse, where no end is to be found or seen or imagined in eternity, neither below nor behind nor in front of oneself.

VALENTIN WEIGEL

✦ • ✦

CHAPTER TWO

On the greatness and smallness of the globe and on the entire world and its eight visible spheres

An egg [is] composed of yolk and albumen. The yolk is situated in the middle of the albumen and touches no side but instead hovers in the middle; so is our world like an egg.[44] For it, too, is round and has two spheres, the upper and the lower. The upper comprises the air, together with the firmament; the lower is the earth and the sea; [together they] make up a round globe, [and] hover in the air amid the heavens and touch no side, like the yolk inside the egg. And just as the albumen surrounds the yolk, so also the eight spheres together with the air surround the sea and earth like a ball. Now, as I have said, the lower sphere or globe, the earth or sea, is like a center within a circle, and the upper sphere is the air together with the fire and firmament, which is also called the heaven by the simpleminded.[45] This heaven or firmament is divided into eight visible, distinguishable spheres on account of the seven planets, each of which has its own circle or course. The lowest planet is the moon, the closest above the earth; the second is the star Mercury; the third is the star of Venus, [which] stands in the third circle counting upward from the earth; the sun stands in the fourth sphere; in the fifth circle the star of Mars goes round; in the sixth the planet Jupiter; in the seventh Saturn; in the eighth heaven are all the stars of the firmament, small and great, together with the twelve celestial signs of the Zodiac, beneath which each of the seven planets completes its course. The ninth sphere is added for reasons of motion by the astronomers, and the theologians add the tenth and eleventh, for which they may take responsibility themselves. For we are not speaking here symbolically of the aquaeous heaven, of the waters above the firmament [cf. Gen 1:6–8], or of the fiery heaven in which God dwells, but only of the circular physical spheres. Thus, if I ascend with my inner eye and with the outer one, then the earth, measured against the firmament or uppermost heaven, is like

70

a center or point and is small indeed. Yet, if I descend from the heavens to the earth, I find the globe of the earth great, broad, and thick. And [just] as the earth is like a small point [when] measured against the firmament, so is the entire universe [when] measured against the depth upon which it hovers, small, indeed like nothing at all, as will be shown in the subsequent chapter.

Therefore, attempt now to assess the magnitude and smallness from these figures.

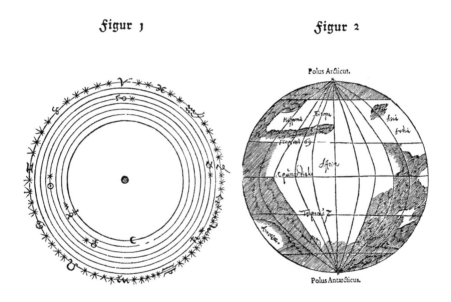

figur 1   figur 2

The earth and the sea together make up a thick round globe, which is divided into five zones in accordance with the circles of the heavens, which [correspond] to Europe, Asia, Africa, and America; moreover, into [the directions of] Morning, Evening, Noon, and Midnight, as well as into other times, months, and years, in accordance with the sun and the twelve signs.

VALENTIN WEIGEL

✦ • ✦

CHAPTER THREE

That the earth is to be divided into five zones in accordance with the circles of the astronomy of the heavens, and that ten circles are to be found on the firmament

After we have seen that the entire machinery of the world [*machina mundi*] is composed of two spheres, of the lower sphere of earth and sea, and the upper sphere of air and firmament; and that there are seven planets with their own spheres that complete their course below the zodiac of the firmament, so let us travel up to the course of the seven planets, excepting the sun, and rise to the firmament, to regard it as do the astronomers in accordance with its ten circles, so that we can measure and divide by means of them the surface of the earth, the lower globe upon which we dwell. For no one can properly know his home [or] in what part of the world it lies, nor will anyone be able to calculate the distance from one land to another without knowledge of the upper astronomical circles; indeed, no one will be able to travel successfully by water or land without having some knowledge of the firmament by means of these circles, in order to see how far toward noon or midnight he travels, and so on.

Upon the firmament the astronomers conceive of six large circles and four small ones, as follows: horizon, meridian, equinox *(aequinoctialis)*, and Zodiac, Tropic of Cancer and Tropic of Capricorn, two *coluri*, the Arctic and Antarctic Tropics. Such circles, I say, are imagined by the astronomers on the heavens; they do not posit them as truly being upon it (excepting the broad circle of the Zodiac, the pathway of the sun and planets); rather, one calculates, divides, and measures by such circles the course of the stars and the sun and the moon, the circumference of the earth, and the distance from one place to another, and so on. Now let us regard each great circle in particular, for this will be useful to us in order to understand and divide up properly the circle of the earth. A great circle is and is designated as that which divides both the heavens and the earth in two. There are six of them.

The first is called Equator or Equinox, which causes day and night to be divided evenly in the entire world, inasmuch as the sun in its course in the springtime enters the first degree of the Ram around March 11 and in the fall the first degree of the Wagon around September 12; it follows the circle on its path and [thereby] makes the day and night equal for us. This circle is divided into 360 degrees, as are all others large or small. It has much utility besides, which you may seek out in the *Booklet of the Armillary Sphere* [of Peter Apianus].[46]

The second great circle on the firmament is the Zodiac, upon which the twelve celestial signs stand. Each sign has thirty degrees, so that the entire circle has 360; [the Zodiac] divides heavens and earth alike into two equal parts; and inasmuch as it is rounded, it has two poles of its own, not with the equator, as you can see in the instrument of the subsequent figure of the entire celestial sphere. And notice here, above all, that only the Zodiac among them all has its breadth at twelve degrees, six on each side. The other circles are only lines without breadth, yet the Zodiac has, as mentioned, a breadth, [below which] the planets have their courses; in the midst of which a line is shown [which] is called *via Solis*, the path of the sun; for the sun alone remains always in the middle of this broad circle, while the other planets deviate to the sides.

The third great circle is called Meridian, the Noon line; [it] divides both heavens and earth into two equal parts right down the middle. Thus it passes through the two poles of the world, Arctic and Antarctic, and through the zenith, that is, the vertical point; where the sun is found in this line, Noon is its dwelling, and for those below you it is Midnight. There are as many lands, places, or zeniths as you care to have or imagine in the Meridian line. As many meridians can be counted as lines run through the poles of the world, [there] being everywhere meridians, as you can see in the globe of earth.

The fourth great circle is called Horizon or *finitor*; [it] divides the entire world into two parts as well. The upper is called *superius hemisphaerium*, the lower *inferius hemisphaerium*. If you were to stand in a flat smooth field, you would see around you that the circle of earth seems to touch the firmament. This circle is called the horizon; and the horizons may be counted likewise many in accordance with the position and place of each in which one finds oneself. When the sun is rising, it stands in the *horizonte orientali;* and when it sets, it is on the *horizonte occidentali.*

Fifth is *colurus equinoctiorum*, a great circle [that] passes through the poles of the world and through the first degree of ☌ and ♎; as soon as the sun traverses these two degrees, it causes the two equinoxes of the year, in spring and fall. Thus are day and night equal throughout the world, which is why it is called *colurus equinoctiorum.*

The second *colurus* passes through the first degree of ♋ and ♑. By means of this circle one can calculate that the sun departs from the equator by 23 degrees and several minutes when it is in ♋ and in ♑. Now four small circles or tropics follow; the tropic ♋, the circle of cancer, is described by the course of the sun when it is at the beginning of the Crab, that is, around Saint Vitus's Day, which is the longest day here in Europe toward

figur 3

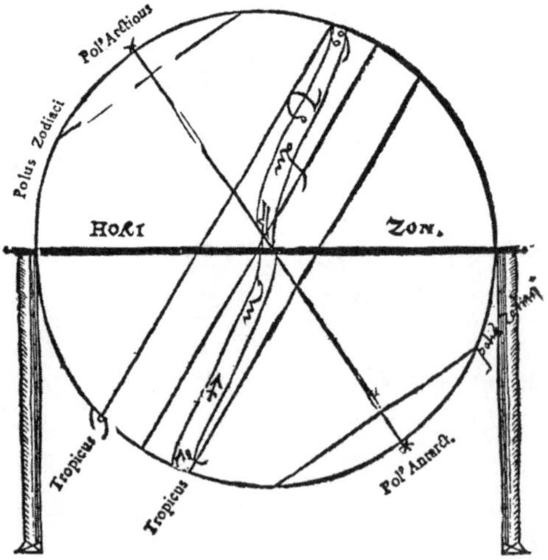

74

Midnight. The other tropic 🐐 of the goat is made by the path of the sun in the beginning of 🐐, on Saint Lucy's Day, when the day is shortest here and the night longest. From then on, the sun begins moving toward us.

The Arctic Circle is described by the pole of the Zodiac, which diverges from the North Pole of the world by 23 degrees and 30 minutes and on account of which it courses around the pole of the world on all days. The same way in reverse the Antarctic pole is described, as you can see in this instrument or figure [see figure 3].

✦ • ✦

C H A P T E R   F O U R

That the circumference of the earth is also divided up in accordance with the circles of the heavens

Now that we have reported on the great and small circles of the heavens devised by astronomy, these are now to be applied to the lower globe that is the earth, so that one may see in which part of the earth our dwelling lies. For the entire earth is not inhabitable due to the immense cold or the immoderate heat of the sun, and in order to show this in the earthly realm, you should regard the zodiacal and equinoctial [circles], as well as the two poles of the world and in addition both tropics. You will find five zones on the earth, [each] like a wide belt that, toward Midnight, beneath the Arctic pole, is called *frigida zona* on account of its great cold, so that it cannot be inhabited. Likewise, beneath the Antarctic pole, within the *Circulus Antarcticus*, is also found a *zona frigida*, for the sun cannot reach it. But between the Arctic and the Tropic of Cancer, or similarly between the Antarctic and the Tropic of Capricorn, lies a temperate zone *(zona temperata)*, a moderate place for dwelling, which is neither all too hot nor all too cold. And in these parts, lies the region [of] Europe, Asia, Africa, and America. Yet below the *Equinoctial* and on both sides [of it] lies *zona torrida*, where everything is withered *[verdorret]* on account of the [ever] present sun. The broad and curving circle of *Zodiacus* is divided by the great equatorial circle into two parts; it dissects the Zodiac at the beginning of the Goat and the Wagon, so that six celestial signs lie toward Midnight, the remaining six toward Noon. And when the sun passes through these Midnight signs, we who dwell toward Midnight have the longest days and the shortest nights. In addition, those in *Hybernia*[47] are without any night; they have day constantly for almost six months. And when the sun comes above the equinoctial line to the Midnight sign, we have the shortest days and the longest nights; indeed, the Hybernians have for six months pure night and no day.

♑ / ♌ / ♊ / ♏ / ♌ / ♍ : These are Borealic and Septentrionalia for the reason that in these signs the sun departs from the equator and approaches toward Midnight, the Crab.

♎ / ♏ / ♑ / ♌ / ♐ / ♒ : These are called Meridionalic signs, for the reason that in these signs the sun departs from the equator and approaches the Goat toward Noon. And inasmuch as the sun's course ceaselessly passes through these twelve signs, and it does not depart from this circle to either side, so it follows that below the equator and alongside it there is the torrid zone

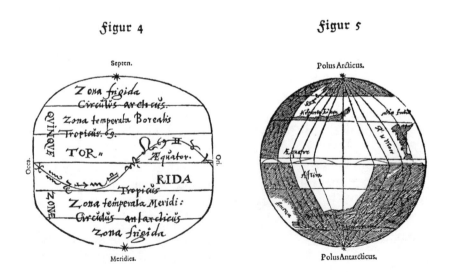

figur 4   figur 5

76

where neither leaf nor grass can be found, but only sand and stone and that no one may live there on account of the great heat. The people who live there around it are black and brown on account of the great heat of the sun. From this it can be seen how small [is] the place on earth [that] can be inhabited by human beings; for toward Midnight below the Arctic Pole and within the Arctic Circle, or similarly toward Noon within the Antarctic Circle and [beneath] its pole, no one may dwell on account of the great and powerful cold.

Furthermore, right beneath the Equinoctial and alongside it, the perpetual heat of the sun forbids it. Except for whatever is permitted [to be] in its proximity, as in Ethiopia and Africa, whatever is *zona temperata* [lies] between the Arctic and the Tropic of ♒, or between the Antarctic and the Tropic of ♑, as you shall now see.

✦ • ✦

CHAPTER FIVE

On the four parts of the world, counted in accordance with the lands

If one contemplates the circles of the heavens and the course of the sun, there are four parts of the world: the Beginning, as the place where the sun rises on the horizon for each land, and Evening, where the sun goes down for every place and introduces the night; Noon, when the sun stands, for each, pointed vertically, the Noonday Line; and Midnight, when the sun is found at the bottom of the heavens [*in imo coeli*], or at the edge of the world [*justa Plagam mundi*], where one recognizes the Arctic pole and Noon the Antarctic. Inasmuch as the heavens and the globe of earth are both round, the rising and setting can be posited everywhere, for the reason that the sun is rising and falling all the time, inasmuch as it progresses round in a circle, but not in each land every hour; when the sun is rising for people in India, those in Spain might have Midnight; and when for the Spaniards the sun stands at Noon, the Orientals might have Evening, and so on. Therefore, although the sun in its circle rises and sets all the time from the diverse perspectives of the inhabitants [*divers(o) respectu habitantium*], that is, as the people on earth see it, nonetheless, it rises or sets for one people or land before the other, and so on, as the celestial globe [*globus coelestis*] shows. But about these four parts of the world we are now speaking, not in accordance with the circles, but only in accordance with the land [-masses], of which there are four. The first part of the world is called Asia, after the son of Manaeus Lidius, Asia; [it] lies toward Morning, with respect to us who live in Saxony, Europe. However, there are two, Asia Major and Asia Minor, in which are situated Pontus, Bythinia, Phrygia, Cappadocia, Licia, Caria, Phamphilia, Misia, Lidia, Gallacia, Cicilia, Colchis, Galilea, Idumea, Jerusalem, Syria, Media, Persia, Hircania, Armenia, Scythia, Turkey, Babylonia, and so on. The rest you'll find in Peter Apianus, in his *Abacus*, and in the *World Book (Weltbuch)* of Sebastian Franck.[48]

The second part of the world is called Africa, after Aphrus,[49] a descendant of Abraham; it lies toward Noon in our eyes or from our location. The greater part of Africa is uninhabited and a desert, partly because of the proximity of the sun, especially toward Noon, and in part because of the infertility of the drifted sand. However, toward Europe, Africa is well populated and very fertile. In it lie Libya, Ethiopia, Mauritania, Egypt, Carthage; that precious River Nile flowing out of paradise; [and] the Atlas Mountains, in which are found Moors so black that they glitter with blackness from the heat of the sun, on account of which they live underground. This region fell to Ham, Noah's son, as Asia fell to Shem, and Europe to Japheth. Whatever else can be known about it you can read in the *World Book* of Sebastian Franck.[50]

The third part is called Europe and stretches toward the setting sun at the Atlantic Sea, toward the rising sun at the River Tanai [Don] and at the Riphet Mountains. And although it is the smallest part of the world, nonetheless, in fertility, moderation of atmosphere, in cities and castles, [and] above all in its artful, friendly, virtuous folk, it surpasses all other parts of the world, which is to say, Asia, Africa, and America. In breadth from Noon to Midnight, Europe is nowhere greater than 225 German miles, states Apianus;

in its central part it extends and forms itself in two wings, quite like a dragon. But the length of Europe from the River Tanai to the Sea of Cadiz, where it is longest, extends to 750 German miles.

Now the beginning of Europe and head of the dragon beginning in the Occident is Spain, which has five kingdoms, namely, Galicia, Navarre, Castille, Catalonia, [and] Aragon; after [Spain], there follows Gaul, Italy, Brabant, England, Scotland, Gelderland, Holland, Germany, Swabia, Saxony, Wallachia, and so on.

The fourth part is called America, it is named after Americo Vespucci, who discovered it by sea voyage in the year 1497. On order of the King of Castille it is called the New World, [and it] occupies in its breadth 525 German miles, in length, however, 750. In this island or world, all the inhabitants go naked; [it] lies in the globe alongside Europe and Africa, toward the setting sun. If you care to know more about this part, you can read of the sea voyages in the *World Book* of Sebastian Franck.

✦ • ✦

CHAPTER SIX

How the length of the earth is measured from
Evening to Morning by the Equator
and its parallel lines, but the breadth from
Noon to Midnight by the Meridian

Although there is no beginning in a circle or a round sphere, nonetheless the astronomers with their cosmography posit one, so that they can measure the earth in length, breadth, and depth; indeed, one can posit a beginning in a circle wherever the one will. But they take their beginning to the west of us, in Spain at the Isles of the Blest *(Insulis fortunatis)*, close to Compostela; from that point, they count the miles in length toward Morning following the equator and its parallels. And not without reason does one begin counting the degrees of the heavens and the miles of [the length of the earth] from Evening to Morning. For all the planets with the sun pass in their course toward Morning, notwithstanding that to the inexperienced the opposite appears to be true, that is, that the stars pass from Morning to Evening, and that such people feel as if they [could] palpably confirm that the sun and all stars rise in the East (Morning) and set in the West (Evening). The following conclusion can be drawn from this: There is a twofold course or movement of the heavens, an outer foreign course through the uppermost firmament, and an inner native course of each planet and star. God has ordained that all spheres and their stars pass around the earth in twenty-four hours from Morning to Evening with great speed, yet, this notwithstanding, each planet or star has its particular course from Evening toward Morning beneath the curved circle of the Zodiac. Take the example of a wheel or millstone: If you turn such a wheel, a fly might have its own path on the wheel, so that if you were to turn the millwheel from Morning to Evening, the fly might crawl [in the opposite direction] from Evening to Morning. Consider, so it goes with the course of the heavens: The uppermost heaven speeds clear around in twenty-four hours from Morning to Evening, and makes for us a natural day, taking with it all the lower spheres, and within that each star has its own course through the Zodiac from Evening to Morning. For, out of the ♑ passes the ♄ into ♒; and out of ♒ into ♐, it completes its course through the Zodiac in thirty years. The ♃ passes through these twelve signs in twelve years, from Evening into Morning. The ♂ in two years. The ☽ in one year, likewise from Evening to Morning, even though it is each day thrust from Morning to Evening by the uppermost heavens. Thus the moon is the lowest planet [nearest] to us; [it] traverses the Zodiac in four weeks; [and it] comes together with the sun twelve times, [whereupon] each time a conjunction occurs, that is, a new light of the moon, and so on. And just as the latitude of the earth is calculated from Evening toward Morning in accordance with the path of the stars from the equator and its parallels; so is the longitude of the earth calculated from Noon to Midnight, that is, from the Antarctic pole toward the Arctic pole, or from the Equator toward Midnight, and this by means of the meridian that must be drawn above each dwelling through the zenith and both poles of the world. And just as the length, longitude of place [*longitudo loci*], is what indicates to me whether a place lies closer to Evening or Morning, so that latitude is what indicates whether my place is closer than another to Noon or Midnight. Thus, latitude shows me how high the Arctic pole of the world stands from the horizon of my home. For example, if I wanted to know in what relation to one another Leipzig and Venice stand, which is more toward Evening or Morning in longitude, and which is situated more toward Noon or Midnight, then, in order to discover this, I would consult the *Abacus regionum* of Petrus Apianus and look up the longitude of Leipzig and then do the same for Venice. I would note them for myself as follows:

	Longitude	Latitude
Leipzig	29° 58'	51° 24'
Venice	32° 30'	44° 50'

From that I see that Venice is situated a few German miles more toward Morning than Leipzig and that Venice has a greater longitude from Occident toward Morning; 32 degrees are more than 29 degrees, from which I see that Venice lies several German miles more toward Noon than Leipzig, since Venice has a small latitude, inasmuch as you see that Leipzig stands 51 degrees above the Equator, so that the altitude of the pole is greater than at Venice. If you want to know exactly, you must learn to calculate the distances of places. That is not my intention here.

✦ • ✦

CHAPTER SEVEN

That it is useful for a human being to regard
the height of the Arctic pole, for it shows
him where he is at home in the world

On the firmament there are two points that remain still and unmoved. They are called poles for the reason that one draws a line from these two points right through the world, around which [axis] the firmament passes, like a wheel around its hub. The one pole stands at Midnight and is called Arcticus for the reason that it is seen from the Little Bear [that is, the Little Dipper]. The other, in the direction of Noon, is not visible to us and is called Antarcticus. If one could live precisely below [that is, at] the Equator, one would have both poles on the horizon, as you can see in the [subsequent] figure; but the more one would move from the Equator toward Midnight, the higher [or nearer] would be the Arctic pole. On the other hand, the Antarctic would be entirely concealed beneath the horizon. Now we dwell in our part of the world, in Europe, far from the Equator, indeed above the Tropic of Cancer. Therefore, for us the Arctic pole is high on the earth, that is, from the horizon; for example, at Leipzig it stands 51 degrees, 58 minutes, from the horizon; the closer one moves toward Midnight, the higher it is seen, up to the 57th, 58th, 59th, 60th, 61st degree, and so on. The higher this pole stands above a land, the more it is toward Midnight and the further it is removed from the Equator or Noon; thus the altitude of the pole is one with latitude. All navigators need this pole in order to cross the sea, to orient their voyage by; without any knowledge of it, they would not know whence or whither they proceed. The magnet in their compass always points toward this pole, and all Noon lines pass through it, and through the other one. Whoever does not have this knowledge of the celestial circles and the poles will not know upon his voyage which way is which; even if he can distinguish one place from another, he will not know whether he's traveling toward Morning or Noon. But whoever lets himself be guided by the altitude of the pole will be able to assess quite correctly the four parts or places of the world and what lies between them. For example, if I wanted to travel from Rome to Jerusalem, I would not know how to proceed. This is why I [would] have with me the *Abacus* of Petrus Apianus along with a compass. I would ascertain the longitude and latitude of each place. I would make notes from it for myself, having laid out the tables in the compass, dividing them into the four directions of the world [*Plagas mundi*], as follows:

figur 6

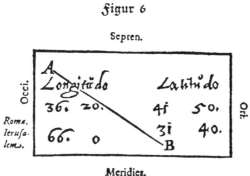

Here I see clearly that Jerusalem lies several hundred German miles toward Morning, and Rome in Evening toward Midnight with respect to Jerusalem. Therefore, I recognize that from Rome, as from Evening, I must travel along the line AB, that is, half toward Morning and half toward Noon. To know this is not merely pleasurable but useful as well. But if I wanted to know how many miles it is, I would have to calculate it according to an art that I do not intend to teach here.

Moreover, if I wanted to travel from France to Cracow in Poland, I would take the compass and regard the directions of the world [*Plagas mundi*], Ascendant, Descendant, and so on, and seek the length and breadth from the *Abacus*.

figur 7

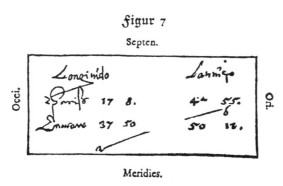

Thus I would find that Cracow in Poland lies very far toward Morning (if I happen to be now in Paris), and that Cracow is also toward Midnight. Therefore, I would have to travel half toward Morning and half toward Midnight along the line Ab. So, from that you can see how one place is situated with respect to another and whither your journey should proceed, whether on land or water, so that you should not be an ignorant simpleton, like a wandering spirit who didn't know where on earth he dwelt or had been at home with his mortal body or hut.

✦ • ✦

CHAPTER EIGHT

On the form, figure, thickness, and circumference of the earth and on the four winds of the world

The earth and sea together constitute a globe; some people compare it and its lands to the human body, the earth being the flesh, the water blood, the stone bones, the mountains arteries, the head being the beginning or Asia, the feet the Descendant [Niedergang] or America, the right arm [reaching] through Africa, the left through Europe. All of this we'll leave to itself. We have a different view of our own and want to recount it. In actuality, though, the earth with the sea is round and has fifty-four hundred German miles in its circumference (according to the art of calculation) and in its diameter 17,181.5 German miles, as we can recognize from the celestial degrees. Furthermore, one demonstrates it to have four prominent corners or parts in accordance with the four winds: From the Orient blows Subsolanus, which has alongside of it two companions, one on either side, Caecias and Eurus. From Evening blows Zephyrus, with its two companions, Corus and Favonius. From Noon blows Notus, which also has two companions, who are Affricus and Auster. From Midnight blows Boreas, [with] Aquilo and Circias. So that you can name all the names of the winds that blow at any time, consider the following table of the names and circuit of the winds.

Eurus,	Auster,	Favonius,	Corus,
Eastnorth/	South/	Westwind/	Northwest/
Subsolanus,	Notus,	Zephyrus,	Aquilo,
Easterly Wind/	Southeast/	Westsouth/	North Wind/
Vulturnus,	Affricus,	Circias,	Boreas,
Eastsouth/	Southwest/	Westnorth/	Northeast/

There follows the figure of the diameter of the earth and its curcumference together with the twelve winds.

figur 8

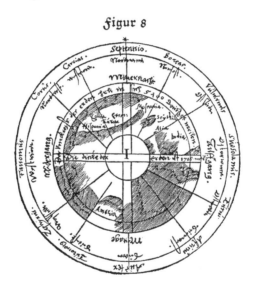

Now if you want a thorough knowledge of which wind is blowing at any time, take a compass and place it upon the world of this wheel of winds so that the points in the compass meet; when you have discovered in this manner where Noon should stand in the wheel, let the wheel stand thus aligned with the pole or axis of the world [*axis mundi*]. Then put the compass away and take a flag and a wire and stick [it] in the middle of the world of this wheel of winds: whichever way the flag points, that is the correct wind at that time.

VALENTIN WEIGEL

✦ • ✦

CHAPTER NINE

That the earth with the sea forms a globe and stands in the middle like a point in a circle, and why it cannot fall or be displaced

From the considerations of the foregoing chapters it is sufficiently evident that the earth and sea form a sphere with a circumference of fifty-four hundred German miles and a diameter of two
thousand German miles; when one regards the earth and its circumference with the sensuous eye from one's own vantage, it is a
very great body, but if it is compared with the upper heavens, it is
like a point or center compared with its circle. This fact may be evident and obvious even to the simplest minds, namely, [from the cir-
cumstance] that the star that rises in Morning and stands above
one's head at noon remains in the same relation to the earth. The
same is true at its setting; if a line were drawn from the center of the
earth up to the stars, so that it would stand in Morning, Noon, or
toward Evening, it would remain the same line [and] of the same
length. From that it follows that the earth stands in the middle and
that it is a center with respect to the firmament. Now we want to
consider the reason why the earth together with the sea does not
fall, as inexperienced minds [would] suppose, and why such a corporeal mass [*moles corporea*] as the great ball of earth and seas is, does
not fall from its location, nor is it removed from its spot, [and how]
this is natural and [how] first of all the cause [of it] is that all creatures stand above themselves [or their place] and nothing hangs
below its [place].

For, stand or sail upon this ball wherever you will, you will at
all times have above you the heavens and will at all times have your
head extending in an upward direction toward the stars. If one were
to ask you how it happens that the earth does not fall, you should
answer, It does not fall for the reason that it cannot fall upward, for
falling down is nothing other than falling upward, inasmuch as all
creatures stand above themselves [that is, above their appointed

86

places]. As impossible as it is that the earth together with the sea should rise and cast itself upon the firmament, it is equally impossible that the earth should fall upward with those who dwell opposite us, or as we say, who dwell below us; for those that dwell under us, and whose feet point toward our feet, can just as well ask, Why does the earth not fall downward? To them one would reply quite rightly that it does not fall downward with us; for we do not stand and look with our heads downward, bur rather upward.

If you were to travel in a ship, you would certainly not be cast with your ship upward into the heights toward the heavens; and just so it is with those who would voyage beneath us upon the water— they cannot fall. For to them up is up, just as for us, since everything stands above itself [that is, its appointed place]. In the same manner the sphere of the earth cannot fall toward Morning or Evening, nor toward the sides against either of the poles of the world, for no matter in what place you stand, you see everything above you. The inexperienced minds say that God or the angels must be holding the earth so that it does not fall from the center. But this is not so. Everything stands [quite] naturally. God is all the more to be praised and acclaimed for being a Creator who can place such a great and heavy sphere into the middle into air, and [thus] the entire world into a nothing. Everything stands in itself, though not outside of God, and has its seat within itself, just as the seat of the [element] fire is nowhere else but within fire, and the seat of the [element] water is nowhere else but within water, and the [place] of the spirit nowhere else but within the spirit. So, too, is the seat of the earth nowhere else but in the earth, that is, within itself, as the following chapter will demonstrate. The simpleminded might imagine that one could fall downward into the heavens, if one were to dig a hole clear through the diameter of the earth. But this is not so. For just imagine *per impossibile* that one had dug from the Antipodes all the way through the earth and had come to our surface and had finished the hole so that one would see the heavens just as we do, we could then bend over and pull him out of his hole, but we would hardly fall with him into the heavens. So also would it be with us, if we were to dig our way to the Antipodes. We would not fall on the other side to the heavens; indeed, we might find that we would not fall down through the hole toward the middle [*ad mediam*]. Moreover, for the same reason the earth itself falls to no side, small as it is compared with the firmament. For how should a point fall out of a circle? It must stand still and deviate in no direction. Were it nevertheless to be shattered, then the stars and the firmament would descend upon the center, and [yet even then] nothing would fall out. This will happen on the Final Day, when all physical things shall melt and burn.

✦ • ✦

CHAPTER TEN

That this whole great world of heavens and earth stands at no place and can fall nowhere

It is miraculous, think the inexperienced, when one says that angels are in no place, [or that] a spirit is in need of no space but instead dwells in itself in no place, [and that] God is in no place. But then why should a spirit or an angel be enclosed by a physical place (though Lucifer does lie bound and enclosed in these four elements, but then that is his torment of hell); yet this great world stands in no place that one could refer to [by asking whether it is] here or there. For outside the world there is no physical place. Now this great world, being that it is a creature [that is, a created thing], is finite, that is, limited and comprehensible, for no physical thing can encompass its infinitude, [and] so too are the spirits and angels limited, comprehensible, and finite, inasmuch as no one can deny that the world must have an end or a terminus. It is equally clear that it can stand in no place, but instead, being itself a place and comprehension of all places and physical things, and being that only in accordance with its internal space places can one designate here and there, and by no means outside the world. However, [inasmuch as] the earth and sea can stand free on all sides as a sphere in the air and fall nowhere, thus too can the entire world stand in nothing and fall nowhere.

This visible world stands in itself, and in accordance with its external aspect it stands in the depths, within the abyss of infinity [*abysso infinitudinis*], a depth that is in height without end and in breadth without end and in length without end and in depth without end. In such a void the world stands, for no one can in all eternity fathom, plumb, comprehend, or conceive the same [void]. Whether in height, depth, breadth, or width, no end to it shall ever be found. All physical things are enclosed and comprehended in this visible world; outside of the world there is no physical thing, thus neither is there any location or place. Locations and places are only internal to the world, in the way that the earth is a place of trees, animals, [and] human beings; [and] water is a place of fishes and nymphs. The heavens are a place of stars and air, [and] the air indeed encompasses all corporeal things, as Theophrastus [Paracelsus] asserts.[51] Thus, the earth is divided into Asia, Europe, Africa, and America; Europe in turn into Spain, Anglia, Gaul, Germany, and so forth; Germany in turn into other places such as forests, cities, castles, villages; and in turn the cities into streets, houses, and so forth. The houses into rooms, chambers, kitchens, cellars, and so on. Those are all places and locations and indicate a distance from one [place] to another. Thus each tree, animal, [and] human being has and requires its own place, location, or space. For all physical things must be here or there comprehensibly surrounded by the air; as the fish [is] by water, bodies cannot be without place. Now the world [itself] is the greatest of bodies, a great visible thing, and yet it is [enclosed] in no place, for the light of nature does not allow that a physical creature is without end; if the world is finite and comprehensible, it must be in no place, for if the world were enclosed by a physical thing, whether air (which, though, is impossible), then one would proceed to inquire upon what the latter stood, [or] who supported it; from this thing, in turn, one would proceed to ask what supported it; to infinity [*usque ad infinitum*], one would proceed to inquire, which cannot be: Hence the world stands in nothing. Similarly, the external circuit, breadth, or convexity of the heavens stands among all physical things in no place and comprehends all places and all physical creatures. In just this way God is enclosed by no term or place and comprehends all invisible things; outside of this God there is no spirit, or angel, or devil, neither world nor visible nor invisible being, just as little as there is a physical creation outside of the world. Just as the earth and the sea form a sphere and stand in the air and cannot depart from their place, so also do the heavens and the earth, and this is the entire machine [of the world]; the clay of the earth [*limus terrae*] from which Adam was made stands in nothing and falls nowhere. For just as the earth floats in the air and [yet] remains in its place, so also does the entire world float in nothing and falls nowhere, [and this] in a natural manner, not that it is standing on supports or that someone is holding it; rather, it stands naturally, of itself, this way. And, indeed, the Creator is to be praised for being able to place such a great edifice into nothing, so that it remains standing unmoved upon the depths. However, it does not fall down for the reason that it cannot fall above itself; for all creatures stand above themselves inasmuch as the world is round. Thus, on all sides of its rotundity it stands above itself. For, just as little as it is possible that the earth with the seas should rise above itself and cast itself into the heights, just as little and much less would the entire world rise up and throw itself upward. Instead, it would have to fall below itself; however, nothing is under it but rather everything above it. Look upon the globe wherever you will and you shall find that at all ends the convex rises over itself, just as at all ends the concave [sinks] below itself to the center. That is the reason why this great world does not fall, neither toward Evening nor Morning, neither toward Noon nor Midnight. Such parts of the world are proven and noted in all places only within the world.

ON THE PLACE OF THE WORLD

✦ • ✦

CHAPTER ELEVEN

That the earth hovers in the air and the entire world is in nothing, in itself, and cannot fall down

Though in the preceding chapter the chief reason has already been recounted as to why the world may not fall down into nothing, nonetheless it is hardly useless to say more about it, so that our inner eye will be instructed and confirmed in this truth from which many other things can be deduced.

For it is not in vain that we regard so intently the reasons why the world has no place and [yet] does not fall; nor do we do this for the sake of the world but rather for the teaching that flows from it, which is useful and necessary for [understanding] the Holy Scriptures; for from it can be seen what heaven and hell are, what sin, damnation, and salvation are, how heaven or the true fatherland is not to be sought here nor yonder but rather within us, [and] that the kingdom of Christ on earth is not bound to particular places, locations, persons, or gestures.

Inasmuch as the earth and the sea together form a sphere, people can dwell and voyage on all sides while having their heads upward toward the heavens. They see everywhere that the heavens stand at the same distance from the earth. For just as it is the case here in Meissen that the heavens are far above us over the earth, so it is at the Antipodes with those people who live precisely below Meissen with their feet toward us. One of the teachers of the church by the name of Augustine writes in the sixteenth book, chapter nine, of his *City of God*, that it is not possible for people to live both above and below [the earth]; for those who lived below it would fall down. In this he was following his carnal sensuous eye, namely, the imagination, which cannot behold such things. Had he left behind his imagination and followed the rational eye, reason would have spoken in him just as it does in me [to the effect that] falling in this place is the same as falling up, for all creatures stand

91

above themselves. Since Augustine did not understand such things about the Antipodes and the earth, about how it stands in the air and falls nowhere, how then should he have understood that the entire world stands in nothing and may fall down? On the contrary, as little as a ship can rise up and cast itself onto the firmament, even as little can the earth rise up with our Antipodes and cast itself toward the firmament. For to them it is not below but rather just as much upward as it is for us. Therefore, to fall downward is not different from falling upward, as the round sphere sufficiently demonstrates. The astronomers posit in the round sphere two points: The upper one at the top is called zenith, the vertical point [*punctum verticale*], and the opposite one is called nadir. Thus, if you stand at Leipzig, you have the zenith above you on the firmament, the point precisely above your head; and thus below Leipzig on the firmament is your nadir, and similarly at all points of the world. Just as little as I can rise up and cast myself to the zenith, just that little can those Antipodes who live below Leipzig rise up and cast themselves at their zenith, which for me in Leipzig is called nadir; for what is to me zenith, the same is to the Antipodes nadir; and what is to me nadir, the same is to my Antipodes zenith. For the same reason the earth and the sea can fall nowhere. Rather, it must stand at rest in itself, freely in the air, on all sides. What is said here about the earth and the Antipodes, about how on all sides of the earth they stand above themselves amid the heavens and do not fall, the same should be understood with respect to the entire round world: It floats in nothing, in itself, and does not fall. For it stands on all sides in accordance with its convex above itself, just as in accordance with its concave it looks below itself to the center. Similarly, when one considers the finite and the infinite, the limited and the limitless, it is clearly apparent that this world floats in nothing, in itself, and cannot fall down. For how should the finite, corporeal, destructible fall into the infinite, incorporeal, indestructible? For without there is nothing destructible, and even if it were to fall down (which is impossible), it would have to fall into the infinite and would fall without end and cessation, for the fall would find no bottom upon which the world would finally [come to] rest. Therefore, the world floats in itself, and in this it follows its invisible Craftsman, who likewise dwells in himself and is in need of no sustainer or external place outside himself; he is, so to speak, his own dwelling and place.

God is in no place but rather floats in himself. The angels are in no place and in need of no place but rather float in themselves, though not outside of God. Thus is the world in no place but rather is for itself the place, and floats upon the depth in itself. All creatures follow after their Creator and likewise desire to live within themselves with God or in God, just as the seat of fire is nowhere else but in fire, and the seat of water nowhere else but in water, and the dwelling and seat of the spirit nowhere else but in spirit. For outside of it, it is in need of no place. Thus, the seat of the entire world is nowhere else but in the world; that is, it floats in itself upon the depths and is a place to itself. It encloses all places and locations without any external place and location. That which is in no place but is rather a dwelling and place unto itself, the same can fall to no place, for that which is nowhere falls to nowhere. The world is nowhere, for outside of the world there is no place, neither under it nor above it. For this reason the world can fall neither down nor up, nor deviate to any side. Within the world is posited *Ubi*, that is, here or there, *terminus a quo et terminus ad quem*, from one end to another, from the earth to the heavens, from a mountain down into a valley, from Spain to Saxony. Moreover, Ascendant and Descendant is demonstrated, Noon and Midnight, to the right and to the left, behind and before, and so on. But outside the world, one has no *Ubi*, that is, no here or there, no Evening or Morning, no behind or in front. For this reason the world can fall neither toward Morning nor toward Evening, neither down nor up, but rather must remain still in itself. Now whoever would not be instructed and informed of this, but rather, through imagining, thinks and esteems that the earth with its Antipodes might fall down, or that the entire world might not stand upon the depths, that it would [instead] have to be enclosed within a place, [so] that it does not fall down—this person thinks and posits impossible, self-contradictory things. For, just imagine that the earth with the Antipodes would fall downward: [In that case] it would also fall upward, toward

Morning and Evening, and indeed toward Midnight and Noon, inasmuch as with its rotundity it faces [equally] to all sides, as if one who dwelt below the Arctic pole toward Midnight could say [from his vantage] that the earth does not fall down, then impossible things would follow: that a corpus such as the earth would at one and the same time fall toward Morning and Evening, toward Midnight and Noon, above itself and below itself, which cannot be the case. So it is too with the entire world that one could find places, Morning, Evening, to the right and to the left, that would fall simultaneously toward all places, as much to Ascendant as to Descendant, as much downward as upward, to the right as much as to the left, which is impossible; therefore, it must be the case that it hovers upon the depths in nothing and does not fall out of itself, much less hither or thither, inasmuch as no place is to be found outside. Thus, we see in the great world how all creatures have their seat and stool in themselves with God, and remain in the will of God. It is only the devil and the sinner who have deviated and seek their bliss from without in the creatures, thus tormenting themselves. For in the spirit in ourselves is heaven, Christ and the true fatherland in the will of God.

Oh, how wretched are the human beings who seek satisfaction and their good life in the world hither and yonder. They seek in vain and remain exiles even in a kingdom. If they would abandon this world with Christ and go into themselves, they would find God, the true fatherland within the spirit that needs no place or space, as does the mortal carcass in this world. The spirit resides in itself in God, and whoever goes within himself goes to God; whoever beholds himself in his spirit, beholds God and dwells in his fatherland in God and beholds in him the world and comprehends the world and all places with God. Finally, the world cannot fall on account of its smallness in comparison with the incomprehensible depths, for as great as the world is to our corporeal eyes, it is equally small in the eyes of the angels, as will be shown in the following chapters.

ON THE PLACE OF THE WORLD

✦ • ✦

CHAPTER TWELVE

That the physical things are great and incomprehensible to the outer eye, but small and comprehensible to the inner eye

In the spiritual invisible being greatness and smallness are the same thing, of *magni et parvi eadem est mensura et divinitas*, [of the great and the small measure and divinity are the same], and so forth. Hence, a spirit or angel is great and small, for it is not physical or visible, for there is nothing so small among physical things that the spirit is not even smaller, and there is nothing so broad and great among physical things that a spirit is not far greater,[52] and there is in its essence nevertheless neither greatness nor smallness, for example, a pin point is small indeed, yet an angel is smaller, for it can be in it; and, inasmuch as a spirit takes up neither place nor room, many others can be with it without obstructing the others. Thus the world is the greatest corpus, yet an angel is far greater, for it comprehends the world; no circumference is so great that a spirit could be enclosed by it. [The spirit] encompasses all places (although Lucifer must be locked, or, as scripture says, bound with chains to this world, which is his pain and torment of hell). From this we learn that for a spirit removal [*remotio*] and nearness of the places [*propinquitas locorum*] are one and the same; that is, near and far mean the same [and] are the same to it; as Mercurius[53] and Eckhart[54] testify that, to my soul, a thing two thousand miles across the sea is just as near as the body in which [the soul] dwells. This world is to the external eye too great and incomprehensible, but to the inner eye it is small and comprehensible. Whoever wants to study and measure these things with the external sensual eye and the five senses does not belong in my *Sophia Christiana* and remains altogether inept, for it is not written for cows and calves but for human beings. Whoever wants to comprehend such things only with his carnal eye behaves like a cow contemplating a new gate. But the human being should be much better than a child or an animal and should strive to seek out his inner eye, about which enough has been said in the first book.[55] With the same [eye] one sees that this great world is small. To the physical eye the earth and sea are great indeed, having a circumference of fifty-four hundred German miles; such cannot be taken in by any physical eye. Now, great as the earth is, yet compared to the firmament, it is a center or minute point, just as this entire world with earth and heavens, great as it is, is nonetheless similarly small, indeed nothing whatsoever, compared to the incomprehensible depths. A droplet of water compared to the great sea has a relation or comparison, for both are *finita*, that is, finite and comprehensible. But this entire world is not only small, it is like nothing at all compared to the depths. For how should one compare the finite with the infinite? Yet, by means of these and similar examples, one can make an approach and exercise oneself until at last is understood better all that one must know concerning the place the world. It is as if a mustard seed were to be suspended in the hollow center of a great wheel: Just so is it with the world as compared with the depths in which it stands, or like a drop of water against the sea; [just] so does the entire world stand in comparison with the incomprehensible nothingness, for, if I rise with the inner eye above myself into the expanse, the world seems small to me, and the higher I rise above myself [ascending] above the world, the smaller it becomes, indeed, until finally it becomes like a bean or mustard seed, indeed [like] nothing at all. But how dare we compare *finitum cum infinito* [the finite with the infinite], that is, the incomprehensible with the finite? There is, after all, no relation or comparison of the finite and the infinite. Thus, one discovers that the physical world has been made out of nothing and has been placed within a nothingness. A superb craftsman is God. He is in need neither of material from which to build, nor of a location into which to place his building. I praise you, God in eternity, that you reveal to me how the world has been made by you in your word out of nothing and placed into nothing, and [how] you allow it to hold sway within itself.

✦ • ✦

CHAPTER THIRTEEN

How this visible world has been created without material into a material, and how it will again return to nothing in the end

This great visible world, heavens and earth, the clay of the earth [*limus terrae*] with all corporeal creatures, has a material and yet was made without [any] material; it is of sulphur, salt, and mercury.[56] For God had no physical material to make it from, but rather it is made from nothing. It is indeed material [and] visible but not originating out of any material, but rather out of that which is invisible; namely, the earth has originated from and consists of the water beneath the heavens (2 Pet 3[:5–7]). This entire world and everything that one sees was with God and invisible in his word, incorporeal. And as it was with God, so too was it given in the creation to the angels when God spoke: "Let there be light [*fiat lux*]." So, too, all physical creatures were in each angel invisible, incorporeal, incomprehensible, and wholly one. Just as an entire tree, with roots, trunk, branches, leaves, twigs, [and] fruit, is concealed within the seed or nut, and the seed is the entire tree though in nutlike or seedlike fashion,[57] so also the entire world was in the angel in angelic fashion; the angel has within itself and with itself everything that is in the entire world. Now, before the creation of the creatures, all creatures were in God, invisible. Through his word he created the angels. In these the world too was invisible and wholly one single thing. But after the fall of Lucifer, God wanted to have the human being as well. Therefore, beforehand, he created the clump of earth, that is, this visible world with all [its] creatures, a world that is an excrement or expulsion from the invisible stars. These stars are essences of the angels distributed into the four elements, that is, into the matrices of all visible things. Now that which was eternal in God came into the angels through the word; what was there in the angels, this passed over into the invisible four elements and [the] stars; and what is in the stars, that comes under our eyes, visible, into this world. All corporeal things are an excrement or coagulated smoke, *fumus coagulatus,* of the invisible *astra* [stars]. This same smoke has three substances in it, the sulphur, the salt, and the mercury. Just so, a tree is coagulated smoke, set in these three substances. And so as well, the human being, in accordance with his body, is nothing other than such coagulated smoke, an expulsion from its internal sidereal corpus or *astrum,* and so on. Thus, all physical things come forth from the invisible, for each *astrum* would have its body. Thus, the physical things have been made out of nothing, just as this world itself has been made out of nothing; [it is] only an expulsion from the invisible elements and stars (for the elements are invisible and spiritual, as are their *astra,* but the *corpora* in which they dwell are visible); and just as [the world] is made out of nothing, so it will return to nothing, and do so in the following manner.

Just as a great forest, felled and ignited, would be incinerated to coals, and the same coals turn into pure ashes, and the ashes into a transparent glaze, and the glaze would be turned into a wind or thin air, and finally the air into nothing. So too, will this great world with all [its] creatures melt away, burn up, and pass away, for all physical things transpire again as they have come into being. Just so can it be stated how the world has been made out of nothing and how it stands in nothing and how it will again turn into nothing.

✦ • ✦

CHAPTER FOURTEEN

How it was before the creation of the world,
in the world, and after the destruction of the world,
and where at this time paradise or Christ is to be found,
and what heaven and hell are, and where our
fatherland is

Before the creation of this physical world there was no place but rather the abyss of infinitude [*Abyssus infinitudinis*], the eternal expanse, but now, while the world still stands, there are places and locations, space and place for retaining the physical things, and this only within the world, [for] outside of the world there is no place, as has been stated above. Hence, after the destruction of the world there will be no more place either, for when the world is gone, all places and locations will be gone as well, and things will be as they were before, when there was no physical world.

Now one might inquire: How was it before? I answer to this: Just as it is now. For that which is unalterable never changes. There being a world and creatures has neither given anything to nor taken anything away from God in his depths, just as the sun shone the same before living creatures were created as it has afterward. It always remained a sun in its light and its being. Nothing is given to it, though all eyes look upon it; nothing is taken away from it either, even though it gives sufficient light to all eyes. Thus, too, the depths of the divinity remain unalterable before the world, in the world, and after the world. And though you might think that it is not now as it was before, for the reason that the world now stands and hovers physically upon the depths, nevertheless you should know that your inner eye, sunk down too low, lies steeped in the visible corporeal things; if you were to raise it [the inner eye] up above yourself into the expanse, you would ascertain at once that things are now just as they were before the creation of the world. So I say that the world and all creatures have taken nothing from and given nothing to the eternal expanse; rather, it remains as it always was, as you can see from this example. If you were to suspend a tiny, hollow mustard seed into the center of a great [and] excellent wheel or sphere, what would you give to the wheel or what would you take away from it thereby? Nothing whatsoever. Though in so doing you might have given it a center that is visible and that had not appeared there beforehand, nevertheless, we must take into account that both the wheel and the center are finite things [res finitae] and are therefore comparable to one another. But the eternal expanse, which is infinite, cannot be compared with the world, which is nothing at all compared with the incomprehensible depths of God. You might compare a tiny droplet of water with the sea, inasmuch as both of them are finite, but the world cannot be compared with the depths, for it is nothing at all in comparison. Therefore, just as it was before the world, so shall it be again after the cessation of the world; it is already for the angels and in the eyes of God just as it was before. But [it is] not [so] for the devils, for they are still bound to the place of this world and must remain locked into it; nor is it thus for the godless, unbelieving human beings, for they persecute the pious in this world and can expect the eternal fire and torment; nor is it that way for the faithful, for they await in this time the salvation of their bodies from this prison. But that things are always already as stated above for the angels can be recognized from the fact that [the angels] are not subject to any temporal change and are not enclosed within the circumference of the world, as are the devils, but instead dwell freely in God, seeing through and passing through all things, and are detained by no corporeal things. The solidity of the earth does not stand in their way, nor deep sea, nor the rapid heavens, nor the dark night. They pass through all things without hindrance. But as for us human beings, we must be aware that after the destruction of the world nothing corporeal shall remain, neither earth, nor air, nor anything else; rather, there shall be an eternal expanse without an end, in which shall be the blessed and the damned, the angels and the devils. Just as might be [assembled] together in one place or hall the joyous and the mournful, those who dance and those who weep, the hungry and the satiated, the beautiful and the ugly, healthy and sick, blind and seeing, strong and weak, and so forth. So it shall be after the world has passed away: the blessed in God, the damned outside of God. Not that they will be found in some separate place external to God (for nothing can live or move without God); rather, they shall not dwell in the will of God, in the true paradise. But first of all, paradise is this visible world in which the human being stands [positioned] between time and eternity, for all creatures are beautiful, lovely, and good, and [they] are truly called paradise, as the *Theologia Germanica* testifies.[58] Moreover, each believer is a paradise of God, a dwelling and temple, as well as the heavenly Jerusalem. Just as, in turn, God is also a temple, dwelling, and paradise to the human being; that is the true fatherland and paradise for which we have been created, as well as [for which] we have been redeemed by Christ, and so on. Hence, paradise or Christ or the kingdom of God is not outside of us but rather within us; therefore, we do not need to seek heaven here or there. If we do not find, feel, and taste it within us, we will seek it in vain and find [heaven] nowhere. God comprehends all things, and all places are for him a single place, and he is with us at all times, indeed, in us. He is our paradise, our heaven and bliss, not outside of us but rather in us, therefore bound to no locale, place, ceremonies, gestures, or persons, as some people teach against God [that the kingdom of God] is linked to ceremonies; it is instead in us, in the inner ground of the soul. In spirit stands the kingdom of God, and not in the body. Moreover, just as heaven or Christ or the kingdom of God is in this world in no place outside us, so much the less after the destruction of the world, when all places have been annihilated along with the visible world, will it be in any place outside us, whether here or there.

Thus, it follows from this that we will not see God in that [other] life outside ourselves at some particular place; rather, in ourselves we shall see him face to face. Many people believe that heaven or hell is a physical, finite place, [or] that the blessed will be in a beautiful conclave, and, in contrast, the damned will be likewise in some enclosed location. Oh, indeed not! Neither heaven nor hell is a comprehensible physical place. Instead, both [are found] in an expanse without any physical or material finitude, but with such a chasm distinguishing [between the two of] them that the damned can never pass from hell into heaven. But as little as this chasm is physical [and] material between angels and devils, blessed and damned, just as little is heaven or hell a finite material place. Were wood, stone, steel, [and] iron like a thick mountain, nonetheless the spirits would not be imprisoned therein; the damned would pass through, as the sprites [*Schrötlein*], nymphs, and water people in our world can pass through a wall and make no hole. It is rather a different sort of chasm through which there can be no penetrating; it is the separating wall and the flaming sword that remains suspended before paradise against all those in eternity who do not unite themselves with Christ by faith. Everyone among the damned carries hell around with him, just as everyone among the holy carries heaven with him. Whosoever does not know himself does not know his fatherland, namely, heaven, paradise, the kingdom of God, Christ within. For our fatherland is not this world, not Europe, not Germany, not this or that principality, not Leipzig or Worms; neither is this or that house our home and habitation. For from it we may be hounded by a mortal man, a poisonous worm, or death. Hence no external place, not even our mortal body, is our true dwelling, but rather God within us, and we in God. Whoever lives in God and God in him is at home in his fatherland and cannot be driven out, no matter in what place in the world he be. Nor can he lose the word of God, even if there should be taken away from him Eucharist, baptism, the oral sermon, books, and all ceremonies; he has lost nothing, for Christ is within him, Christ is baptism, Eucharist, and the word itself. Whoever says in such an event that he has lost the word of God has never properly known and tasted of it. And whoever in such an event says that he has been driven out, as an exile in wretchedness, because he is driven from one place to another by a tyrant, does not know nor recognize his fatherland, heaven, Christ, [and] the kingdom of God. Therefore let us close with Boëthius, [who says] that no wise man can be driven into wretchedness.[59] However, a Christian is the wise man. Even should he lose and leave his child, wife, house, hearth, and farm, nonetheless he has lost nothing.

✦ • ✦

CHAPTER FIFTEEN

Where hell is now, and that this visible world is a hell of the devils that are compelled to live in the four elements

It has been shown in the preceding chapter that each damned human being will carry along with him hell and the devil after the destruction of the world, when there will no longer be any physical place. However, it might be properly asked where in the world at this time the hell of Lucifer is, [and] whether it is a physical place and location, as is believed by some. For many people are so naive that they believe hell is a place beneath the earth, inasmuch as at certain places fiery flames and hot water shoot out [as if] it all came from hellfire. Similarly, many have taught and written that heaven is an enclosed residence beneath the firmament, inasmuch as Christ ascended visibly into heaven. Such people teach as well the opinion that the world will not be destroyed, cease, or burn with fire but instead only be renewed and purified, so that all the stars, sun, moon, and earth shall remain. Oh, the great foolishness! For whom should the sun shine, for the blessed or for the damned? The blessed [who are] with the angels in heaven are in need of no external sun, [for] God will shine in them and be their sun. Moreover, for the damned it is no longer of any use, any more than it would be of use to the devil, who has just as little need of light from without. Furthermore, the damned are in no need of any fields, meadows, vineyards, or fruits that grow; for in [their] kingdom one does not eat, drink, or do anything of the kind. And so we return to our question: Where is hell now as the world stands [*stante mundo*]? For the simpleminded might wonder how this world could be the hell of Lucifer, when a spirit cannot be enclosed or comprehended within physical places. So you should be aware that in the time in which this visible physical world still stands, the devils are not free or on the loose but rather bound by chains to the darkness, as Peter has testified; that is [to say], Lucifer is enclosed with his own within this visible world, and thus some dwell in water, others in fire, some in the air, and [some in] earth, not in the visible, physical things but rather in the four elements, which are also spirits. For spirit must live in spirit. For that very reason, even if the devils live in the elements, in fire, water, air, and earth, it does not obtrude on the elements at all and does not harm them either. For a spirit has no place, and occupies no space. And thus this dark world is a hell to Lucifer. He is called a lord of this world and prince of darkness. He rules as well in the air below the firmament. But there could be no greater hell or torment and pain than that an angel should be expelled from the celestial light and thereby in addition remain enclosed in a shattered place. The heavenly light [of] paradise was changed for Lucifer by his fall and turning away into a dismal darkness; and what caused this was not God, but rather [that] he himself willfully cast himself into this darkness and prison. Therefore, when God created this visible, corporeal, destructible world, Lucifer was enclosed there in these four elements, to dwell there until the Final Judgment, after which he [will be] let loose and thrown into the darkness together with all the damned. Therefore, while this world still stands, before the final day, hell is a physical place to the devil indeed, [or] so to speak, even though a spirit can be neither detained nor enclosed, neither by steel nor by iron. Nevertheless, after the Final Judgment Satan will be let loose and not enclosed as now.

However, although the devils dwell in all four elements, it is nevertheless not to be believed that hell is located precisely below the earth, or in a mountain or hole from where fire often flashes out. For such things have natural causes. Nor should one believe that the warm baths grow hot in the earth from the infernal fire. [It is rather] the case that the waters that flow through the earth strike heated stone masses and are heated thus. Such a phenomenon does not come from hell but rather has natural causes, of which Paracelsus in his *Philosophical Writings* has treated rightly enough. The earth would be far too trifling and small for hell, even though it doesn't matter to the spirits whether a physical thing is narrow or wide, large or small. For they are in need of no physical seat, nor do they possess any place or take up any room. They pass through all things, as do the other damned ones.

But that Lucifer has to be bound within the four elements now for these six thousand years: this is an enormous hell for a spirit, and a greater torment than that he cannot experience. But he shall be set loose, notwithstanding that he will remain damned and will bear his hell and damnation within himself, as do the other damned; they shall be tormented with one another from eternity to eternity.

ON THE PLACE OF THE WORLD

✦ • ✦

CHAPTER SIXTEEN

That many different useful teachings
follow necessarily from the above-mentioned things

When one assiduously considers the preceding chapter on the place or term [*terminus*] of all beings, it will be discovered that splendid and useful teachings proceed from them, that, first of all, this physical world stands in no place, and much the less do angels and their creator God.

2. That the world, like the earth, can fall in no direction, neither downward nor upward.

3. That it is held by no supports, but instead naturally hovers and stands freely within itself, in the same way that God also moves, stands, lives, and hovers within himself.

4. That after the destruction of the world no place or corporeal, material thing shall remain, but rather a simple expanse, even as [it was] before the creation of the world; and in this expanse shall be heaven and hell, [the places] of the pious and of the wicked, yet [they will be] distinguished by a chasm that cannot be crossed in eternity.

5. That all places and locations are only one single place before the angels and God, inasmuch as one spirit encompasses all places.

6. That one may not approach or come to God by reason of place [*ratione loci*], that is, in accordance with place or location, but rather by reason of faith or affect [*ratione fidei seu affectus*], since God is near us at all times and everywhere present, even if we are not always present to him in the way that we might think, on account of the separation between God and us, or our turning away.

7. That to me and all human beings, God is just as near in this world as after the destruction of the world, in the life to come.

8. That one shall not see God in the eternal life at a particular place, whether here or there, but rather each shall view God within himself in heaven, and that our fatherland, the heavenly Jerusalem, is within us and not outside us. For just as in this physical world the kingdom of God is not in a particular place, much less shall it be possible

for God or the kingdom of God to be in a particular place after the destruction of the world, for with the destruction of the world, all place will be taken away [*nam sublato mundo tollitur omnis locus*].

9. That heaven, the kingdom of God, Christ, paradise are bound to no external ceremonies or persons or places, but rather alone stand in the spirit; therefore, the external only signifies, shows, and leads into the eternal ground.

10. That a true Christian cannot be robbed of the word of God by any human being or even by the devil, even if the sacraments and the office of oral preaching are taken away. But whoever in losing the external ceremonies says that he has lost God's word, and that Christianity has been undone, speaks against the foundation of truth and has neither had God's word ever nor has tasted Christ.

11. That heaven, both in this world and also in the future one, is not outside us, but rather always within us; [that] wherever a true Christian is, he cannot be chased into exile, even if he is driven from one physical place to the other, for he has his fatherland within.

12. That that person behaves very foolishly by striving in fear for kingdoms, cities, fields, houses, meadows, gardens, money, and the like. For the earth is only a point compared to the firmament; the entire world is nothing, and becomes nothing as against the eternal heaven; and everything that is outside us is not ours, does not make us saved. Indeed, the body itself is not our dwelling place, since it can be killed by human beings or [eaten by] worms; rather, our fatherland within encompasses all things.

13. That the heaven of the blessed and the hell of the damned are not physical, enclosed places. Rather, as each human being turns aside through sin and each turns back [toward God] through faith, in that same way shall he also feel and find his hell or heaven. Therefore, the godless carry hell within them, just as do the pious their heaven.

14. That the world in vain seeks wisdom, heaven, or Christ in external things, hither or yonder, but rather that all wisdom or perfect bliss must flow and spring from within outward, out of the heaven of God within us ourselves.

15. That all creatures, angels and devils, [and all the] saved and damned necessarily must stand, go, live, and hover in God, since he

is an encompassing of all creatures, of the visible and invisible [ones], and [that] this does not serve to save the damned. This will be explained in the next chapter.

16. That Christ's ascent into heaven did not occur in terms of place [*localiter*], nor his descent into hell; rather, he ascended into heaven to his Father, who fills all creatures and is bound to no place. And his descent into hell is his letting himself enter into our earthly flesh, into misery, fear, suffering, death, and [his having] by this work destroyed Satan's kingdom.

17. That in the spiritual [mode of] being, and after the removal of the world, the six parts or characteristics of places are not considered or shown: above, below, before, behind, right, left; however, where such things are stated in scripture as above and below, to the right, and so on, they are to be understood *ratione dignitat[i]s et excellentiae aut beatitudinis*, [that is], in accordance with the dignity [and excellence] and blessedness, not, however, in accordance with place, [not] so as to mean: God is above us; Christ sits at the right hand of God; the devils and the damned are under the feet of the blessed— not in terms of place or space [*non loci aut spacii ratione*].

✦ • ✦

CHAPTER SEVENTEEN

That nothing may be blessed or have calm unless it is at its certain and ordained place; and [concerning] that which is a definite place of the rational creature, in which it possesses calm and bliss[60]

It is always certain and true that no thing finds calm or bliss until it arrives at its certain and predestined place; and since the will of God or Christ is a place of all the blessed in which they find complete calm and bliss (John 10[:9]), so it follows that the damned will never again find calm or peace, since they cannot come to Christ and live in the will of God. Whoever is not in Noah's ark must go down and be ruined by the waters of the flood. Whoever is not in Christ must be damned. Christ is the will and the law of God: Whoever lives within it lives in no specific place. Should a creature be outside of its natural, specific, and ordained place, that is its sorrow, wretchedness, and ruination. As if the fish were to be on land and the birds in water; the deer in the air. They would not abide there for long. Thus too is the rational creature ordained to walk and live in its certain place: in Christ, that is, in the word and image of God, not in the creature, that is, not in itself. Now God is an all-capacitating tabernacle [*omnicapax tabernaculum*],[61] an all-encompassing Being, who encloses all creatures, the visible and invisible, [so] that outside of God not even a fly or gnat can stir or live without him. And since all creatures go and stand, live and hover in God, whether good or evil, angels or devils, it might be thought that the devils and damned in hell are just as blessed as the angels in heaven, for not even hell can be outside of God. Now hear the reply to that. Yes, it is true that no creature can be or live outside of God, as Paul himself has said (Acts 17[:28]; Gal 5[:25]): In him we live and are; and inasmuch as we live in the spirit, let us also conduct ourselves according to the spirit. But the fact that I stand, go, live, hover, and move in God does not make me saved, for this is natural and creatural; and all the devils and all the damned go stand, live, and hover with their hell in God, and there can be outside of God no hell or devil or any creature at all. But when I have been so far removed and saved from myself by faith, so that God stands, goes, lives, and hovers, rules, governs, and becomes all in me—from that I am blessed; for I live in *proprio loco*, in the ordained place, namely, in Christ, in the image of God, which is the immutable will of God. God is a being of all creatures and also encompasses with his being all creatures, but with the rational creature there is this determination, that it has a free will, as does God, to choose as it pleases, without any compulsion.

God's being is not distinguished from his immutable will (though God wants nothing for himself; only in the creature does he become volitional and [become] a will). Inasmuch as God's Being encompasses all and is the Being in all, so too, he wants to be the very will in the rational creature; [just] as the latter, namely, has its being from God and nothing from itself, so too, it should have its will from God, and nothing from itself. That is, it should not be presumptuous of the will, as if it were its own, but rather let [it] remain in its noble freedom. Then God will want all things in it; moreover, the very best. For it would have lived in its predestined place and been blessed. But the rational creature, such as Lucifer and Adam, lives in its own will. It indeed lives from God, but not in its predestined place, in the will of God. They do not behave in accordance with the spirit, though they lived in the spirit (Gal 6). For the rational creature is ordained, called, and chosen that it might live in the will of God, subjecting itself to the will of God, in abandonment [of self], hovering only under God, falling away from its own self, denying itself, which is the same as believing in Christ, and so on. But inasmuch as the creature lives in accordance with its own created will, it does not stand in its ordained place. Hence, it finds no rest, or satisfaction, or bliss, even though it is from God and has its being, life, and motion in God.

Nevertheless, it is only creatural and natural. But creature and nature do not bring salvation; it is not sufficient in itself. For this only comes from grace, rebirth, faith, or Christ, as he himself says of himself (John 10): I have come so that they have life and complete satisfaction. The will of God or Christ is the predestined and certain place of the blessed in this and the future life. Now Christ or grace do not want to act or rule where nature or creature act or rule. [For] wherever the created will acts, the will of God cannot take place there. For this reason the devil and all who are evil are not blessed, even though they stand, go, live, and hover in God. For that is an obligation to all creatures as a duty to their Creator. Otherwise, there would be no creature, and God would remain alone of himself and with himself. Rather, rebirth is what saves here as well as there, for in the reborn it is God who has his being, lives, shines, spirits, rules, and is everything in them. Just as the creature has its life and being from God, so also it has its will; but to presume its will and being as its own property causes sin, falling away, [and] transgression. For inasmuch as the creature presumes its will (which is not supposed to be its own, but rather surrendered unto

God), the creature acts against the will of God and does not dwell in its appointed place, but rather outside God, so to speak, [as] if this were possible. That is, it wants to live alongside God and sit next to God with Lucifer, instead of living under God in self-abandonment and obedience. And inasmuch as it lives in its own will, it finds no rest, peace, and bliss, no more than does a fish on dry land, or the like. Therefore, were there no self-will, there would be no hell, but rather the purest heaven. Heaven, however, is the will of God or Christ, for Christ is the true Noah's ark. In the same way that Noah and his people were sustained in God's ark [*in arca sua*] from the waters of the flood, so too will all those who are found in Christ remain safe from hell and eternal damnation. This Christ, however, [does not come] from without, but rather [is] the word or image of God in each and every believer.

✦ • ✦

CHAPTER EIGHTEEN

*That Lucifer has been chased and driven out of heaven
and Adam out of paradise without any change of place;
they remained where they were before, from which it
follows that sin is not substance but accident*

The scripture that is directed at our heart states that Lucifer has been thrust out of heaven and Adam chased out of paradise. This you should not understand as meaning from one place to another, as happens with physical beings, as when one chases a human being from one land into another, or from one group into another, and the like, but rather in accordance with the spirit, which is in need of no place and is [instead] cast from one state of blessedness into another. A shadow or image is not of itself; it is rather the shadow and image of another [being]; [it] cannot be or persevere without the one of whom it bears the image. Now, inasmuch as the creature is a shadow and image of the eternal self-sufficient infinite being (this is especially true of the rational creature), so too it must remain within that being and cannot live or be without him, that is, without God, whether [the creature] is evil or good, permanent or transient, obedient or disobedient. And though it can neither be nor live outside of God, it is nonetheless the case with the rational, free creature, angel or human being, that, without compulsion, without force, freely, it can direct [itself] to the right or to the left, to the knowledge of good and evil, and eat of it; that is, it lies freely in its own hands to remain in the middle, in the created image, and to retain the property of the image, to live within it, or to fall outside it; that is, to turn to the right or the left.

The eternal, inactive [*wircklose*], self-sufficient, infinite, true, uncreated, unborn Being or Good has given birth of itself, from its own Being, to another Being [in order] to reveal itself in it and through it and by means of it, and to call all things into being, whether visible or invisible. This born Being, inasmuch as it is not of itself, and not its own being, as is that which is not born, is properly called an Image, a Son, a Brightness or Radiance of the Divine Majesty, a Word, Arm, Will, or Law of God; for in it can be seen and contemplated that which is eternal and inborn face to face, as in an image and mirror, through [which] and by which God makes, effects, rules all things, as by his Arm, Hand, or Tool; through which he judges all creatures, and so on. Such an image of the inborn highest good is called the Firstborn before all creatures because God, through him, gave birth to all things as an image and likeness, especially the angel and the human being, the rational, free creature. Now it is resolved in eternity who shall not be found [to be] in conformity to this Firstborn and remain as one with him, that the same one [who is not in conformity] shall be thrust out of the heavenly paradise. This Firstborn is the Word of God, the Will and Law of God, the true image of the eternal and invisible God, in which the creature should live. That is, it should retain and keep the nature, kind, and property of an image, namely, it should not be of its own self. For it is not of itself. It should not love or seek itself, but rather him of whom it bears the image. It should not presume for itself everything that is pronounced and called good. It should not presume the will, but rather let it be free, [let] it hover under God, so that he shall will what he wants through it and with it. For what is free belongs to no one. The will has been created free. Therefore, the creature should not assume it as its own but rather leave it to God. But what does the angel do in heaven? It presumes the will and imagines it belongs to itself and not to God. It imagines its being, ability, knowing, and being able is its own and not God's. Because of this, it is cheated out of itself, freely; [it is] chased out of the heavenly paradise. That is, it falls out of the free image of God, out of the will and law of God, and should remain instead in Christ, in conformity, out of the Firstborn. Behold, that is sin and its fall from heaven into hell, from light into darkness, from truth into lies, from life into death, from blessedness into damnation, and so on. And all these things are not [to be] reckoned in accordance with place or being but in accordance with the will. For Lucifer remained at the very place where he was before, and remained in his being what he was before. God is a concept and place of all spirits, outside of which neither devil nor angel can be or live. Everything must have being and life from the One; otherwise, it would be nothing at all. From this it follows that Lucifer after his fall into sin likewise remained in God and has retained his being and life as before, but with this difference: In accordance with the will he has become untrue and disobedient, [he] has abandoned the property of the image. Hence, sin is not a substance or being but an accident, [having occurred] through presumption of the will that should have remained free. For, should sin be a being, Lucifer would have become nothing, and something would have been lost to the one Inborn Being, which is impossible. In terms of being, the devil remains good. But in terms of the will, he is ruined and spoiled. This circumstance or accident is the sin, which causes no change in the untouchable God. It is only to the disobedient creature that it is a terror, torment, pain, and damnation, as is proper that evil should punish itself. Thus Lucifer has not been thrust from one place to another, even though he remains locked into this visible, physical world, as his place, until the Final Judgment. Rather, he has remained where he was before and has not altered the world of place, anymore than his being has changed. Rather, where this world stands now is where Lucifer was with the other angels in heaven, and his heaven was changed for him into such a dark world. It is indeed true that before this world was created, Lucifer was not bound to the place of the world and yet was in his hell, for he carried his hell within him. And when after the Final Day this world together with place is removed, he will nonetheless remain damned in hell. For it is not a matter of place. Place neither saves nor damns. It is only a matter of the presumption of the will, through which the image is lost. Understand that it is the same way with Adam, who after being driven out of paradise remained in the same place where he was before. For this great world was his paradise, viewed externally; in the same way that his inner and heavenly paradise was the image of God in him. He lived in the spirit and not in the flesh. But after presuming the will, he lost the image, fell out of the spirit into the flesh, from God into creature. He also retained [his] being, but not in accordance with the will. Therefore, sin is not a substance but a circumstance or accident. And inasmuch as the angel or human being is changed only in will or accident after the fall, but not in being (for it remains the same angel or Adam), it follows that all inner gifts of God are still present in each. But the turning away from the light to the darkness, from God to creature, causes one's own blindness and ignorance of one's self and God, [which is] meant and intended [with the statement that] all is lost through sin, which is nonetheless not the case. For simply turn back inward through Christ, into the inner ground by dying unto yourself, and so on, and you will have to confess that the kingdom of God is within you and all things in Christ, about which it is proper to say no more. Let everyone experience it within himself.

VALENTIN WEIGEL

✦ • ✦

CHAPTER NINETEEN

That all the wishing, sighing, and pursuing by the creature occurs for the sake of calm, in order to possess it, and that it cannot be overtaken externally, but rather must be overtaken at ease and awaited within, through Christ

God is the eternal rest, blessedness, and the end of all creatures. He is inactive [*wircklos*] and a pleasant sweet repose [*Stillstand*], who makes all those [be] calm and quiet who do not presume the will, that is, who remain in the image of Christ. The same [ones] walk in the will of God, as God has become all; therein is blessedness, calm, peace, and complete sufficiency. Thus it happens that as soon as the rational creature is robbed of such calm by the presumption of its own will, it becomes restless and fearful of itself; [the creature] runs and races after calm, seeks it hither and yonder, in this and that place outside itself, as all those who have turned away prove. But the faithful do not run out; rather, they await peace within themselves through Christ. We see in this time in the unfaithful what a fearful running and scurrying there is, what care, trouble, and labor are undertaken to achieve and carry out this and that, to turn hither and yonder bodily, all of which happens for the sake of calm or in order to possess satisfaction. Is it not so that when you are in a place where you experience aversion, difficulty, and unease, you covet another place in order to flee from all of that, or better, in order to possess calm or happiness, as, for example, from one house into another, from one city into another, from one village into another, from one office to another, from one land to another, and so on? And you do this, as I said, because from your natural inborn constitution you pine for the proper place or fatherland, for calm and blessedness, [for a place] in which you can be joyful without restlessness, unease, and disquiet. And you expect to find this here or there, externally, among creatures. This is why

114

you do not know your true fatherland, your home, the kingdom of God within you, the calm and joy in God, within yourself.

Our home or fatherland is not outside of us but rather inside within the spirit. Hence we are not at home in Spain or Germany or in Leipzig, or in this or that house, and so forth. For whence another mortal can chase and drive me out is not really my home. It must be such a place or home from which neither man nor animal nor worm can chase or expel me in eternity. But from such a place that is outside you and not found or possessed within you, you can be expelled and driven, whether a castle, village, city, principality, or kingdom—as daily experience teaches. A powerful lord can expel you by war; a wretched human being may strangle you [though you are] a powerful potentate. Hence, all places outside of you are not your abiding stead nor home nor fatherland wherein you possess calm. Indeed, your body is closer to you than all places. Nonetheless, if you know nothing but your body, which is a hut or mortal dwelling of the inner human being, then you are still an alien and not at home in calm, as Paul testifies when he says (2 Cor 5[:4–7]): While we dwell in the body, we wander as pilgrims to the Lord; for we walk in faith and not in seeing. While we are in our hut, we walk and are strangers of the Lord and long for our lodging, and so on. From that it is to be concluded that heaven, home, fatherland, calm, and blessedness are not to be sought hither or yonder outside of us. But rather in ourselves Christ must be awaited and gained at ease, so that no one else can chase or push us from our fatherland, since it is not outside us and stands in the spirit and not in the body or physical dwelling. Anyone who wants to get there and possess calm must leave all places and physical things, [must] cling to nothing and even deny and hate his own life, [must] die altogether with Christ and await God within himself. Then he will hear what God himself says about this home and fatherland, about calm and bliss in a sweet condition. Furthermore, though after the destruction of the world the damned spirits will have need of no external place; nonetheless, they will not be at home in calm. The reason is that they seek incessantly in great fearfulness for calm, the eternal good, which nonetheless cannot be found or possessed outside of them. For it is incomprehensible and intangible to all creatures. But if it were possible for the damned to stop all their sighing, running, moving, to depart from their will and desire, to hate and deny themselves, and to die entirely with Christ, then they might recognize the inner fatherland of heaven and enter it. But it is hard to abandon and hate oneself. All desire and movement must cease in order to taste that which is immobile and within. Heaven or calm is not overtaken but earned at ease and awaited within in Christ. This the godless, restless, damned cannot do. Hence, they carry damnation and hell within them, as will be explained in what follows.

✦   •   ✦

CHAPTER TWENTY

That the eternal hell for the damned is their own love of themselves and their hatred of the highest good, which they desire without end but in vain

The human being cannot resist love; it is inborn that [the human being] must love when he encounters the beloved and he experiences well being, and when he is deprived of the same, he experiences pain and suffering. No more than he can cast aside the immortality of the soul can he cast aside the natural love of the good. Boëthius says that everything desires its origin and does not achieve repose until it has possessed its assigned goal and ordained end. This is especially to be understood as true of the rational creature, which hastens to the highest good. But that is the highest good that one has and can no longer covet [anything]; and this is nothing other than the good that is the highest of all goods, which comprehends all other goods within it: the blessedness that is God himself. Now though all creatures love the highest good, even the evil ones, nonetheless, the disorder of love causes in the evil creatures only pain and torment and not peace. For they intend and seek themselves through self love and not the pure God. Hence, this perverted love is that of the spiritual chill or fever that torments human beings above all other ills, into the inner hell above all hells. And believe me that there is no greater sorrow of the heart than that one should hate that which is dearest of all, that which is best of all, the infinite good that is God, and that cannot be hated. For the good is the object of love; [if it is] love, and God alone is the proper, true, infinite good, then [this] is the sole good for the rational creature, who has been created to be receptive of it. Hence, to want to despise the same good is against the nature [of the rational creature]. Hence, it cannot be without pain if one hates it. Rather, it is a spiritual fever, which one calls the chill or cold. In this fever the heat and the cold are disordered in the human being, and both torment him. So, too, the love of God torments the human being even in hatred, and it torments him all the more, the more he hates the one who is more lovable. Do not be astonished that I write that the creature both loves and hates, and so on. For if you know Christ, the wisdom, then you understand his statement that all creatures seek and love themselves, by which they think they approach the eternal good, [but they are] cheated by themselves. For whoever loves himself must hate God, and whoever would love God must hate himself. Whoever is able to deny, lose, and hate himself is found and loved by God and is blessed. But the evil ones do not want to hate themselves. Hence, they hate God and love themselves. And if one does not hate God because he is good, but because he is just and a stern judge who punishes evil and torments wickedness, though all is good within himself, and the wicked hate this too because they recognize that it is good; then their own hatred torments them. For they must see in the little spark of their mind that their hatred is evil. For the little spark of the light of truth and of natural love of the good has not been extinguished in them, so that they recognize that they do wrong (Wis 5). And insofar as they know that they do wrong by hating the justice of God and [by hating] the one who is the very best, and [in so doing, they] blaspheme him that no one can praise enough. Their blasphemy and hatred cannot trouble him; rather, they will be tormented all the more by it. For the more impatient and impetuous they are in their torments, the more their

117

pains harm them. And all of that serves to the honor of God and his justice. And their torment and blasphemy is his great honor. For it pains them so bitterly that (were it possible) they would shatter and break from wickedness, and they would like to be not at all (for in regard to their being they remain good and cannot become nothing, but on account of the will, they are evil and spoiled), so that they would not have to suffer. And yet they must be, so that they can be tormented to honor him whom they have reviled and whom they hate so much that they would like to go against nature, so that he would not [have] the nature of the [very] being from whom all being is. This is the inner hell, this is the hell of all hells: to be thus eternally deprived of the infinite good on account of one's own wickedness, and to nonetheless love it because it is the end of the rational creature, which it nonetheless cannot have. For it has brought it about and must bear his power and punishment, whom it has hated for being just, and must rage against him whom none can resist. Having angered him because grace and favor is life, indeed life itself. He is higher than the heavens and deeper than the abyss and broader than the earth. Who would do anything to him or take something from him? Who, with his wickedness, would touch the Untouchable? And who would move the Unaffected with his blasphemy? Even the damned will be pained by their self-love and tormented in eternity by their hatred of the eternal good.

✦ • ✦

CHAPTER TWENTY-ONE

How three hellish furies torment the damned and give them no rest on account of their hatred of God and their love of themselves

You should not be amazed that love and hatred is instilled in the damned, for if there were no love in them, neither would there be any hatred in them. That is, if they were not self-seeking and self-loving, but rather were to abandon self and let themselves go, there would be in them no hatred of God. Instead, God would become the love within them, and from it they would be blessed. But indeed they seek and love themselves by desiring to be freed from the hellish pain, torment, and suffering; the more they desire this, the greater their torment becomes. From this self-love arises also their hatred of God's justice, which, notwithstanding, is good and from God himself. This is why it is said that if there were no love in the damned, neither would there be any hatred, for we hate nothing but that which is against what we love. You may say: If that were true, God would have to be against himself, for you say that one only hates that which is against what one loves. If one then hates God, and loves him, and [if] that which is hated is against that which is loved, then wouldn't God have to hate himself? The answer: It doesn't follow that God should be against himself for the reason that he is hated and loved; it should instead be concluded from the above that those who hate him and those who love him are against one another. But if love and hatred subsist together within one single person toward God, then that person is against himself, and for that reason peace and repose can never be together in a damned person, for he conducts and suffers a perpetual controversy against himself. God, the highest Good, remains always as he is, immutable; whether you love or hate, curse or pray to him, you will neither trouble nor please him, neither give to nor take from him; he sits too high up for you. Hence, all change occurs only in the creature and not in the immutable God; therefore, within the perverted and damned human being love and hatred are against one another. For whoever turns away from one and toward himself, which happens through presumption of the will, so that he does not remain of one will with God, that person becomes split and divided within himself and carries on a perpetual struggle with himself. Thus the good and evil becomes internal within him. For reason and the spark [of conscience] say that one should love justice and truth in God. But the evil, which doesn't want to be punished, disposes and drives the human being as long as he is on earth [toward] the other side. Thus, a struggle comes about in the evil human beings, [a struggle] of the evil inclination against the conscience, and neither gives in. And thus there is a constant ongoing unease within him and therefore a constant torment. For what God has planted into nature no one can root out: the spark and worm of conscience [*vermis conscientiae*]. For inasmuch as the evil people willingly choose evil, and subject themselves to it, [evil] is left to them for their pain, so that they will be tormented by it. Thus, the evil does not subside but rather incites those who possess it against God and his justice and moves them to hatred and anger against this same strict justice. Therefore, neither does the spark of the divine light subside, so that it contradicts the evil. Thus there is no calm or peace for the damned. The ancient poets wrote poetically that Acheron [the river in Hades] and Night [*Nox*] gave birth to three daughters in hell, the first called Tisiphone, the second Megaera, the third Allecto; [they] are the three Furies in hell who eat at the damned [and] torment and punish them ceaselessly in darkness and sadness. In these hellish Furies [the poets] were describing the inner hell, the bad conscience of the damned. *Acheron* means in effect "without joy." [*Acheron*] gives birth by the sad dark night to three dogs of hell, three daughters. *Tisiphone*, [consisting of] *à tíno* and *Phoneo*, has as its name "revenge" and "punishment" by the ruin of death. From these Greek roots arises the word *tisiphone*, meaning the ruinous deadly vengeance and punishment. *Megaera* comes from the Greek word *megairdon*, "hating, punishing, eating at," so that the damned in the dark, sad hell are bitten and eaten at by the love and hatred within themselves. *Alecto* comes from the Greek too: *leio*: "to cease, rest, remain still"; and in front is placed the letter *a*, *privandi particula*, thus *alekto*, [means] as much as "ceaseless," "restless." Accordingly, this hellish punishing, eating, hating, and biting within the conscience goes on without end. And these three dogs of hell are not outside the damned but rather inside, within the conscience of each, which no one can escape. This is because of love of self and hatred of God. In the damned, there is not a love from friendship but rather a covetousness. Nor is it a love from grace but rather from nature. Nor is it a voluntary love; it is rather from inborn curiosity. Nor is it a love for virtue but rather a love that is suffering.

Nor is it a love with joy but rather with sadness. This is caused by the self-will that burns in hell. That is the proper way to put it. For only God is being, and the being of all beings, and neither this thing nor that thing. Otherwise he would not be all and above all. Nor is he either today or tomorrow. Otherwise he would not be eternal.

But that which is this thing or that thing, or today or tomorrow, is not true being, but [instead] nothing in itself; thus the disobedient creature that covets this or that, today or tomorrow, this [creature] is nothing and remains abandoned to itself. This nothingness burns in hell, that is, the self-will of the creature that covets this or that, [which] wishes to be saved today or tomorrow, that is, by loving and seeking itself. Yet precisely in so doing it only increases its torment. Therefore, whoever would escape the hellish flames must be as nothing, that is to say, must lose, deny, and hate himself, as Christ has instructed us sufficiently.

✦ • ✦

CHAPTER TWENTY-TWO

*That in that other world there will be no
natural, elemental body that occupies a space
or expanse and that looks this way or that way with
physical eyes, but rather a supernatural celestial body
incarnated from the Holy Spirit, which is in need of no
external place*

When this world along with time will have been superseded after the Final Day, all natural and physical things will cease as well, and there will be no more place that detains us from without, but rather an eternal expanse in which there is neither stars, nor sun, nor moon. Neither water nor air nor any element will then be present. In this expanse we will hover in God, not with a natural, comprehensible, elemental body, but rather with a supernatural, new, celestial, clarified body, which is no longer in need of any external

place or element. But what else is a new supernatural body but a*
spiritualized and deified one that has grown from the new birth,
from the flesh of Christ, and not from Adam. For the flesh of Adam,
that is, the natural human being, will not possess the kingdom of
heaven; [for this, there] must be a celestial and supernatural flesh
from the new birth. If we are supposed to have coarse, material, tangible bone and a natural flesh, with external eyes, ears, noses,
tongues, and with the members needed for natural life, such as the
heart, lungs, stomach, and so forth, then it would not be a new,
supernatural body, but rather it would still be under [the sway of]
nature and in nature. Hence, it would have need of air in order to
take breath, and of the sun to see externally with its eyes hither and
yonder, [and] of ears to hear [sounds] from without, [and of] the
physical tongue to speak to another. In that case heaven would not
be spiritual but rather natural and physical. God would be seen here
or there, externally with our outer eyes, by the medium of light, and
so on. Then God would also be physical as we are (for thus states
scripture: We will be like him, and we will see him face to face
[1 Cor 13:12], and so forth). But no! The kingdom of God does not
stand here or there in the spirit; God is and remains a spirit in eternity. For this reason we must have a new, celestial, spiritual, supernatural body that is clarified, spiritualized, and deified, so that it will
be in no need of any natural, external help, neither light, nor air,
and so that we will not see God externally, with physical eyes, in a
particular place, but rather in ourselves, face to face. What is of
nature is earthly, bestial, and temporal, and must cease along with
nature: the beast does not enter heaven, but rather the human
being. The body from Adam is not the [whole] human being; he is
made of the clay of the earth [*limus terrae*], mortal, perishable. The
inner human being from the mouth of God is the human being.

---

* Without interrupting the sentence, a commentary, presumably carried over from
the lost manuscript source into the printed work of 1613 on which this translation
is based, inserts the following indented remark after the line ending with "a": "Just
as Christ is God and human being in heaven without deification of his humanity, so
also do the believers retain their humanity without any mingling with the spirit, in
contrast to the angels."

The latter must be incarnated by the Holy Spirit through the new birth [and] bring a new flesh to heaven, so that we have altogether a supernatural, celestial, clarified body, which is not in need of any external help, but rather dwells in itself, as does God. For were our bodies to have in heaven coarse, material, Adamite bones and members, made of the clay of the earth [*limus terrae*], this would go against faith and scripture, which always directs us in time toward the spirit, toward our true fatherland in the inner ground, to God. Though the inexperienced ones, and especially the creatures of flesh, want to understand Holy Scripture only physically, just as Job says, I shall see God in my flesh and [just as the article of faith states], I believe in a* resurrection of the flesh. In these statements they can only think that they are going to be resurrected with their natural, coarse, Adamite bodies and have such external, natural members as to be able to sit and do other things in some place.

However, the word of scripture does not apply to the flesh from Adam but rather to the flesh from Christ the Redeemer by the new birth.† For this reason Job does not speak of God the Creator, who created the flesh of Adam from the *limus terrae*; rather, he speaks of God the Redeemer, of the Son, through whom we are reborn in faith [and] receive a new flesh in which we will behold God; in such flesh we must be clothed from the new birth. Otherwise, we will not be able to enter the kingdom of heaven. There is a great difference between the flesh of Adam and the flesh of Christ, between the old birth and the new birth; for the flesh from the clay

---

* Without interrupting the sentence, a printed insert carries over an indented comment into the 1613 version, as follows: "The flesh of Adam is awakened to the Final Judgment in the good and evil [human beings]: All of us must come before Judgment in our mortal, Adamite flesh, with our good rational faculty and senses, but after the completion of Judgment, this Adamite body falls away, and only the new celestial body proceeds with Christ into his kingdom. Nor in the damned does the Adamite body remain; it falls away, passes away with the elements, and [the damned] are thrown with their eternal bodies into the fiery pit."

† As above, a printed insert reads: "As for the arising, that is, the awakening to Judgment, Job is speaking of the Adamite body, but as for the resurrection, it is only the new body that enters heaven and not the old one."

of the earth [*limus terrae*] is not meant by Job, but rather the flesh from the new birth. It would be unbecoming that the kingdom of God in that other world should be seen and discerned with external eyes and ears in this place or that, although it must now be seen and known [only] in the spirit. For if we had external, comprehensible members, then our bodies would lack for the air through our lungs and the respiration, for the external light through our eyes, the voice and the speech through the air and our ears, and there would [then] be set limits in that world, the limit from which and the limit to which [*terminus à quo, terminus ad quem*], from here to there, [all of] which is nonetheless entirely against the sense of the spiritual and celestial Kingdom. All natural means and sustenance must be discarded, such as eating, sleeping, traveling from one place to another, [and] speaking with a physical voice to another. For take as an example the speech by means of our tongues. My dear fellow, what would you say to some acquaintance or friend? What would you ask in that other world, when it is not time but rather eternity that prevails? Whatever you would say to that other, he would know it as well as you. From God, in himself. For God would tell him everything as he would you.* Hence you would be in no need of instruction from anyone either. For God is your instructor in you, from within, and not from without. Should you want to ask something or other, as is the case on earth, the entire world with its time would be gone. Should you want to hear something about the future from someone else, there would be eternity there, which has nothing future in it, and in the same you have everything present.

---

* Without interrupting the sentence, the following commentary is inserted in an indented space: "Theophrastus [Paracelsus states] in [his work] *Sagaci:* There is a difference between rising up and being resurrected. Rising up: that is, we will all be awakened. For the mortal body must again come to the soul before the Judgment, without any flaw, entirely strong, with its senses in order, and so on. Resurrection: that only applies to the believers who go with Christ into the kingdom of God and abandon the Adamite body."

The insertion is an imprecise paraphrase or interpretation of certain discussions found in Paracelsus's *Astronomia Magna oder die ganze Philosophia sagax der großen und kleinen Welt*, in Karl Sudhoff, ed., *Medizinische, naturwissenschaftliche und philosophische Schriften* (Munich: Oldenbourg, 1926), 12:322–23.

We see the same thing in this world with the prophets: they do not need to learn or hear by means of the external physical tongue; rather in God himself, within themselves, they hear. Behold what God speaks and says. From this example, take note that our bodies do not hear or receive in that other life by means of the five coarse external senses, rather from within it will see, hear, and grasp God, and the like, face to face; and will hover within itself and dwell in God, being spiritualized and deified. For everything that is natural and bestial [and] sensuous can no longer exist. Otherwise this would be a failing and wanting, and a long while.

✦ • ✦

CHAPTER TWENTY-THREE

That in that other life there will no longer be a knowledge of languages, arts, and faculties; otherwise there would be no perfection in the eternal kingdom

In 1 Corinthians 13[:8–9], the Apostle says of the future world that in it there will be no more prophesies and tongues and no more of [our human] knowledge. Just as there will be no natural, external body present in that world, but rather a supernatural, celestial, new body, which has its dwelling within itself without any external sustenance, in the same way there will no longer be any practice of prophesying, the arts, languages, and faculties, that is. One will need neither preachers nor prophets, who have been sent in this time only on account of the external witness. Nor will one have any need of language teachers or translators, who were invented and practiced on account of the external human being. For if we had remained inner human beings in paradise, there would not have been languages either. Nor will one need grammar, dialectic, astronomy, arithmetic, medicine, [or] jurisprudence, for such things are intended for the temporal, mortal human being. Knowledge of all natural things will also cease, for nature will be superseded along with the world. Before Adam fell into sin, [but instead] walked in paradise in God, he had no need of languages, arts, or faculties, nor did he inquire about the knowledge of nature [or] about astronomy. For he lived in the manner of an angel and was in need of no piece-work, just as the angels in heaven are not in need of languages, arts, and the like. And had we remained in paradise, the natural arts, languages, and the like would not have been necessary. No doubt all would have been concealed within us but not needed for use. But after the human being fell into sin, out of the spirit into the flesh, from God unto creature, he was subjected to the stars and to nature and forced to discover and practice natural arts, languages, crafts, and the like. From the bite of the apple of the forbidden tree come the languages, and they lie in the stars of the firmament [and] lie concealed too in the human being. For [the human being] is made of the great world, of the clump of earth. Hence, all must lie within him. But when the heavens with the stars with the entire world disappear, and our natural Adamic body ceases to be, along with the world, there will be no more languages either, nor arts, nor faculties, for they serve only the natural and transient, not the eternal. Though the children of the world seek their paradise in the transient arts [and] in so doing forget Christ, the truth, they nonetheless pretend that the arts are an aid to theology, without which one cannot arrive at truth. I say: They are for many a hindrance for Christian Wisdom [*ad Sophiam Christianam*], inasmuch as [such people] remain in the arts and languages and do not go beyond them.

Christ, the celestial wisdom, is not learned by means of arts or languages; rather, from the Father must he be heard, as [it is] with children. Otherwise, the worldly wise Greeks and Pharasaical Jews would be the best Christians. But one finds the contrary of this at all times: The arrogant world-taught ones do not even want to know Christ [and] are angered by him [and] call him a devil, seducer, sacramentarian, and enthusiast. Open your eyes, you theologians! Look around you, how you know Christ. It is not enough to present his history to the people from without by rhetorical discipline and to be able to dispute about it by means of dialectic. No, these arts and languages do not do it. There has to be a new human being in whom Christ himself is the theologian and preacher. The languages and arts should be indeed for hastening further out of nature and into grace, out of Adam and to Christ, but the greatest crowd of the theologians remains sitting with its languages and arts in Adam, abandon[ing] *Sophia Christiana* completely. And if someone comes taught by God himself and lays out Christ purely, [that one] must be their devil and enthusiast. Woe to you, Pharisees, you will not eat life, that is, Christ, from the poisonous tree, but instead death. You do not want to follow Christ. And those that do want to follow him in simplicity, they are made out to be devils and heretics by you. You don't want to enter heaven and want to prevent others from entering there. Now there will be no more arts and languages in heaven, for in this world they have served their sole purpose. Nor will there be any more faculties, for the jurists will not be allowed to represent causes. God will represent the cause of the just. Nor will there be any need of physician or theologian either. One will not need to explicate scripture. No single letter of the scriptures will remain. Each will understand within himself, instructed by God, how he has behaved in faith here. One will not need to heal the sick. Though in this life it is necessary, in heaven there will be no more sick. One will not need to make the blind see, for we will have no failing, elemental eyes. One will not need to make the deaf hear; for there we will need no physical, external hearing. One will not need to drive out devils. There are no devils in heaven. One will not need to explicate the three chapters of Genesis in which the entire scripture stands composed in brief, of creation, fall, and redemption, and so on. But in this life it is necessary to know, and for this temporal life God has let it be written. Now, the worldly scholars will say: It is not to be undertaken. It is too high. We must reserve it for the eternal academy [*ad academiam aeternam*]. Oh, you wretched theologians! Who is to explicate scripture for you there? It will no longer exist. Have you learned nothing here? One won't keep you there as special professors. One will not preach there. God alone will be from within the preacher, teacher, and professor to us all, for the high and the humble, the learned and the simple. For we must all be taught by God. And what the anointment [of the spirit] teaches us is correct. This does not apply to the eternal but rather to the temporal life; in this life I must be taught by God, and what I learn here will be useful to me there. But if I am to reserve it, as you say, for that other world, I would act against Christ, [just] as you do. For I would make out of Christ a liar, as if he were speaking incorrectly [in] (John 6[:65]), [that] we must be taught by God and must hear it from the Father, and so on. Should such statements, in your opinion, apply only to the future life, and should you only hear it and know Christ? If so, then all who are godless and damned will likewise hear from the Father in that other life and be saved. No indeed! Whoever does not know Christ here through the spirit of the Father will receive nothing there. Therefore, learn from the Father in this world what *Sophia Christiana* is. Then you will be freed from many errors, and you will properly lay out and understand this matter concerning resurrection.

✦ • ✦

CHAPTER TWENTY-FOUR

That in the kingdom of heaven there will be neither emperor nor pope, neither king nor bishop, neither prince nor preacher, but rather only one Lord of all lords over all, namely, God

In this transient world one has regents of the worldly and spiritual estates, that is, emperors, kings, princes, lords, judges, officials, popes, bishops, teachers, preachers, and so on. And of necessity one must have government, and one should hold the same in honor and obey it in accordance with the Apostle's command: Let everyone submit to the governance that has power over him; for there is no rule that is not from God; but rather, where there is government, it is ordained by God. Whoever opposes the governing power defies the divine order. It has been placed there to instill fear in and punishment upon those who are evil, and for the protection of the pious [Rom 13:1–4]. Now in this life, governing authority exists, and one has to accept it according to its order, estate, dignity, and nature. But in that other life, there will no longer be a governing authority. All worldly rule, governance, and power will cease. Had we remained in innocence in paradise, there would have been no need of regents, spiritual and secular. For no one would have risen above anyone else. We would have all remained one in Jesus Christ. No one would have been above or below, first or last. We would have all remained subject to the one God without external commandment, order, statutes, and governing regime. Everything would have remained in common; no one would have possessed anything of his own, whether countries, people, fields, meadows, houses, or the like. But after falling into sin, when each chose his own property and became an external worldly human being, and evil on earth grew more and more, then there had to be regents on earth, and there also arose a multifarious order and distinction among peoples, countries, and villages, and the like. The people of God, the Israelites, were governed by patriarchs, prophets, priests, judges, kings, and so on. And likewise for other peoples, by their regents and governments. As long as this world lasts, there will likewise be spiritual and secular governments. But after the elimination of the world, all order, principalities, governments, authority, and power shall also be eliminated. For in heaven there shall be no need of these. Things will be as they were before. Then we will all be one in Christ Jesus. Then there shall be neither Jew nor Greek, neither slave nor free, neither woman nor man, neither Persian nor Scythian, and so on [Gal 3:28], but instead all one in the Lord. There, goods will no longer be owned as they are now. One will no longer forbid [the use of] or capture animals; nor will one enclose [and limit access to] birds or fish against the rights of nature, as they do now when they declare waters with their fish to be property, or the birds. Even though the human being should rule over fish, fowl, [and] beast [in common], and no one should have them as property, but rather all the blessed will have a common good, so that there will no longer be any need of governmental rule. In particular, authority or government, both spiritual and secular, arose and was instituted after the fall, on account of the external human being, who then began to live in evil and according to his own will. For it is precisely for this reason that there are priests, teachers, and prophets—so that the outer human being will be instructed, initiated, and led to the inner [human being] from whom he has fallen. That is the point of all of scripture, of the law and ceremonies; namely, that the outer human being may be bound, tamed, and brought to faith, that is, to Christ, the inner human being. However, inasmuch as, in the eternal world, the outer human being will no longer be (for he will be entirely drawn into the inner human being, [and will be] celestial, deified, and spiritualized), for that reason one will no longer be in need of teachers, preachers, or priests in heaven, nor of prophets, and even less of emperors, kings, princes, judges, or other estates for punishing evil. For there will no longer be evil in heaven; evil will only be in hell. All potentates, regimes, and all who use force, from the highest to the very lowest, belong only in this world. They are only applicable to the outer human being, only to the lesser part of him, namely, to the mortal body, and to material goods. In accordance with the inner human being, God alone is the Lord, in this world as well as the other one in the blessed. For it is to the outer human being that worldly authority is assigned. So look up, you kings, princes, and regents on earth: see to it that you conduct your office in humility [and] do not acquire damnation with your injustice by fulminating and raging against the anointed of the Lord because you do not listen to your godly preachers. For what you do unto them you do unto Christ himself. You certainly have no cause to be arrogant in your power. [This is so,] first, because your authority does not extend to the inner human being, but rather applies only to the least part, namely, the body, which you are able to kill. But the true human being you must leave unkilled. Second, your power does not extend over the great[est] good of your subjects, namely, the inner treasure, but rather only [covers] the least, small, alien good, mammon. You may seize the physical goods with injustice, but the kingdom of God neither you nor the devil can take from the simple. Third, your rule does not last long, and you are subject to the same death as your subjects. And finally, in the kingdom of heaven your rule and estate is quite finished. No one will say then: You are emperor, prince, pope, or priest. For in Christ Jesus nothing counts but the new creature, neither emperor nor king, neither prince nor peasant, neither doctor nor magister. They all stand equal before God; they are all the same before God. Thus all estates, orders, and names will cease. God alone will be and remain Lord of all creatures in eternity and no one else.

✦ • ✦

CHAPTER TWENTY-FIVE

That in that other life human beings will have no more titles, names, or human offices drawing distinctions of kind among them

In this world people use a name and a title in accordance with office and family. Thus some Jews are of the tribe of Levi, some from the tribe of Benjamin, Juda, Napthali, and so on. Thus this person is called by this family [name], another by another. One is called Peter, a second John, Conrad, Martin, Elias, Ambrose, and so on. But in that life of the future world, there will remain no such difference of names. No estate or family or title will be found in heaven. No one will be called Paul or Mary, neither Francis nor Gertraut, or the like. For these things are only temporal and cease with time. They only apply to the least part of the human being, that is, to the earthly body, not to the inner human being. In accordance with the body alone human beings are called by name and not in accordance with the spirit. The soul or the spirit has no name. It is called spirit and soul, and not Conrad, Peter, Andrew, Martha, Catherine, Anna, or the like. To take an example, Moses is not called Moses in accordance with the inner superior part, but rather solely in accordance with external mortal human being. For the names are found only in bodily things, in order to distinguish them thereby from one another, as Moses from Aron, John from Paul. In the spiritual being no name will remain in heaven. We will all be one in the Lord. And should you care to say that Elias and Moses have returned from paradise, and Christ has appeared on Mount Tabor, and have retained their names? The answer is that, insofar as they appear bodily, they have to be called by name for the sake of distinguishing them, for the sake of the disciples, who saw them on the Mount, and so that they can appear yet in the world. But if the world should be superseded, no name will remain. The reason is that the external being will no longer be but will be transported* into the inner spiritual being who may not be thought of as distinct by means of a name. If Adam had not sinned, no titles of men or families would have arisen; but because of the fall into sin, when the human being became external, there arose the giants, tyrants, [and] judges, and one wanted to be greater than the other, considered himself nobler than the other. From this arise the families and nobility, from sin, that is. That one gives to the one one name and title and to a second another—this happens on account of the external human being, in order to distinguish the one from another. But when in that other life after the end of this world we will be drawn into the inner human being and will live in accordance with the new human being in heaven, there will be no titles or names anymore, no nobility and no commoners, but rather all [shall be] one in the Lord. Even Christ will no longer be in accordance with the flesh,† but rather shall instead yield the kingdom to the Father, so that God shall be all in all (1 Cor 15)[:28]. The difference of title, name, and family is only ordained for this time and assigned to the external human being, to distinguish one from another. But the body and time must cease and be consumed by death, and with it title and name of family and human estate. Oh, you fools! Why do you boast of your name and title and swell in pride of family and nobility? Behold the toad, which likewise swells up. But it is only of the earth, and your body too is only of the earth, you who call yourself John,

---

*An inserted text commentary reads: "Cast off like an old garment, and only the new human being will remain."

†Text commentary: "That is, in accordance with his state of humiliation, as he was in this world."

Dick, Peter, or Nick of N. You want to have a great and illustrious name with your posterity with a fine house, with high arts, with great titles and epitaphs. But everything corporeal comes to nothing. Do you have no more hope for your name of high or low estate? If not, it will soon be all over with you. See to it that your name is written in heaven into the book of life. Learn *Sophia Christiana*, and your name will remain eternally. The fact that the angels in heaven are also called Seraphim, Powers, Principalities, Archangels, Cherubim, [and] Raphael, Uriel, and so on—those are not names. They are but designations of offices or orders thought up by human beings. Human beings have to measure to distinguish everything temporal. The human being simply invents names for the angels, even though spiritual things have no name. Only the physical, visible things are called by people by names, so as to distinguish one from the other, like one plant from another, and the like. Neither do the stars have names, yet since they appear physically, the human beings gives them names such as Jupiter, Mars, Saturn, Venus, Cancer, Ceph[e]us, Orion, Pegasus, and the like, to distinguish one from the other, though the stars know nothing of these names. Human beings have merely made them up for them. And if the celestial bodies hardly bear names, so much the less will human beings have names in eternal life, when no physical thing will be present.

✦   •   ✦

CHAPTER TWENTY-SIX

***What it means to be in heaven and in hell,
and that the immutable will of God is the particular place
in which all the blessed come together and dwell***

Since in this book we treat of the place or term [*terminus*] of all beings, visible and invisible, and insofar as we have concluded that God can be comprehended in no place, we must consider what being in heaven and hell means. A point or center is a concept and place of all lines, and [the number] one is a place of all numbers, for it conceives all numbers. The will of God [is] a place of all the blessed; it encloses all believers within itself, and they are of one will with it. Now, however, the will of God is nothing other than Christ, the Word born of the Father, which is a being of all creatures. God is for himself in eternity as much without will as without affect. He wants nothing, but in him and through the Word and creature he becomes a will for us and becomes willing, to wit, in the firstborn Christ. There he lets himself be seen, [lets be seen] what he wants eternally, and so on. And just as he has created all things through the Firstborn thus too he encompasses all creatures and wants that the rational creature should be one with the Firstborn and live according to him and remain in him. For he alone is the law, word, and will of God. Through him one must come to rest.

Now this will of God is a word of all creatures; just as in a center all lines are conceived, so too God encompasses all creatures, whether good or evil, devil or angel. However, though all creatures are encompassed in God and cannot stand, go, live, or hover without him, nevertheless, as was explained above, the devils and evil people are not blessed. The reason is that the rational creature has a free will, which God does not force, but rather would have be free, without any presumption, so that the creature gives and abandons itself to God, so that God thereby would see all things, as is seen in Christ of Nazareth. He had the very freest will of all, and through it allowed the Father to want and be all. There God himself was human. There God and human being were one. Now let us posit Christ or the will of God as a single center, and the unitary [*das einig*] is [identical] with this center; the same is in its proper place, is in heaven, and finds calm, complete satisfaction, life, and bliss. But whatever deviates from this center, from its assigned place, and lives in itself—that is, what does not want with God—has deviated from the center, from its assigned place, and lives in accordance with its own will, and for that reason it can possess neither peace nor calm. For in the creature of and by itself no calm is to be found, but rather only in the single center which is the immutable will of God. Thus, to be in hell means to live according to one's own will, to be turned away from the center, just as to be in heaven means to live in the will of God, to be one with God, to remain in the center, which has as its proposed goal Christ, the expressed will of God. Whoever is and is found in this remains one with God and is in heaven, at his predestined place. But whoever lives according to his own will is not in heaven, but rather outside, of which the Book of Revelation reports: Outside are the dogs and murderers, the thieves and liars and magicians. The nearer to the center, the more blessed, and the farther from the center, the more restless and unblessed.

✦ • ✦

CHAPTER TWENTY-SEVEN

That for me it depends on will and not on being, whether one is in God in heaven or whether one is in the devil in hell

It is the same whether you are in the world or outside of the world, since in the future life we must be without the world. In either case you cannot be without God. For God is not only a center but a circle of all creatures, that is, God and his will or Word is not only in all creatures but also outside of them,[62] conceiving and encompassing them, so that not even a fly can live outside of God. Everything has to be in God in accordance with being but not according to will. In physical things place is one thing and that which is contained in place another, and these are not the same or comparable. They cannot become united with one another. They are locally unequal to one another, so that the wine is in the keg, but the keg is not in the wine, the beer in the jar but the jar not in the beer, for they are not of the same kind. Hence, though I can say that flour is in a sack, I cannot say that the sack is in the flour. I am in the garden, but the garden is not in me. However, with spiritual, invisible things there is equality, and an equalization may soon occur, as soon as one wills it. And in the spiritual one thing is in the other. Thus, I am in the kingdom of God, and the kingdom of God is in me. I am in Christ, and Christ is in me. I am in the Holy Spirit, and the Holy Spirit is in me. I am in God, and God is in me. I am in heaven, and heaven is in me. I am in the will of God, and the will of God is in me. I am in the word and law of God, and the word and law of God is in me. Thus Christ too says in John 14[:11] [and] 17[:21], I am in the Father, and the Father is in me. I and the Father are one. In these spiritual states of affairs one should notice, moreover, that there is also a difference on account of the will or on account of faith or absence of faith. Thus spirit can easily unite with spirit and be of one will. The devil is everywhere present with us in this world, just as the sunshine passes through the world and alongside us. So too the spirits are alongside us, around us, and with us. They are not superseded by physical things, in the way that the sunshine is superseded by a garment or roof. Rather, without hindrance they pass through clothing, iron, steel, flesh, [and] through our bones, legs, [or] body, so that they are alongside our spirit always. And thus inasmuch as we are in faith and remain in Christ, they do not harm us, even if they are right next to us. For our will is not united with the evil spirits. But if we walk in unbelief and evil, they are no longer alongside us, but rather indeed in us and we in them. For spirit then unites with spirit and [they] are of the same will. It is no longer a matter of *juxta*, that is, alongside and with us, but rather in us and we in them. Thus it is said truly that the devil is in the godless, and the godless in the devil, so that both are one and of one will. For the devil was in Judas, and Judas in the devil, for he acted according to his will. For the blessed and believing ones, it is *juxta* to me and not *In*.* Thus, the devil is next to the pious, and the pious are next to the devil, and are against one another. The devil is next to the believer, and the believer next to the devil, and there is no believer in the devil, and no devil in [the believer], even though their two spirits are right alongside one another. Thus too Lucifer and God are alongside one another, for the devil is not in God, and God is not in the devil. Hence, the devil and God are not one but rather contraries of the will [*contrariae voluntatis*]. It is entirely a matter of will and not of being or spirit. So, for example, Christ is

---

* An inserted note reads: *Juxta aliquem, in aliquo.*

alongside the devil in the desert, and the devil is next to Christ, and they are against one another, not as one. For he [Christ] does not want as the devil wants. As [Jesus] says: Whoever is not with me, […] he disperses [Matt 12:30; Luke 11:23]. That is to say, whoever does not want as I want, is against me, as is the devil, even though he is next to me. When one says that the devil is next to Christ, or next to the believer, one should not understand this to mean next to the body or flesh. For no physical thing hinders the spirit. But rather spirit is next to spirit. Before Lucifer fell into sin, he was in God and God in him, and God and Lucifer were of one will, as it is with the other angels. But after his fall into sin, Lucifer was no longer in God, and God [was] no longer in him, but rather alongside him. Not that he fell out of God in accordance with being. For that would be impossible. And Lucifer [then] would have become nothing. But rather in accordance with the will he deviated from God and fell away from him. This was the expulsion of Lucifer from heaven: his deviation from the will of God in that he ate of the knowledge of good and evil. Thus too Adam was driven out of paradise, not in accordance with physical place, but rather in accordance with the will. He was no longer of the same will with God as before. He was divided in himself and split by this disobedience. There still remains indeed after as before the fall *GOD*: the Word, light and life in all things entirely without distinction. For the light shines in the darkness and is in all things like the life (John 1[:5]). But before rebirth one does not know God's will; one knows nothing of God's will in oneself. One does not know Christ, the path of life.

Therefore, though God is in the old, unbelieving human being, he is not in God. Thus, although the kingdom of God is in such a one, he is not in the kingdom of God. Though God still loves him, he does not love God. And although God seeks him, he does not seek in God. And although God shines in him, he does not shine in God. For God favors all equally with his grace without exception. It is only a matter of the abandonment of will.

VALENTIN WEIGEL

✦ • ✦

CHAPTER TWENTY-EIGHT

*Though the union of spirits is precisely a matter
of the will, nevertheless no one can by his own will
effect or give to himself rebirth [or] faith, that is,
the unification with the spirit of God; rather, God himself
must give it without any of our doing*

So far it has been proven that there can occur no unification in
corporeal things on account of their unlike nature. But in spiritual
things one can be in the other, so that God is in me and I am in
God, and I and God are one in will. Christ lives in me, and I live in
Christ; I and Christ are one in accordance with will. I am in the
kingdom of God, and the kingdom of God is in me; one is in the
other. For such things stand in the spirit or faith. Furthermore, it
has been proven that in Christian things one is alongside the other,
and not one in the other, which is entirely a matter of will, so that
the devil is alongside Christ, and Christ is alongside the devil, and
one cannot stand in the other, though both are spirits. This is
caused by the unlike will of the two. Thus the believers are alongside the devil, and the devil alongside the believers, and one is not in
the other. For the devil may not be or rule in the believers. He may
not and cannot dwell in the pious but indeed in the children of
unbelief. This is caused by the willing. It is entirely a matter of the
will whether one is in God in heaven [or] in the devil in hell, and
that one carries heaven or hell within oneself. Though it is true that
every human being carries within himself heaven and hell, blessedness or damnation, nonetheless one may not find both at the same
time. Inasmuch as you are in God, you cannot be in hell or in the
devil. One has to cede. Therefore, although God remains in all
equally with his Word or kingdom before the fall and after the fall,
nonetheless, they do not all remain in God, but rather next to him.
Before the rebirth one does not know anything of it. The evil people do not remain in God, as God remains in them. The evil people
do not live in God, though God lives in them. The evil people do

not love God, as God loves them. The evil people do not seek God, as God seeks them. They do not find God, as they are found by God. They do not think God purely and simply, as God purely and simply thinks them. They are not born of God as children of God, as God wants to be born a human child in the human being. They do not give themselves to God, as God gives himself to them. They do not abandon themselves to God completely, as God offers and abandons himself to them completely. It is entirely a matter of will. In sum, as long as the human being lives of his own will, he is without faith, without Christ, without God, without salvation. He bears heaven within himself and cannot enter into it. God has to serve in him as an enemy, death, darkness, and damnation, though he would and should rather remain his friend, life, light, and eternal blessedness. This happens through no fault of God's. The turned away human being damns himself. Now you might say that inasmuch as the rebirth of faith is not in the being, but rather only occurs and is brought about in the will, what I wish for, God will also want, and the same holds true for all the damned in hell, who would exchange heaven and blessedness for damnation. Accordingly, can I not want, effect, overtake, give, and take the rebirth [or] faith for myself by my own powers? The answer is that it is indeed a matter of will, and that without the will or willingness no unification of spirits will occur, [and the fact] that the evil people are no longer next to but rather in the devil is a matter of will. But to give the new birth or faith is not within our own will or pursuit but rather in God's will. He must do it, not the human being. Rebirth is not the work of the creature, but rather God's work in the abandoned human being. God does not want it without the human being, and the human being can do nothing without God; rather, both with one another, God effecting it, the human being suffering it [to happen]. If the human being is damned, it is not the fault of the good God, who at all times wants to effect it, and so on. Rather, it is the fault of the human being, who does not want to suffer God, to rest or to keep the Sabbath. Nature does not do it here but grace. What must happen is, in short, to be as if dead, to hate and abandon [self] entirely. For it is not a matter of the wanting or pursuing [human being], but rather of the pitying God. God through his grace that runs ahead must give and effect the will. It must not come from flesh and blood of man (John 1), but rather immediately from God. Should it be a matter of the creatural will, all devils and the damned in hell would want nothing other than bliss. No, there must be a dying, there must be an abandoning of self within and without, in spirit and in nature, if God is to become human in you, that is, should you be born of God for heaven. The new birth takes place only in the children, that is, in those who are poor in spirit, who hate, abandon, [and] deny themselves and lose themselves in God, not when they desire and want to have it, but rather when God wants, which is without any desiring, wanting, pursuing, knowing, and recognizing of theirs, God himself effects the new birth, faith. Nature is dead, knows nothing about it. But you do hear the rushing of the wind, that is, you feel and experience the renewal in yourself. However, you do not know whither or whence, as Christ testifies (John 3[:8]). The children are the best at this; they should remain a pattern and model for us all.

✦ • ✦

CHAPTER TWENTY-NINE

That heaven, the kingdom of God, the true fatherland, is much closer to us than we are to ourselves; hence, we do not need to seek for it outside of us but rather to await it in the spirit, within

If only one knows the saying of Christ and has faith in it, that, as Christ says to the Pharisees, the kingdom of God does not stand here or there in external demeanors but is rather inside within you, one would then be sufficiently convinced that neither place, ceremonies, nor other external things make us blessed but rather only the true faith in the spirit. For though in this world there are still places, the kingdom of God stands in no particular places, nor

140

much less is it to be found here or there when the world with all its places has been superseded. Nor does it stand in the body, but rather within in the spirit. After the disappearance of the world one will not need to move from one country to another, from Europe to Asia, from one place to another. For it would be an imperfection to be moved from one place to another, hither and yonder, and not to possess all things in the spirit, as do the angels and [as does] God himself. It will be an eternal Sabbath, upon which one may not travel but rather will wait within oneself for God and hear what he speaks, and so on. Whether you are in Africa or America, whether you are in the world or outside of it, you will nonetheless find the kingdom of God, heaven, your [true] fatherland, not outside you but within you in the spirit. Should you seek a physical place outside yourself and think that you would find edification and satisfaction or bliss, then you do not know yourself, and do not know where your true fatherland is found. Since this great visible world is in no place, rather it hovers within itself, and has all things within it, outside of it is nothing, why then would you seek satisfaction or bliss, or possess it in a place outside yourself? You are, after all, the image of God, a temple and dwelling of God. The angels seek nothing outside themselves; rather, they possess all things in themselves like God. In short, you will find no peace, satisfaction, or blessedness outside of yourself, neither in kingdoms, nor in precious dwellings, nor in songs, nor in harps, nor in melodious instruments, not in feasts of joy, not in merry societies, not with wine, not at a full table, not in lust of women, not in royal pomp or honor, not in dancing and playing, not in poetry, not in books and writings, not in the healthy body, not even in the entire world, but rather only in God in yourself, and by no means outside of you. Whoever does not see all places as a single place, but rather expects to find more pleasure and joy in one place than in another, does not yet know what Christ is, or where his fatherland is. In the true fatherland in myself there is no consideration of the limit from which [*terminus à quo*] and the limit to which [*terminus ad quem*], that is, of hither or yonder, nor of the property of place, such as above, below, behind, in front, to the right, to the left, as is customary to point out within the world;

rather, there is a still sweet rest and peace in an eternal Sabbath, when God has become all things in me, when no more acting or going out is necessary. For the perfect has arrived, [and] that which is piecemeal is done for. And that is also the reason why in heaven neither God nor the angels effect anything, for there is no deficiency or susceptibility there. The closer anyone is to it, the more complete and blissful [one becomes]. If you can go into yourself, you will come to God in your fatherland. The clothing is close to me, but the body is much closer, for I can let the clothing go, and walk away naked with John. Therefore, the body is dearer to me than clothes or houses. For of what good would the clothing or houses be to me, if I had no body? In the same way, bodily things are of no use to the devil; he has no body. The body is close to me, the soul much closer still. For of what good to me is my body without a soul? Therefore, I can let my body be killed, as did Paul, in order to escape only with my soul. A Christian lets the body go, but not the soul. The soul is close to me, but God is much closer to me. For what good would my soul be to me without God? Therefore, I would rather hate, deny, and abandon myself so that God will become and remain all to me. I want to be nothing and to lose myself, so that God becomes all and finds me. Therefore, I will not ask for heaven and earth, in order only to remain concealed within You. Amen.

END.

III

VALENTIN WEIGEL

*T*he Golden Grasp

For Discerning All Things Without Error,
Unknown to All the Universities,
Yet Necessary for All Human Beings
to Know

Written in the year 1578

*

Register of this little book

I.
That the contemplation of the eternal deity and of the six days of creation, and also the knowledge of oneself, are most useful.

II.
To know nothing of the eternal deity and its works and not to know oneself are the cause of all seduction and darkness.

III.
That two things are needed for seeing or judging, namely, the eye and the object.

IV.
On the eye and the object, what they are, and how diverse.

V.
That in the human being there are two kinds of wisdom, a natural wisdom for mortal life and a supernatural wisdom for eternal life, and that the one far surpasses the other.

VI.
That one must necessarily posit a twofold knowledge, a natural, active knowledge for this life and a supernatural, passive knowledge for eternal life.

VII.
On the distinction of the threefold knowledge or comprehension in the natural eye, and how the one encompasses within itself and surpasses the other.

VIII.
That the uppermost, innermost eye can always act without the help of the lowest, but the lowest, outermost can accomplish nothing without the uppermost or innermost.

IX.

That all natural knowledge does not proceed from the object, but rather from the eye itself, and to what end such consideration is good.

X.

How all natural knowledge is transformed or becomes various from the nature of the eyes and not from the nature of the object, from which it is again concluded that knowledge comes from the eye itself and not from the object.

XI.

That the human being is the eye itself, through which all visible and invisible objects are seen and known.

XII.

What natural and supernatural knowledge mean, and that the latter is always passive, but the former active, and to which end such a consideration serves.

XIII.

That in the supernatural, inner knowledge God is the very eye in the human being, [so to speak] his instrument, from which pure unity proceeds in heaven.

XIV.

That among the pious unity and peace prevail because of the one will of God, which they bear and suffer in heaven and on earth.

XV.

That in the human being both kinds of wisdom or knowledge come through the birth from within and not through the shadow from without.

XVI.

That books do not effect or make any being in the human being but should only be written and used as a keepsake, reminder, memorial, or testimony.

XVII.
On the twofold contemplation or judgment of scripture by the outer and by the inner human being.

XVIII.
Whence one customarily seeks and takes judgment.

XIX.
That no one should take or make a judgment based on other people's persuasion or consideration, for it would be taken in from without and against the light of nature.

XX.
That one should not draw the judgment in knowing all objects from the letter of scripture.

XXI.
That knowledge does not proceed and come from the thing known, from the object, but rather from the knower himself.

XXII.
That the object does not bring in the judgment or knowledge from outside into the knower is proven with Holy Scripture.

XXIII.
That faith alone is the right judgment, and the knowledge of God, and the testing of spirits.

XXIV.
That one should not seek nor can one find the testing of spirits in external books of human beings, but rather in the spiritual book of the heart from within, and [by] taking Holy Scripture as a testimony of this.

XXV.
That this book is God's word, or kingdom, or wisdom in all human beings, and [that it] has various names.

XXVI.
Why the inner book or word has become visible and external, and how [this occurs] in three ways.

XXVII.
That the short, trifling, worthless joy of the world hinders and cancels the eternal, infinite treasure.

XXVIII.
That one must learn of God in this time and not wait for heaven to do so.

✦ • ✦

THE GOLDEN GRASP

For Discerning All Things Without Error,
Unknown to All the Universities,
Yet Necessary for All Human Beings
To Know

In the name of our Lord Jesus Christ I write this little book in which simple souls should be brought so far in understanding that they can overcome and banish all the high doctors and worldly scholars. [I do it] also in order to convince [the reader] that all universities reside in blindness and darkness, in all three faculties. So come hither and look upon the works of the Lord, listen quickly, speak slowly, learn beforehand, judge afterward. Do not dampen the spirit [cf. 1 Thess 5:19], but instead test and see what it speaks [1 John 4:1–2]. Come and see with your own eyes and not with other people's eyes. Come and listen with your own ears, and don't believe what others have heard. Come and taste with your own tongue, then you will become comprehending, clever, and wise, and freed from all darkness and error. For from now on, you should not believe because of what others tell you but see for yourself that truth is truth. You will become witnesses yourselves and no longer believe so as to please anyone. The time has come to no longer restrain the truth but rather to write [it] publicly, and such truth is in you. You will thank God in heaven that through such a trifling instrument as me you have been led and brought to the very thing that is most necessary of all, which is the highest, and which is in you; however, you knew nothing about it, and have not known yourselves. Not to know oneself and God is the highest blindness and darkness. But to know oneself and God expels all darkness and assures the human being of not being seduced by anyone else. But those who do not want to favor themselves that they may learn, how shall they be favored by this book? [There are] those who say, What do you want me to learn, or what can you write, that I should then learn from you? The answer is, I cannot teach you anything new, but rather that which is within you, which you carry with you without knowing it, which must amaze you. Will you say: What need do I have of your report? I don't have any need of your golden grasp; I already understand all things better. The answer is: If you already understand all things, then read this little book, and it will certainly agree with your understanding. If it doesn't agree, then understanding is not yet in you; you are still blind. Simply admit your ignorance and blindness, and you will be helped. But if you say that you are not blind but rather seeing, there will never be help for you, for this little book will be presented and given for judgment, so that those who are thus blind and unseeing should become seeing and comprehending. But those who are seeing and knowing will either be confirmed in their knowledge, or [as] blind and unknowing and remain so both here and there in eternity (John 9:39). Take note, dear fellow, this little book should make the blind and unknowing seeing and comprehending. Those [who purport to be] seeing and knowing will find themselves to be blind and ignorant. They will remain that way in all eternity, failing to recognize that knowledge is not drawn from the object (which would be counter to what I write). To the contrary, [here] it is written and presented for judgment that those who [come to] recognize themselves as unknowing and blind will be saved from error. Those who regard themselves as the knowing and seeing ones, without being that way, will remain ever in darkness, here and in eternity. For that reason, mild reader, judge with modesty. Do not reject this little book, and you will not be persuaded perniciously. For whoever rejects this little book gives testimony about himself that he is a liar and intends to remain an enemy of truth, and so on.

✦ • ✦

CHAPTER ONE

That the contemplation of the eternal deity and of the six works of creation, and also the knowledge of oneself, are most useful

Whoever often contemplates the eternal God, how he in the beginning created all things through his Word and Spirit of his mouth, from nothing something, as the angels arose from nothing through the word of God, whereupon the other five days of creation followed, as through separation all things have come forth to light; [whoever contemplates these things knows that] God possesses all things in himself; he created the angels as well so that they have all things within themselves. From the waters emerged the four elements and [the] *astra* [the stars as relays of the divine creative power];[63] from the elements and *astra* emerged the elemental bodies [*corpora*]; from the bodies grew forth fruits. Whoever contemplates this must admit (I say) that everything became something out of nothing, through the Word, from that which was concealed into being, [that] all things have emerged from the invisible into the visible, from the spiritual into the physical, and remain one within the other.[64] Thus the visible physical tree remains in the invisible spiritual tree. Thus all external things flow from within outward, not from outside in. Just look, whence does the tree come? Indeed, from the *astrum* or invisible seed. Whence comes the pear? From the tree. Whence come the snow, hail, rain, fog, and the like? Not from earthly vapors, as Aristotle claimed, but rather from the invisible *astra* of the stars that make the invisible visible. Whence the human being? Out of the *limus terrae*, which is to say, from the clump of earth that is the entire world.[65] Invisibly Adam lay in the world, and [then] became *visible. Spiritually, he lay within the world*, and [then] became physical. That out of which one has been made one has and also bears within one: the pear is of the tree, the seed of the pear. Therefore, a tree can grow again from the seed, together with other pears, whereby all proceeds from within outward, from the invisible [outward] into the visible. Adam was extracted from everything in creation, and all creatures lie within him. His spirit is from the firmament or stars; hence, Adam has all arts, crafts, languages, faculties of study, and all bestial human wisdom within him, for that which is in the firmament is also in the human being. Beyond that the human being also has the eternal soul, from the inspiration by God, along with the divine spirit. For that reason the eternal celestial wisdom also lies within him, from which it can be concluded that all knowledge of all things is not taken from books, but rather flows out of the human being into the letter. Therefore, whoever often contemplates the eternal deity and its works and also learns to know himself obtains complete wisdom, and his study comes easy. What someone else cannot learn in thirty years such a one can learn in three years without error. Oh, if only the universities and worldly scholars knew this grasp and small ground, they would not hope in vain to read their wisdom from books with trouble and toil and would not lead themselves, along with others, into such darkness.

Oh, eternal God and Creator, the works of your hands testify sufficiently that all things come from the invisible into the visible, from the spiritual into the physical, and all things flow outward into visibility. Thus the letter comes from the inner spirit, Adam from the world, knowledge or understanding from Adam. For the human being comes before all books; the books are from the human being. Illuminate me further, you True Light, that I may only know you and myself. Then the knowledge for all things will be revealed to me. Amen.

✦　•　✦

CHAPTER TWO

*To know nothing of the eternal deity and its works
and not to know oneself are the cause
of all seduction and darkness*

The assiduous contemplation of the works of God and the knowledge of oneself leads to God and makes the eye clear and bright;[66] [it] also testifies that understanding or knowledge flows from within outward. Such a one is not to be seduced by anyone else, for he has the judgment or the knowledge within himself. But whoever does not consider the origin of all the works of God, and also does not want to get to know himself properly, [to know] what he is, whence he comes, and what he bears within himself, and so on, must necessarily fall into various sorts of error and blindness, and in addition must also be seduced and deceived by human beings and false books. He must hear and believe what others say, and must believe upon hearing persuasion, whether true or lies. One thinks that knowledge flows from the object; that is to say, this is the opinion of the worldly scholars, as if the books could carry the understanding into the human beings, as if the human being could read his understanding out of the book; and [they] do not want to see that all knowledge flows not out of books, but rather from within out of the human being. They speak against themselves in saying: I take my understanding out of the book, and [they] say: I do not understand it. But if the understanding came from the book, then they would also get this understanding from it. But to the contrary, if the understanding is not already in the human being, then he will not get it from the book. All things come from within outward and not from outside inward. For, truly, if I am to see, an eye must be in my head; had I no eye in my head, I could not see. Am I to hear, the hearing must be in me. If I were deaf, I would hear nothing, regardless of what one spoke. If I am to smell, then taste must be in me; if the taste is not in me, then I can smell nothing. If I want to know what is written in the book, the understanding must have been opened up in me beforehand and must be within me. If the understanding were not in me, I could not understand the book. If the book is supposed to bring the understanding into the human being, that is, if knowledge is supposed to be taken from the object, then it must follow that one hundred readers extract a single undivided understanding from it. But no! We experience the opposite, to our detriment, and must confess that the understanding flows from within outward and is not carried from without, out of the book, into the human being. As many heads, as many understandings, and as many readers [as there are], that many senses are applied to the scriptures. Holy Scripture is a single object. If the scripture is supposed to bring the understanding into the human being, or effect [it], then all readers would have to receive only one single understanding from it and not become so split or divided in their understanding. The worldly scholars themselves say (whenever they see an uncomprehending person), *Caret iudicio, caret intellectu.* That is, this person is not gifted with any judgment; he has no understanding within him. He can neither judge nor decide about any matter; [they say this] in order to demonstrate that understanding must be in the human being beforehand, if he is to decide properly or judge of things. And even though they speak such things, they know neither God nor themselves. Therefore, both the teachers and the pupils remain blind, and both fall into great darkness. For the one believes the other on hearsay and knows nothing of the inner testimony. There can be no greater seduction than not to know oneself and to know nothing of the inner ground.

Oh, God, awaken me to see and contemplate the works of your hands, so that I will recognize that all things flow from within outward into the external, and not from without inward, and that all Wisdom lies concealed within me, which I would not need to bring in from without, from the object, but rather the knowledge flows from the knower into that which is known. Amen.

✦ • ✦

CHAPTER THREE

That two things are needed for seeing or judging, namely, the eye and the object

When we want to recognize and see a thing with our physical eye, three things are necessary for doing so. The first is the instrument or tool for seeing, the eye itself. The second is the object or thing vis-à-vis, the tower, the tree, the stone, and so forth, that is

154

seen. Third [is] the lighted transparent air, or appropriate distance between the eye and the object. For if the air were dark and full, one could not see the tower, the tree, the stone. Nor if I were to place my eye too close to the tower, the tree, the stone, so that no medium remained between the eye and the object, would I be able to see. For that reason there must be a lighted air, and the eye needs an external medium or light to see the object. What I have said about the eye applies also to the hearing. In order that I hear sound through the medium of air, three things are necessary as well; likewise for the sense of smell; and so on. However, all of this has been said about the animal eye inasmuch as the other animals need the same things as we. But insofar as the human being is above the animals, to that extent he has a better way of seeing: with the inner eye. Therefore, we should dismiss the outer and [instead] treat of the real eye in the following manner. If I am to see or comprehend a thing, then not three things are needed, as with the animal sensual eye, but rather only two: the inner eye and the object, for example, the book, and so forth. If I am to know or understand what is in the book, then the understanding must be in me: *I cannot take the understanding out of the book. If I am to see, then the eye must be in me.* If I were blind, I could not see. I would have no *iudicium* or understanding in me. Hence, I could not judge or know what is in the book.

The inner eye or understanding needs no external light or air. It has its own light within itself: the eye is the light itself. For if my eye were dark, I could see nothing (Matt 6[:23]). To this the simpleminded and inexperienced might retort and say, If I am to read the book, then I must have an external light such as the sun or a candle; otherwise I couldn't see the letters. Therefore, here too three things are necessary, and not two. The answer to that is: Yes, indeed, if, with your physical eye you want to behold the visible letter, then you do need three things, the eye, the external light, and the book. But I'm not talking about seeing in the way that cows and calves behold a barn door, but rather about the understanding or inner eye, which understands the book without external light. For to read without understanding would be not to read, *legere et non intelligere est negligere*, say the worldly scholars. Therefore the inner eye has its light within it and is itself the light (Matt 6[:22]); [thus] only two things are necessary for seeing or judging, namely, the eye and the object, the seer and that which is seen.

Oh, Lord God, you who makes us more learned than all animals on earth, and wiser than the birds, and who teaches us human beings all that we know (Job 35[:11]), and who lets books be written on account of our weakness, so that we will be reminded, warned, and convinced thereby: illuminate the eye within me so that I see; open up the understanding within me so that I understand; and sharpen the [power of] judgment in me so that I rightly test all things. Then I will not deny the inner testimony, as do the Pharisees, but rather I will confess with the pious that understanding does not come from without, out of books, but rather springs and flows from within outward. Amen.

✦ • ✦

CHAPTER FOUR

On the eye and the object, what they are, and how diverse

Inasmuch as two things are necessary for judgment or knowledge, the eye or tool and the object or thing vis-à-vis, it must first be understood what I mean by the eye, and [it must be understood] how varied it is, and [also] what is meant by the object, and how varied it is. And let us begin with the external eye: The eye is a tool with which and by means of which the human being sees a thing, which also requires an external light. But seeing of this sort applies rather to the animal and [thus] least noble aspect of the human being. Therefore, in speaking of the tool or instrument, the human being must be divided in accordance with three powers. For in the human being there is found a threefold comprehension: the sensual, the rational, and the mental [powers of] comprehension. If the soul goes outward to the senses and acts only through them, it knows a thing only in the animal or bestial manner and comprehends a thing just as the other beasts do. If, however, it turns instead toward reason, to the arts, crafts, [or] languages, then it learns and comprehends a thing as does a human being; [that is,] it uses the rational eye. But if the soul proceeds into the innermost part, into the understanding or [inner] mind, it sees and comprehends a thing in a spiritual manner, angelically. Therefore, a threefold eye may be assumed in the human being.[67] The lowest, least noble is *sensualis*, the sensory eye. *Imaginatio* [imagination] may be included with it, whereby one only sees, hears, grasps, tastes, [or] smells physical things. The middle eye is *rationalis* [rational], with which the human being rises above sensuality and uses reason, with which one can conclude one thing from another. The third and highest eye is *intellectualis* [intellectual] or *mentalis* [mental], with which the human being beholds and knows the object in angelic manner.

The object or thing vis-à-vis is the thing that is seen and known, as, for example, with my eyes I look at the house and the moon in the heavens. In that case the house [or] the moon is an object of the eyes. With reason I know and behold the art of dialectic, arithmetic, and other arts and crafts. Thus the arts are an object of the rational eye, for by means of and with the reason I comprehend such things. With the understanding of the mind I recognize and behold the angels and the eternal God. Thus is God and thus are the angels objects of the mental eye. And everything that one looks at, hears, judges, understands, [or] recognizes is called an object [of it]; thus, the Bible is an object to whomever reads and understands it or regards it, and so on. However, it is a twofold object (for it is two beings: God and created thing), a comprehensible, finite, and circumscribable object insofar as it is a created thing, whether visible or invisible. For everything that God created can be comprehended by the understanding. The other object is infinite, immeasurable, and incomprehensible, insofar as it is God, who cannot be comprehended through human understanding; only from a distance is he known. For just as our sensual eye beholds the wide sea but can neither encompass nor comprehend it, so too is the incomprehensible God immeasurable and infinite to the inner eye.

For that reason, seeing, hearing, understanding, recognizing, comprehending, judging, and so on, I refer to here as the eye, and it is in the human being. But that which is seen, heard, grasped, understood, judged, or recognized I refer to as the object or thing vis-à-vis, whether it is finite and comprehensible, as is the creature, or infinite and incomprehensible, as is the eternal God.

Oh, eternal God and Lord of all goodness, you have favored the human being with such light that he may behold your creature as an object that is finite and comprehensible, and in order that the human being may be led thereby to you, the immeasurable object, so that he may be satiated by you and not remain in the finite creature. Draw me, dear Father, so that I may come to the Son, and with the Son to you into eternal life. Amen.

✦　•　✦

CHAPTER FIVE

That in the human being there are two kinds of wisdom, a natural wisdom for mortal life and a supernatural wisdom for eternal life, and that the one far surpasses the other

Insofar as all things that have flowed from God, the eternal Font, are known, either from the light of nature from assiduous researches or else from the light of grace, in a still Sabbath in which one effects nothing but rather suffers it, [and] in which God knows himself through himself: to that extent one can properly posit a twofold *philosophia*, that is, a natural one from the light of nature and a supernatural one from the light of faith and of the spirit in Christ. The natural *Sophia* or wisdom encompasses the works of nature, namely, the whole Adam before and after the fall and the entire order of the creatures. The supernatural *Sophia*, however, encompasses the whole of Christ in accordance with both states of being, that is, the Creator of the new creature of heaven. Thus one might refer to the *Sophia naturalis*, that is, the natural wisdom of

God and of his creatures, as *philosophia;* and *Sophia super naturalis,* that is, the supernatural wisdom of Adam and Christ, of the old and the new human being, of the letter and the spirit, and so on, one might call *theologia.* The supernatural wisdom or theology teaches us to recognize what is Adam and Christ in ourselves and outside of ourselves; [it is] encompassed in the scriptures of the prophets and apostles; [and it] serves for the eternal and heavenly life. But the natural wisdom or philosophy teaches [us] how to know the entire nature of the visible and invisible light; [it] serves for the temporal short life and ceases with the world. And although *theologia* explains nature and grace, the earthly Adam and the celestial one, and [though] *philosophia* accounts for all natural created things, nevertheless the two should not be entirely separated one from the other. Nor should they be mixed with one another without proper order. Rather, both should be cultivated, conducted, and understood in a modest manner. The one extends its hand to the other, and if they are conducted properly alongside one another, without mixing them up in a disordered manner, we can understand all the secrets of natural and supernatural things. For it is a poor and simple-minded *Theologus* [theologian] who only knows the external Christ and Adam, as the *Historia* is spelled out following the letter of scripture, without [reference to] the power, life, action, and spirit in the celestial or inner being. But if, however, one is to properly know and explain nature and grace, Adam and Christ, on an apostolic and prophetic foundation, without error and darkness, then one must be instructed by the Holy Ghost from on high how to understand the nature and order of the created things or beings: whence, why, and to what purpose the world and the human being were made and ordered. This is called *philosophia naturalis,* a natural wisdom, and it is encompassed and briefly recounted by Moses in the Book of Creation [Genesis]. Hence, if a *theologus* is to understand Adam and nature, he must understand the entire world and all created things or beings. In that event he can confirm that the human being is the small world, created from the *limbus.*[68] To know and understand such things is the sphere of the natural philosophers. What sort of *philosophus* is it, then, who would dare to interpret the created things or beings of God or nature without Christ? Whoever does not proceed with wisdom, that is, with Christ, must err and go astray in his objective. Christ is the wisdom of God, a beginning and an end of all creatures. Therefore, if someone wants to explain nature and to philosophize without error, he must begin with it in Christ and end in him. Otherwise his philosophy is worthless. All of our study must proceed from Christ and lead and direct us to the one and only Christ. Whoever is not found in him proceeds in darkness with all his philosophizing and will be in the end regretful of having lived in this world. Therefore, [the dual gift of] *philosophia* and *theologia* is and remains a gift of God, both from God, the one for this time, the other leading to eternity. And whoever conducts *philosophia* in nature in order to come to Christ and employs *theologia* in grace in order to understand Christ and to walk in him will have sufficient light, delight, and joy in this time and in the end die in peace as well.

Oh, eternal God, one discovers great delight, joy, and edification in your creatures and creations; they are the purest works of wonder. But one discovers infinite edification in your eternal wisdom. Like a drop of water against the wide sea, so is the earthly wisdom compared to the celestial. Both are from you and [both] are in us. Oh, let me not dally with the transient wisdom, but rather [grant] that I might leave the temporal behind me and follow the eternal, all-powerful One. Amen.

✦ • ✦

CHAPTER SIX

That one must necessarily posit a twofold knowledge,
a natural, active knowledge for this life
and a supernatural, passive knowledge
for eternal life

Let us grant that there is a threefold comprehension found in the human being. By this I mean that there is, first, a seeing in accordance with the senses a sensual knowledge, and second, in accordance with the reason a rational knowledge, and third, in accordance with understanding an understanding knowledge. [Insofar as] this three-fold knowledge is either natural [and] active or supernatural and passive, one must also concede a twofold eye or faculty of knowledge, namely, a natural knowledge by one's own powers and progression, for which the human being behaves actively by speculating, imagining, considering, researching, and the like; and a supernatural knowledge or wisdom, for which the human being does not act toward the object, but rather awaits his knowledge in a passive manner and receives [it] from the incomprehensible Object, from God himself, who pours himself into the passive eye, and thus the human being effects nothing in this knowledge. He stands still with all his thoughts and is as if dead. Eye, comprehension, and knowledge are here all taken to be the same thing; for with the eye one sees and recognizes something, and just as with the physical sensual eye one sees the object or thing vis-à-vis, so too, with the inner spiritual eye, one sees and knows the objects or things vis-à-vis. And this eye of the inner human being should be understood, exercised, and used in both lights, of nature and of grace. Hence, inasmuch as one experiences, sees, grasps, and knows all things with an inner eye of this sort, the eye or the comprehension and knowledge remain one thing, which nonetheless (as I have said) must be used in a twofold manner, that is, in a natural [and] active way for *philosophia* in this life, and in a supernatural, passive way for *theologia* toward the celestial life. For there is indeed a twofold wisdom, from Adam and through Adam, [which is] natural [and] temporal, and from Christ and through Christ, [which is] supernatural [and] eternal. There is also a twofold light, the light of nature for the temporal life, and the light of grace or of faith for the eternal life. Therefore, there are also two Adams in the world, an earthly one, with the entire nature, visible and invisible, and a celestial one, with grace from Christ. There is also a twofold faith, that is, the natural inborn faith, from the almighty Creator in all human beings, and the faith of grace or of the spirit from Christ, which makes the human being eternal when the natural passes away with the mortal life. There are also two objects, that is, a comprehensible finite object, as all created things are subject to the human understanding, whether [they are] in heaven or in hell, or in the elements, and an incomprehensible, unfathomable, invisible object, that is, God, who resides in a light into which no one can pass and whom no human being has seen in eternity (1 Tim 6[:16]). From all of this it necessarily follows that one should assume a natural knowledge, which relates in an active way to nature, and a supernatural knowledge, which relates passively to grace subject to God. For God or his Word remains unfathomable and incomprehensible, and that is our infinite bliss.

This incomprehensible and unfathomable God be praised and exalted from now to eternity. Amen.

✦ • ✦

CHAPTER SEVEN

On the distinction of the threefold knowledge or comprehension in the natural eye, and how the one encompasses within itself and surpasses the other

Natural knowledge or comprehension is brought about by the *oculus carnis* [the eye of the flesh], that is, by the senses; by the *oculus rationis*, that is, by [the eye of] reason; and by the *oculus mentis* [the eye of the mind], that is, by the understanding. However, we want to reflect further on the distinction of the threefold natural eye, and how one encompasses the other within itself and far surpasses it. From that we will be able to understand that all natural knowledge must change in accordance with the kind, property, or facility of the eye, and not in accordance with the object. For it is not from the object but rather from the eye that seeing and knowing flow. If then the seer or knower is acute and just, the knowledge will be acute and righteous, and vice versa. The eye that is lowest and of the flesh is twofold, that is, external, of the five senses, seeing, hearing, touch, smell, taste, [and] internal, the imagination by which one sees a thing in its absence without the external senses by the inner eye of the imagination, without external light, even in the dark night. Thus I see before me a castle and go several miles away from it; nonetheless, I see the same castle as if it stood right before me; [I see it] not with my eyes, but rather with the imagination. However, inasmuch as the imagination cannot ascend above physical things, but instead is only exercised in physical objects or things vis-à-vis, one can assign it to the *oculus carnis*, that is, to the sensual eye of the flesh. For in the inner being imagination is in place of all the five senses, and [it] encompasses the five senses within it: it sees, hears, smells, tastes, touches within itself, without external light or air, and does so much more quickly than all five senses. It [the imagination] is the sidereal spirit and has its light within itself. Among the external senses, one is also quicker and more noble than the other. *Visus*, the seeing with the eye, occurs quickly in a glance, and [it] peers up as far as the firmament. No other sense can extend so far. *Auditus*, hearing, surpasses smell, for I can hear something farther away than smell [it]. For if a thing is far away from me, I cannot sense it with [the sense of] smell. *Olfactus*, [the sense of] smell, surpasses *gustus*, the sense of taste, for I can smell a thing far away but not taste it far away. Thus, *gustus* or taste surpasses *tactus*, that is, feeling. For I can sense a thing by taste without physical touch, though not far away from me. But I cannot feel or grasp a thing without it touching my body. Therefore *tactus* or feeling is distributed over the whole body, in all members, and is everywhere in the entire body. But taste has its special place in the body, namely the tongue or gum. And smell has its special place in the body, namely the nostrils (for I cannot smell with my fist). Hearing also has its particular place in the body, that is, the ears (for I cannot hear with my feet). Vision, through the eyes, is the quickest and most facile among all the external senses. Even as in a moment, like a flash from heaven, thus [is] the seeing with the eyes. But these external five senses are not surpassed singly by the imagination, but rather all of them at once, and [it] does its work with great facility, for it is spiritual, and has and does everything in it. It sees a thing where no [other] sense can go. It can see, hear, touch, act across several hundreds, even thousands of miles. It has no need of an external physical instrument for its operation.

The imagination is the sidereal spirit; it is the star within the human being. It is all the stars and performs like the firmament. Read Theophrastus to see what he writes about the imagination.[69] Nevertheless, as excellent as the imagination is in effecting all its works, whether near or far, nevertheless, *oculus rationis*, the eye of reason, [goes] beyond the imagination. For reason, or [rather] the human being by means of reason, sees and knows things that are impossible for the imagination to know. Thus, reason sees that the world stands in no place and yet does not fall. The imagination cannot see that; it cannot apply itself to nonphysical things. It operates with physical forms and figures. But reason is higher. For higher still and far more inner is *oculis mentis seu intellectus*, the eye of the mind, of the understanding, as the figure reproduced here shows.

The first, or number one, is the innermost and highest eye, designated by the letter a. The second, or number two, is the middlemost, designated by the letter b. The third, or number three, is the lowest and coarsest [and] most external, designated by the letter [c].

h	8	tactus
g	7	gustus
f	6	olfactus
e	5	auditus
d	4	visus
c	3	imaginatio
b	2	ratio
a	1	mens

understanding	1	a
reason	2	b
imagination	3	c
seeing	4	d
hearing	5	e
smell	6	f
taste	7	g
touch	8	h

The more inner, the more spiritual and noble; the more external, the coarser and weaker. This figure testifies also that the eye or knowing is in the human being, and [that it] proceeds from within, and that the object is outside of the human being.

Oh, eternal God, you font and source of all science and knowledge! You have equipped me with a threefold eye, that is, with senses, like the beasts, with reason, as a human being, and with understanding, like an angel. Oh, let me use the inner eye, so that I will have to confess that all science is within me, and flows from within outward, and cannot be brought in by the object.

✦ • ✦

CHAPTER EIGHT

That the uppermost, innermost eye can always act without help of the lowest, but the lowest, outermost can accomplish nothing without the uppermost or innermost

The eye of the senses or of the flesh is the lowest; [it] is circumscribed and encompassed by the imagination. And insofar as imagination is internal, it is also nobler and more worthy than the external senses. For the more internal, the more forceful and powerful; and the more external, the weaker and more trifling. Reason, the middle eye, encompasses the imagination and insofar as it is more internal, it is also much higher and more powerful in its action or comprehension. Above reason there is still the *oculus intellectus* or *mentis* [the eye of intellect or mind], the highest and innermost. For this reason it is also the most acute and the quickest in its comprehension. For just as external, visible things are seen by the eye in the blink of an eye, so too the invisible, spiritual things are seen in the blink of an eye. Whoever can keep all the external senses still along with the imagination or reason and turn inward into the innermost ground of the soul, awaiting God within himself in quiet abandonment, and can enter upon oblivion of himself and of all things, he will be illuminated by God in his understanding, and this means learning from God, hearing from the Father, and yielding room for the movement of the Father. Everyone can experience such things within himself.

The uppermost, innermost eye can certainly exercise its power without the help and cooperation of the lower eyes, but the lowest can effect nothing without the help and light of the uppermost. About this take note of the following rule: *Quicquid potest potentia inferior, hoc idem potest potentia superior, et multo excellentius, sed non e Contra,* that is, whatever the lower comprehension is capable of, the same can be accomplished by the higher comprehension to a much higher degree. But not the reverse. For the upper eye can do many things that are impossible for the lower eye. Note for example this rule, too: *Unitas omnis est in sua Alteritate, Ceu lux in tenebris, et omnis alteritas est in sua Unitate Ceu tenebrae in luce.* That is, the unity, as the innermost eye, is in the alterity [otherness], as in its lowermost eye,

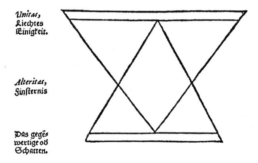

Reproduced from the early printed version of *Der güldene Griff* (1616). The words on the upper left side signify "Unity. The Unity of Light." The words "*Alteritas,* Finsternis (alterity, darkness)" should be grouped with the words at the lower left. The latter signify "The opposing (or the present) or shadow." In the Leiden manuscript version, the same words read "the divided (*das gezweyete*) or shadow." The two interpenetrating triangles signify that the divine unity of being is a light radiating into the darkness of the divided or created being (cf. John 1:5), which in turn casts a shadow back into the divine unity. The figure recalls the geometrical paradigms of Cusanus, even as it anticipates Jacob Boehme's notion of interpenetrating worlds of divine light and creatural darkness.[70]

like a light in darkness. Thus, the understanding is unity compared with reason. Reason is alterity compared with the understanding, and so the understanding in reason is like a light in the shadow or darkness. Thus, reason is unity compared with the imagination; imagination is the shadow or image of reason, and this unitary reason shines into the imagination like a light into the darkness. And imagination in turn [projects itself] into reason, like a shadow into the light. The imagination is unity compared with the external five senses, and is a light compared with them; the external senses, however, are a darkness and shadow compared with the imagination.

Unitas   1. Light unity
Alteritas   2. Darkness, the divided or shadow

This figure reveals how the light shines down into the lowest eye and how the lowest eye casts its darkness or shadow into the upper eye, that is, into its light. The outermost, lowest, brings about nothing without the light of the highest. But the highest can certainly act without the help of the lowest. In the decease of the human being, the outer senses fall away—feeling, smell, hearing, taste, touch; after that the imagination and thoughts; after that reason; and the eternal remains collected in the innermost spirit. Often the middle eye or reason is drowned by too much imagining, and so too the highest eye is often drowned and stifled by the strict action of reason. So too, the spirit of God, the illumination within us, is drowned and hindered by our understanding, if it behaves actively. If the higher is to act, the lower must remain still and passively accept. Thus imagination should effect its works of *cabalistica magia* [cabalistic magic];[70] the external senses must remain still and the imagination may not be extended by the five senses. It must remain collected in itself. In that manner the lower must remain still if the upper is to act. Moreover, if the middle eye, reason, is to effect its works, it must not be hindered by the lowest eye, as by foreign forms of imagining. If the uppermost eye of the understanding is to know and see an invisible thing, the reason must remain still. If the uppermost eye is to be illuminated, it must do nothing, see nothing, know nothing; it must rest in a Sabbath awaiting God. That is to say, if God is to teach and act as the true illuminator, the understanding must submit and suffer. Oh, whoever would be blessed so as to imagine sitting in eternal rest under God need not worry about arts and wisdom; he would learn all things without effort and work. But it is difficult for the natural human being that it should die and not constantly act by fantasizing, discoursing, imagining, seeing, hearing, and so on.

We also learn here that, although the uppermost eye is so high and noble that it can act without the help of the lower, it can nonetheless be prevented and hindered by the lowest. That is why we can read of a philosopher that he had his eyes put out so that his inner eye would not be held back from truth.

1 Understanding mind	*Mens seu intellectus* is angelic, spiritual *divine*, on account of the spirit of God	the highest innermost
2 Reason	*Ratio* is human and [also] angelic on account of the understanding that shines into it	the inner middlemost
3 Imagination seeing, hearing, smell, taste, touch	Is bestial and [also] human on account of the reason shining into it	the lowest outermost

From this, the naive should learn not to judge and condemn others based on their own inability or incomprehension. Just because their naive minds cannot conceive of a thing, they should not assume that others are as coarse as they. It does not follow that this person is a great theologian without having understood the first chapter of Genesis, and that for the same reason, others should not understand it either. [Or] thus, too, imagination cannot grasp how the world stands in nothing and does not fall, but reason sees sufficient cause why the world should stand in nothing and not fall. [For this is as] if the lower eye or *imaginatio* were to say, "I don't understand it, and therefore neither will *ratio* or *mens;* must not therefore reason be as inept as I?" No indeed, it does not follow that one should esteem and judge others to be one's equal out of blind [mis]understanding and ineptitude. As if you were to say, "I have a crude understanding and cannot grasp your writing [or] your preaching, therefore other people must be like me." Rather [you] should say in that [event]: "I have the head of a donkey and do not understand it; others have apt human heads and they will understand it." *Ex tua propria Caecitate et ignorantia noli iudicare seu aestimare alios etiam Caecos et ignorantes etc.* [from your own blindness and ignorance, you should not thus judge or assess others as blind and ignorant]. Realize [instead] that you have not raised your understanding by appropriate practice but instead lie like the other human beasts buried in the dust of the senses. Every object is to each human being as that person is; that is to say, knowledge comes from the eye and not from the object. The way one sees and judges is in accordance with oneself. As your eye is, so too is your knowledge. Thus to the Pharisees Christ is a devil. To the universities a God-taught preacher is an Enthusiast. To the apostles Christ is a Son of the living God and not a devil or seducer. To the *pseudotheologi* or *literantes* [pseudotheologians or literalists], the *Biblia* is a poison and a seduction; to the faithful, however, it is a pleasant and lovely testimony. Oh, eternal God, to each human being you have given light and eye enough. It is only that many do not want to know themselves or to believe those who would lead them to the truth.

✦ • ✦

CHAPTER NINE

That all natural knowledge does not proceed from the object, but rather from the eye itself, and to what end such consideration is good

Inasmuch as in natural knowledge there must be two things— the object or thing vis-à-vis that is to be known and seen by the eye,

169

and the eye or knower that sees and knows the object—in the same way [you should] juxtapose with one another the *videns* [the seeing faculty] and *visibile* [the visible], the *cognoscens* [the knowing faculty] and the *cognoscibile* [that which can be known], iudicans [the judging faculty] and *iudicabile* [that which can be judged], *appraehendens* [the apprehending faculty] and *appraehensibile*, [that which can be apprehended], and [thus] examine whether knowledge comes from the object into the eye or whether the judgment and knowledge flow from the eye into the object.

oculus	*objectum*
the eye	the object
videns	*visibile*
cognoscens	*cognoscibile*
iudicans	*iudicabile*
appraehendens	*appraehensibile*
the seer	what is seen
the knower	what is known
the judge	what is judged

Now, examine whether the eye or the knower is active in its knowledge or passive; in other words, whether the thing vis-à-vis effects something in the eye and thus pours knowledge into it, bringing it into the human being from without, or whether the eye is active and takes its knowledge from that which is to be known, in other words, whether sight or judgment judges, acts, toward the object, or whether the judgment and sight is brought to it by the external object. Such things must necessarily be examined, so that much error is discovered and what follows is more readily grasped. If one were to maintain that all natural knowledge flows hither from the object into the eye, then one would have to grant that from a single object an invariant, undivided knowledge would come into all eyes that have this object before them. But we find that the opposite is the case; it is from the eye that knowledge flows into the object or thing vis-à-vis. For it is in accordance with the nature and property of the eyes that seeing or knowing is accomplished in one and the same object, so that one judges this way and another that way. For that from one and the same object there results so many varied opinions and judgments is not the fault of the object, but rather of those who behold it with such varied sorts of eyes. Now if it were the case that knowledge were effected and carried into the eyes from without, then all eyes would have a single undivided knowledge of it, inasmuch as a single object of knowledge stood before the eyes. An example. A color is on the wall. In front of it stand three or four people. One says it is green. Another says it is blue. The third says it is mixed without green or blue. The thing vis-à-vis remains the same. If it were the case that it effected knowledge in the eyes, then these people would have to receive a uniform knowledge of the color and not have so many illusions about it. Or several individuals are sitting in a public place and they hear at the same time the bell striking in the bell tower. There is one and the same striking of the bell, and yet it is heard differently by many. From that it [may be] concluded that natural knowledge does not flow from the object, but rather from the eye or the knower, and that knowledge of this kind behaves in an active manner and not in a passive one. That is to say, if the eye is to see, it must bring about its effect in regard to the object. For knowing and judging about a thing stands in the knower and *iudicans* [the judging faculty] and not in the object, which has to suffer itself to be judged and known. If you say, Oh, but knowledge does not only come out of the eye, out of the human being from within outward, but rather both from the eye and the object at the same time. For, if there were no object there, no knowledge would come about. For example, if this book had not been written as an object, I could not read and know it. To that one should reply thus: Yes, it is true that if the color were not there, I could not see it, but nonetheless the color does not give me sight, unless it is already in me. If this book did not exist, I could not read and know it. Yet the art of reading is already in me, for this book does not give me [such] knowledge. No object can read or know itself; rather, it must be read by the one who reads it, must be seen by the one who sees, understood by the one who understands. Thus, everything flows out from within, and not from the book inward. If you did not have the understanding in you, you could understand nothing. From that it is concluded that natural knowledge comes from the knower and not from the object vis-à-vis. Therefore, *iudicium* [judgment] remains *in iudicante, intellectus in intelligente, visio in vidente etc.* [in the one who judges; the knowing faculty in the one who knows; seeing in the one who sees, and so on]. From that these things surely follow:

First of all, that knowledge comes from the eye and not from the object. Second, that the object or thing vis-à-vis effects and brings nothing into the eye. Third, that judgment or knowledge varies and differs in accordance with the nature and agility of the manifold eyes and not in accordance with the nature and property of the object; otherwise, a uniform judgment would have to enter from one object into all eyes. Fourth, that the natural eye in its knowledge at all times behaves actively and not passively, *nam cognitio perficitur a cognoscente et non a cognitione*, that is, knowledge is exercised in the knower and not in that which is known, *iudicium est in iudicante et non in iudicato* [judgment is in the one who judges and not in that which is judged]. Fifth, that all knowledge of truth and wisdom must first lie in the human being himself, and not be borne in from the object from without. Sixth, that all useful books are written only as a witness, assurance, note, [and] memorial, to awaken, remind, encourage, warn, to convince and instruct the simple readers in their knowledge of the inner inheritance. Seventh, that to all blind and perverted eyes the most useful of all books are only a poison and irritation, as Christ was to the Pharisees and as Holy Scripture is to the pseudo-theologians. Eighth, that one must have the judgment or light in oneself, taught by God, and not take it from the written letters. For a shadow effects no being; it only gives testimony and leads into the inner ground, insofar as the letter is used in accordance with the spirit or inner understanding.

Oh, Lord God, you have planted your word in my mouth of the inner human being and as a witness to it concealed [the same] in the letters. Govern me by your light and I will be able to read without offense the books for assurance, testimony, and recognition and to confess that all understanding comes from within and cannot be carried in from without. Amen.

✦ • ✦

CHAPTER TEN

*How all natural knowledge is transformed or becomes
various from the nature of the eyes and not from
the nature of the object, from which it is again
concluded that knowledge comes from the eye itself
and not from the object*

From the preceding chapters it has been sufficiently demonstrated that the one eye in the human being is higher and nobler than the other, and that the one greatly surpasses the other in acuteness, worthiness, and agility. From that it is proper to conclude that seeing and knowing do not stem and flow from the object but rather from the eye itself, which is to say, that all natural knowledge and seeing come and are brought about by the knower, and not by the object or thing vis-à-vis. Thus, if the eye is clear, pure, and apt, the knowledge will also be clear, pure, and apt. But if the eye is coarse and dark, the seeing will also be dark and false. In all natural knowledge there must be two things: first of all the eye, and then the object or thing vis-à-vis that is to be seen and known. Without these two no seeing or knowing is accomplished, whether in the visible or in the invisible light of nature, or even in the supernatural light of grace. Although here the simplistic Aristotelian philosopher from the university might want to make the objection that he can fault me by pointing out that there have to be three things for seeing or hearing, that is, the eye as an instrument and the object, as well as the transparent air as a medium; nevertheless, I am not speaking at the moment of the bestial, sensual eye that often peers at a gate like a cow through the intermediate air. For if a cow looks at a new gate, it must have three things to do so properly. But those of us who want to forget the blindness of the university and be instructed in both lights do not speak of such an external, bestial seeing, but rather of the inner human seeing, for which no medium of air is needed, as it is for the bovine seeing. We are more than cows and calves. Hence, our seeing should be spiritual and inner, and not external, bestial, or animal, or the like. The invisible, inner, spiritual eye needs no external air or medium, but rather it places its object before itself, comprehending and penetrating it, whereas the external, sensuous eye has to remain outside in *superficie objecti* [on the surface of the object]. My utilization, notwithstanding, of examples involving the outer seeing is done so that you, the simpleminded Aristotelian philosopher, should be led into the inner eye in order to recognize that seeing does not flow out of the eye and is not brought in[to it] by the object. Inasmuch as all natural knowledge is effected by the eye with regard to the object in an active manner, it follows that seeing and knowing vary and change in accordance with the nature and property and agility of the eye, not in accordance with the object or thing vis-à-vis. Moreover, there is not simply a threefold eye in the human being, but rather each eye in itself can have various distinctions. Not only is the sensual, lowest eye trifling and weak compared to reason, indeed even in itself, among several people, it can be in several sharp, sharper still, and sharpest of all, or blunt, blunter still, and so on. So, too, reason is far below the eye of the understanding, and yet it is among several human beings dark, darker still. And so it is, too, with the eye of the mind; there are quite a few distinctions. In some it is pure, bright, clear; in some dark and opaque. [To take one] example: Sight recognizes its object in one flash even at a distance. But touch or feeling recognizes its object slowly by grasping first one part and then another, doing so at close quarters and not in the distance. Thus, by day I see a tower and recognize at a single glance that it has four corners. But at night I come to the tower and feel one part after the other until I recognize that it is a tower and has four corners. Or take another example of the invisible eye that sees the world and knows upon what [the world] stands. Imagination comes along that otherwise can see physical invisible things from a distance and wants to know upon what the entire world is standing. But it imagines that it stands upon supports so that it won't fall. Such things are seen readily by the rational eye: [It] recognizes the causes of the earth's not falling in any direction. But from this one can draw the conclusion that knowledge does not come from the object but from the eye itself. Otherwise, all eyes would have to form the same concept of one and the same object.

Oh Lord, truth remains truth and [remains this] immovably. But as everyone bears an eye, so does [everyone] see and judge. With that we are all convinced that knowledge flows from the eye and not from the object and cannot be borne in from without, and so on.

✦ • ✦

C H A P T E R   E L E V E N

That the human being is the eye itself, through which all visible and invisible objects are seen and known

How I would like to convince the naive so that they will believe me that the human being is the eye itself, yet I have to say, in the sensual mode, that the eye is not the human being, but rather the human being is the one who sees by means of the eye. And the ear is not the human being, but rather he is the human being who hears by means of and with it. And the tongue is not the human being, but rather he is the human being who thus speaks with the tongue. The hands or the feet do not constitute the human being, but rather the human being is represented and constituted by the one who can use the hands and feet. But with this I hope to have sufficiently shown that the tools should not be accounted as the human being; [the latter is not] the outer eye, but rather the inner, invisible one that knows how to use the outer eye or body: that is who the true human being is. But inasmuch as this invisible, inner human being knows and comprehends all things, either by the senses or by reason or by the understanding, and [inasmuch as his] reason and understanding are nothing other than the spirit of the human being or the invisible human being, it certainly follows that the human being is the eye itself, with and by means of which all invisible and visible objects or things vis-à-vis are known and recognized. Just as an angel is itself all that it can, is, and has, if I may speak in the mode of nature (for in another mode, supernaturally, God is everything in the angel), *so, too, the human being is everything himself* that he can do and know, his art, knowledge, and capacities are his spirit, and this spirit is the human being himself in the mortal body. When this spirit has departed in death, then [only] the body or cadaver remains for the worms. Therefore the body is not the human being, but rather the spirit or inhabitant in the body is the human being himself and the knowledge itself. After the departure of the spirit, the body will no longer be needed, and so on. A smith who forges an axe does not have his art in his hands and feet (though he needs hands and feet to carry it out), but rather the art resides in the spirit; the science or art of the smith is the smith himself. This is to say, the external body that you see is not the smith, but rather the inner body in which the art resides, from which alone the art is exercised and used. [It] only takes the external body as its tool, for the external body can do nothing without the inner. A stonemason has in his *imaginatio* or thoughts a picture to be hewn into a stone. Such art is not of the body but of the inner human being. The latter is the stonemason himself. Thus every art, wisdom, understanding, or capability resides not in the external but rather in the inner human being. The latter is the artist, smith, stonemason, painter, and so on, namely, the spirit in the human being, and [this] is the human being himself. For this reason we have said and concluded that the human being is the eye itself, through which and by means of which all visible and invisible, [all] natural and supernatural things are recognized, known, and studied, and it is from this eye that knowledge and judgment flow into the object, and not the other way around. When one says that the *imaginatio* would like to know and see the location of the world or where [it is that] the angels dwell, and cannot [know and see these things], this is the same as saying that the human being would like to see and know such things by means of the imagination, which can do no more than imagine. Such a human being, who goes no further [than imagining], thinks that outside the world there is a fine place or chamber where the angels dwell and sit upon thrones, or

[he] imagines to himself a thin air outside the world or an external light of the sun in which God dwells with the angels. But the eye of the understanding or mind sees that such things are crude and [that it is] a great imperfection to think that God or the angels should be in need of something external. Therefore the highest understanding casts aside all crude imperfection and discovers that neither sun nor air nor place exists outside of the world and that neither God nor angels are in need of a physical throne, nor indeed of anything external whatsoever, but rather that they are neither here nor there, *and yet are* hovering in themselves, as is God, and so on. The body must be in a place, whether here or there; a spirit is in need of no place. Thus the soul remains [and] the body rots. This outer human being is considered by the outer human being to be the entire human being, though it is only a house and an instrument of the invisible craftsman. So [it is], too, when God utters *producat terra herbas et arbores etc.*, [meaning:] the earth shall bring forth plant life, trees, and so on. [Upon reading this] the naive theologian who is no philosopher considers that the visible *corpus* [physical element] is bringing about such things, whereas they are [actually] brought forth by the invisible spirit from the earth, which is the element. That which we see is only the *corpus* and not the one that does the bringing forth. However, the invisible element does such things through the earth. Therefore, the naive person thinks that the earth does it, which is not the case. The earth is said to bear fruit, [but it is] not [the earth] but the element in it that yields the fruit. The human being speaks out of his mouth; it is not the *corpus* or the tongue that speaks, but rather the spirit does this: the flesh in itself is nothing [cf. John 6:63]. But [this happens] with such a mixing up and uniting that the *corpus* is thought to do all things, though it is [in fact] only a tool of the inner spirit, and this spirit is the human being and the life of the body; [it may be concluded that] life and spirit, knowing, seeing, and effecting all things are indeed one and [at the same time] two. That is, life [or] spirit is inseparable.

✦ • ✦

CHAPTER TWELVE

What natural and supernatural knowledge mean, and that the latter is always passive, but the former active, and to which end such a consideration serves

Natural knowledge is all that in which the human being, by his own powers and capabilities, takes up, examines, cogitates upon, [and] experiences the properties, nature, and effects of the same, whether in the visible or invisible light of nature. This knowledge can also be called an external knowledge, not because it is from the object that the judgment or knowledge is borne in from without into the understanding, but rather because of such an inner knowledge the object is awakened and found by great industry and seeking. For it has already been sufficiently proven that the object does not act with regard to the knower in such a way that it gives judgment and knowledge to the human being, but rather that it flows from the human being into the object itself. However, it can be observed nevertheless that the human being is indeed aroused to knowledge by external objects or things vis-à-vis, as if natural knowledge behaved passively and not actively. Nevertheless, it is to be seen that certainly the *cognitio* [cognition] or the *iudicium* [judgment] is not on the side of the object, but rather in and with the human being, who judges and knows what lies before him. For that reason, although the knowledge of the human being is awakened and admonished by the object, nevertheless it does not come into the human being in a passive way, but rather flows in an active way toward the object in accordance with the nature and agility of the eye. Whether it is aroused or called to mind by the object, in whatever way, in all events, it is a natural, active knowledge. First, because it requires the nature of the human being himself and because all judgment stands with the human being, above the object, and in opposition to supernatural knowledge, [which occurs] by way of grace, [whereby the subject] must comport itself passively and not actively. The supernatural knowledge is not based on the capability from nature; instead, grace acts at the point where the human being with all his reason and wisdom comes into a quiet silence, when God himself pours himself into the passive eye, when the human being only waits and receives, and God gives and effects. In *summa*, when it is precisely the *objectum* that acts upon the eye and not the eye [that acts on] the *objectum*, as happens in natural knowledge. In natural, external knowledge, judgment is in and on the part of the human being regarding the *objectum*. But in supernatural inner knowledge, judgment is in and on the part of the *objectum* or thing vis-à-vis, which is God or his word. Though such supernatural knowledge comes from the *objectum*, nevertheless it does not come from outside; God's spirit and word is in us, and hence knowledge flows from within outward and not from outside inward. Therefore, you literalist theologians cannot say that it is received from the letter, thereby denying the inner word upon which everything depends.

Chapter 1 of the *Theologia Germanica* says that the perfect, incomprehensible Good will not come and be known until everything piecemeal has ceased. [The] creature, with all its activity, art, [and] agility, must stand still and become as nothing in itself, so that the perfect will then come, so that the incomprehensible *objectum*, God, that is, will be known. Indeed, it is rather the case that God sees himself through himself, and knows himself through himself. Inasmuch as [the] creature must vanish and remain still for such inner supernatural knowledge, it can properly be called a passive knowledge, just as the natural is called an active [knowledge], insofar as the creature itself exerts toward practical matters all of its capabilities, powers, senses, understanding, reason, and all activity. From all this the following teaching can be concluded. First, that in natural knowledge unity is not to be found nor sought, even though a unitary object is at hand. For from the nature and agility of the eyes flows such a varied, many-headed judgment. Second, that in supernatural knowledge at all times unity is to be expected and found among all. When all eyes do not behave actively but passively, and when God as the one and only object pours himself into oneness, then in consequence among all the faithful there is [to be] found one *concordance*, one faith, one Christ, one God, one spirit, one heart, one baptism. But among the [merely] natural[-spirited] people, there are mobs, sects, heresies, and nothing but schisms. Take an example: The Bible is an immovable thing vis-à-vis or *objectum* of all natural theologians. If it were the case that in natural knowledge the understanding flowed from the object (as it is said) and not from the eye itself, then certainly the Bible or undivided object of all theologians would have to yield a uniform interpretation or undivided knowledge. Yet we experience just the opposite, to our great dismay. Namely, that it is not from the object which is the Bible, but rather from the eye itself, that is, from the reader and human being that knowledge flows, insofar as every reader knows and judges scripture in accordance with the eye that he is and [that he] applies. Yet what is needed for the Bible is not the *homo animalis*, not the natural human being who perceives nothing of God's word (the understanding is not in him, how should he then perceive it?): it remains closed to him. He must dig in it, like a sow in a beet patch, and [must] remain as blind as the Pharisees who search in the scriptures and suppose that they find life in them, and it is indeed the scriptures that testify of life, but they do not want to come to Christ, to have life [John 5:39]. Thus, they do not want to take leave of their natural, active human being and, by denying themselves, commit themselves to the supernatural passive knowledge. By this example all the universities should be chagrined and brought to their senses; [they should] not take up, read, and understand the Holy Bible, as the unitary *objectum*, in accordance with the natural human being, who remains an enemy of God. On the other hand, the faithful and reborn theologians do know that supernatural knowledge does not flow from the eye, but rather from the *objectum*, that is, from God himself by means of the eye. Therefore, they pray to the Father in the spirit and in truth [John 4:23], whereby their eye is passively abandoned to God, illuminated from above. Then the knowledge comes and the light; [it comes] not from the letter, but from the spirit that is within them. Thus, the supernatural knowledge also comes out from within.

For this reason, what they read in Holy Scripture is to them a sweet testimony; [it] agrees with their heart. For the understanding is within them, and also in the Bible, and therefore they know how to use Holy Scripture. These same ones are and remain all united in their understanding; among them, there is one faith, one spirit, one Christ, one baptism. There is no schism in the holy faith. There is also no Antichrist among them (although they must be subject to the Antichrist), for they are all one, bound together by the spirit in the one and only Christ. Therefore, just as in natural knowledge the judgment comes from the eye itself in an active manner, and [proceeds] creaturally toward the *objectum*, and yields many *iudicia* and schisms, so it is as well in supernatural knowledge, so also does the judgment come from the eye itself, through the illumination of God, [and] likewise from within, but not actively, rather passively, not creaturely, but rather divinely. Therefore, the unitary truth remains undivided among all true Christians because they are subject to the single spirit.

✦ • ✦

CHAPTER THIRTEEN

That in the supernatural, inner knowledge God is the very eye in the human being, [so to speak] his instrument, from which pure unity proceeds in heaven

Natural knowledge can be called a creatural, external knowledge because the creature awakens it by its own powers, capabilities, investigation, and industriousness, and crafts it from the external object for itself. And this should be called external knowledge, not because the object brings it in or effects it from without, as the false theologians claim in the universities and from the pulpit that the letter of scripture pours in divine knowledge from without, [or that] the letter is a vehicle upon which God's word is transported into the heart, and the like; rather, [it is] because such creatural knowledge of the external object takes a recollection of [the object] and thus thinks [the knowledge] borne in from without. Indeed, it is true that all *objecta*, which the creature itself takes before itself and knows, are not internal in the human being (except for God and his Word, who is internal in the human being). Rather, they are all external objects of which a knowledge and judgment are aroused and awakened, whereby this knowledge or judgment must have already been in the human being and not only introduced from the external object. The objects are outside the human being, but the understanding or judgment must be in the human being. The eye must be in one's head if one is to see. The Bible in accordance with the letter is outside the human being, but the understanding of the letter must be in the human being and not come from the external object. But the supernatural knowledge can properly be called the inner, divine knowledge, for it does not come in from without; rather, its object is already within, in the inner ground of the soul, namely God's word, will, law, spirit, and so on. As Christ testifies in Luke 17[:21],[72] the kingdom of God is within you, and the *Theologia Germanica* in Chapter 1 [states as well that] God is an unknowable, incomprehensible *objectum* outside of all creatures, and yet inside all and through all, that is, through his word, law, spirit, and so on. Therefore, it is in vain that God is sought externally in this place or that, as the Antichrist binds God's kingdom to certain persons, peoples, places, gestures, and ceremonies. It is in vain that we would seek the saving knowledge outside [ourselves], in the creatures; God is not [to be] found or seen or known there in eternity, but rather only in his image, Word, or Son, in ourselves, that is where he wants to be found and seen. It is only that here in the saving, supernatural knowledge, the human being is not the eye itself, but rather the human being lets God himself be the eye in, with, and through the human being, which certainly must come to pass not in an active but only in a passive manner.

The eye or the human being who wants to see and know God must do nothing, but rather must be [as if] dead, must celebrate and keep the Sabbath, must give and abandon himself to God in the obedience of faith, [must] await God within himself, and [do so] not externally, in this place or that, with thoughts in an active mode, [by] running hither and yonder among the creatures, and so on. To celebrate and keep the Sabbath in this manner is nothing less than to go into death and to die, indeed, to be thrown into hell, and to be entirely consumed in disbelief, and so forth.

In the preceding it has been proven that in supernatural knowledge the human being is the eye itself. But here in supernatural knowledge the human being is never the eye or the knowledge; rather, God himself is the eye in the human being, and [is this] through the human being as belonging to grace and faith. If God is to act in grace, the human being must remain entirely still and keep the Sabbath, awaiting God in himself. For the true faith from the spirit, which is rebirth, does not let the human being remain himself. Rather, he must be of the one in whom he believes, out of whom he is born again, so that the human being no longer lives, but rather Christ in him. The *objectum*, which the human being wants to and should know, is God or his Word. From this *objectum* or thing vis-à-vis, knowledge flows into the eye as soon as it comports itself passively, so that God knows himself through himself. For the new creature is not of itself, but rather of God. For that reason, God sees and knows himself. Thus, he is the eye and the knowledge itself, in, with, and through the human being, as through his obedient tool;[73] precisely because of the fact that God himself wants to be the eye or the knowledge in the human being, he intends and seeks our highest and eternal bliss. The inexperienced may be amazed that in natural knowledge the human being himself is the eye through which all things in heaven and earth and hell are examined. But it is even more amazing still that God or the *objectum* should be the very eye in the human being. Yet whoever knows Christ dare not be amazed at anything, for he sees indeed out of God and in God that the highest bliss is meant by that. Our eyes are God's eyes; they see what God wants and not what we want. Our reason, understanding, [and] imagining should be God's, and [they] should understand, consider, [and] imagine what God wants and not what we want. And just as the body, including the tongue, ears, hands, [and] feet, are a tool in all [their] natural motion of the inner spirit, thus should our inner human being with all its highest and lowest powers be a tool of God. For just as the tangible body can do nothing without the soul, so too our soul should do nothing without the will of God. All of this is brought about by the true faith, Christ in us. Whoever does not understand the chapter on the passive knowledge of God—[on] how God himself wants to and should be the eye—has not yet known Christ and does not know what faith is. But whoever does understand it knows Christ in faith and remains in the unity of the holy church, which is an assembly of all the faithful in the peace of Christ and indissoluble unity.

✦ • ✦

CHAPTER FOURTEEN

That among the pious unity and peace prevail because of the one will of God, which they bear and suffer in heaven and on earth

As in the case of natural knowledge, a contradictory, divided opinion can arise among people about a single *objectum*, and they cannot have peace and unity: This is evident [both] in hell and on earth in the human church. [It comes about] because the eye or the knowledge comports itself actively, and also [because] each and every eye is so manifoldly different. Knowledge is taken from the letter by human powers, wits, intelligence, understanding, and so forth. This is why there is such a quarreling and disputing among the pseudo-theologians. Just as (I tell you) in natural knowledge discord is beyond all measure, so by the same token with [regard to] its opposite: in supernatural knowledge a laudable unity is maintained on account of the fact that all eyes must comport themselves not actively but passively, and the *objectum*, which is unitary, pours itself into all eyes that have rendered themselves passive in this manner. For this reason peace obtains in heaven among the angels, and on earth [there is] peace and unity among the faithful for as long as they live solely in the will of God. Now someone might nonetheless reason as follows: I see that in the holy faith or supernatural knowledge, the single *objectum* pours itself in the most unified way into all passive eyes; for this reason, one eye will have as much light as any other, and in heaven no one will shine more than anyone else. Instead, everything will be equal. The answer to that is as follows: Concerning eternal life, unity, and peace, everything is indeed equal. But [this is not so] as far as illumination is concerned, for with regard to it the Seraphim and Cherubim have more light than the Powers, and the Powers more light than the lowest angels. And so, too, is it on earth among the faithful: One has more light than the other, one greater knowledge than the other, and yet there is no disunity or schism among them. The degrees of faith or of light are simply greater or smaller, and that causes no division.

The cause of this inequality does not, however, lie in the unitary *objectum*, namely God, who offers himself to all equally without regard for person [Acts 10:34–35; Rom 2:11; Eph 6:9; Col 3:25]. Rather, we human beings are the cause of this [inequality], insofar as we do not give and abandon ourselves to the same degree to God. Therefore, in accordance with the measure of one's surrender or one's faith, one receives light from the unitary *objectum*. The dwellings in heaven are distributed to each according to the degree of having abandoned self in faith to God, about which Christ says: In my father's house are many dwellings (John 14[:2]). If you give yourself wholly and completely to God inwardly and outwardly, then he will give himself to you in turn wholly and completely. About such abandonment [of self], read the sermons of Johannes Tauler.[74]

The sun is a nonpartisan light [that] shines on all equally, the good and the evil [Matt 5:45]. So also is God: He is the love and the light itself, [he] loves even his enemies, and [he] is ready to illuminate everyone.[75] Indeed, his light, word, spirit, Christ, law, and so on shine already in the darkness (John 1[:5], Luke 17[:24]), and [he] advances far ahead toward us with his light, if only we were faithful and abandoned hearts. You should hear an example. In a room there is a window with three kinds of glass, one black and opaque, one yellow and thick, and one white and pure. Upon these three the sun shines simultaneously without regard for their susceptibility. But for the fact that the opaque one remains dark and is not illuminated, and for the fact that the yellow one does not receive as much light as the white one, the nonpartisan sun was not at fault. Instead, the glass itself was the hindrance because of its own insusceptibility. That is the way it is for the rational creature that in an unequal way gives and abandons itself to God. For the spirit buried in the sensual, bestial nature knows nothing of the kingdom of God or of the divine light in the darkness, and whoever else diverts his thoughts with his own cleverness and activity will find little of God in himself. But whoever collects his reason and understanding into the inner ground and awaits God in quiet abandonment will experience and confess that what I write here about the inner ground and witness of the spirit is true.

From all these things there also proceed these following sorts of teachings: First, that supernatural knowledge does not comport itself actively but rather passively with respect to its object. Second, that the object pours out its light equally, like the sun its radiance upon all eyes. Third, that the inequality of the light is caused not by the object, but rather by the incongruent reception or unequal attendance. Fourth, that the good God is not a cause of human blindness, but rather the human being due to faithlessness.

Fifth, that nonetheless peace in unity abides among the faithful notwithstanding the unequal illumination. Sixth, that supernatural knowledge is so called, because such an *objectum* is attained neither by the senses nor by the imagination, nor by reason, nor by understanding, but instead surpasses all natural powers and capacities. Seventh, that faith is a work and gift of the Holy Spirit, [given] into surrendered hearts and in no way [a work] of the creature. Eighth, that all supernatural knowledge or wisdom of God must already have been concealed in us, for divine knowledge cannot be carried in from without. It must spring from within outward, from the Father of lights [Jas 1:17]. Ninth, that scripture effects nothing essential in us, but rather is useful as a warning, admonition, instruction, [and] awakening of the treasure, the inner word that God has laid up in us. Tenth, that the faithful person is not his own self, but rather God's, so that God should remain all in all.

✦ • ✦

CHAPTER FIFTEEN

That in the human being both kinds of wisdom or knowledge come through the birth from within and not through the shadow from without

Everything that the human being is and should be, here in this time and afterward in that other life, the human being is and has not from without, but rather within himself. Now, wisdom or knowledge is the best and noblest in the human being. Such things come from within out of the human being, and not from without inward. This is so unless one were to believe that the external objects carried in such knowledge, yet it is only a matter of an awakening through them. What the human being is and should be by nature he must have and possess it within himself and not seek it without. But how it comes about in the human being or enters must happen by means of birth or conception. Every Christian has a twofold conception or birth; the first comes from the seed. The seed is the *limus terrae* [clay of the earth], which is the great world with all creatures, from which Adam was made, and all of us from Adam.[76] Thus Adam is in us and all his nature and properties. In this seed or natural human being lies concealed all natural wisdom for mortal life and everything that has to do with art and wisdom; it lies in this natural birth from the clump of earth. The second birth happens from the seed, namely, from the seed of the woman, which is the *spiraculum*,[77] the spirit of God, the Word of God or Christ in us, indwelling through faith. In this seed, or in the second birth from heaven, lies the entire Christ, with all heavenly eternal goods. There the kingdom of God is entire and complete, but not apparent; it must be awaited, recognized, found, felt, [and] tasted in the inner ground of the soul. This twofold birth encompasses the natural, transient [wisdom] and the supernatural, celestial wisdom, and from these two births it must come to us. Otherwise, neither the natural nor the supernatural knowledge would be in us or be able to be achieved by us. The scripture says that the human being is placed in the midst of the garden. This is to be understood in precisely the sense that the human being is placed in [the midst of] that from which he has been made. This great world and all creatures are the outer garden; from this outer garden the human being has been made, and [he] encompasses within him all creatures with the entire world. For that reason he is called *microcosmos*, which is the little world, and just as he has been created out of it, in accordance with his mortal part, so too has he been placed in the midst of it, and is a *centrum*, that is, a midpoint of all creatures. Moreover, the human being has also been made from the *spiraculum vitae*, with an eternal soul and a spirit from the mouth of God. And just as the spirit has been taken out of God, from the inner garden, so, too, he [i.e., the human being as spirit] must live in God; outside of God he can neither stand nor proceed, neither live nor hover. He cannot do without God his sustainer even for a moment, no more than he can do without the outer garden in his mortal part. Thus, the human being has all creatures and the world within himself and is encompassed by the world [and] cannot be outside of the world, just as he has God within himself through the *spiraculum*, or inhalation, and is embraced and held by God and can neither live nor hover outside of God (Acts 17[:28]). Inasmuch as these two gardens are in the human being, the outer, which is this world and all creatures, and the inner, which is God's spirit, it can undeniably be concluded that both kinds of knowledge and wisdom are also concealed in the human being, though the one is intended for this temporal life and the other for the eternal immortal life; and that both are not borne in from without, but rather come from within out of the human being. This too is obvious from the light of nature and the light of grace. Whence have books been written? Out of the human being. Whence does the tree grow? Out of the seed. Just as there lies concealed in the cherry pit a great tree with roots, trunk, branches, twigs, leaves, and many hundreds of cherries or seeds, and no one would believe or see this if one did not throw the seed into the ground, so that it is sown to grow, so too there lies in the human being a seed (which is hardly the size of a pea), all inner and outer members of the body, [and] in addition all natural wisdom for mortal life in the sidereal spirit, and when it has grown to a rational human being, the human being [still] knows nothing of it unless he is aroused and awakened to it. Thus is the kingdom of God within us through rebirth or faith. But no one knows it unless he is aroused and admonished to it. But there may be a naive soul who asks: If all is within me, and nothing could come in from without, why then do they write so many books, and [why] must one practice at the arts and crafts? Or, if the kingdom and law and word of God is in me, why then is it written with letters and preached? The answer is: One learns arts and crafts because the wisdom and knowledge were already in us, and for the same reason one writes good books, so the naive will be reminded, awakened, encouraged, admonished, and convinced of the natural inborn inheritance in us. For the same reason, too, the law was formed in stone, because it was in our hearts. And for the same reason did the Word become flesh, and did Christ come physically, because his spirit was in us and must now become bodily in us through the new birth. And for that very reason one preaches outwardly the word of faith that was already in our heart and mouth (Rom 10[:8], Deut 30[:14]), so that we may become completely aware of the inner ground and treasure and accept Christ completely, even in accordance with his flesh and blood, in which the new creature from heaven stands. Everything would be written, learned, and preached for naught and in vain, if it were not already in us. Theophrastus Paracelsus in his little book *On the Foundation of Wisdom*[78] says it thus: Wisdom is sufficient in all people, for all inherit wisdom, and no one can claim that he has more than another. For just as little as a human being is made by God with a member less than another, even as little is the human being deprived of wisdom. For just as is the emperor, so also the peasant; as Christ, so also the human being. As you know that just as the body is one thing in all, and no one is poor or rich in it, but rather all equal, so that no one can say that he is more bodily membered than the other, so too in wisdom no one can say that he has been deprived of wisdom and gifted like a simple wretch, and so on. Nothing of the kind [is the case], but rather it is the case that out of laziness we do not want to be awakened to wisdom and [do not want to] seek the

inborn inheritance. It is not the case that when a congregation con-
venes, no one is capable of anything and all people [are] simpletons
except for one who gives the advice and direction; and when he has
proposed something to the peasants, they all say, "Yes, by God, he is
right. It is just as he says." If now this good advice and direction had
not also been in you, as well as in him, how could you have recognized that he was right? You testify with yourself that he was right;
therefore you have the same wits in you as he does. But you did not
use yours and did not heed them, and so you say: "I didn't think that
far." Now you are a witness to yourself in the inheritance you have,
which is wisdom. So says Theophrastus. If God has given us the
natural knowledge or wisdom of the outer garden, all the more has
he given us his wisdom of the inner garden, of himself. Therefore,
the faithful accept Christ as the true witness of God, but the Pharisees and all those who have despaired of God call Christ and his
followers the devil, because they do not know the treasure, the
inner word, [and] the celestial wisdom.

✦ • ✦

CHAPTER SIXTEEN

That books do not effect or make any being in the human being but should only be written and used as a keepsake, reminder, memorial, or testimony

Though this chapter on the utility of books might not seem to
belong in this place, nonetheless one must say something about it,
so that it is thereby shown how it happens that knowledge does not
flow from books, as if from the *objectum*, but instead from the eye or
the knower into the *objectum*. It is said and maintained that books or
the writing of the letter imparts knowledge to the reader, and thus
that judgment and knowledge are carried into the human being
from the book, from outside, which is nonetheless not the case. For
everything that is written externally into the good, useful books is
already in us, and when we read or hear it, there must certainly be in

us knowledge or *iudicium* [judgment] about the book. The book is outside us. It can't read itself. Nor can it speak. The letter is outside us, but the understanding of the letter is in us. In us is the knowledge [and] the judgment, and not in the book. Aroused and admonished we might well be so that we arrive at the inner treasure, [that is] at wisdom, but it does not follow that knowledge or wisdom is carried in from without, through the letter. If that were the case, then all readers would receive understanding from the book and not be able to say, "I do not understand it," "I don't know how to interpret it," and so on. Just as an accident cannot effect substance, and a shadow cannot make being itself, so too a book or writing cannot effect the inner being in the human being; that is [done by] the wisdom or the concealed understanding beneath the letter. A mirror on the wall certainly indicates something and how we are shaped, but it makes no one be that way; even if an art is written in a book, so that [one] can read of it, one is still not the artist unless one practices and learns the same art, which is written up for one and also concealed in one. Thus are all books and writings [there], that [they may] only indicate what we are and how we should be, but no one can read himself pious or adept. For that reason all books are only external things, only there for a warrant, for a witness, for an encouragement, reminder, arousal, and for recognition whether we are that way or not. When Adam was in paradise, he was in need of no books or ceremonies, no written laws, the same as the angels in heaven and the infants on earth need no books, and so on. But after the fall into sin, when he and his progeny became worldly, external, and carnal, the law was written and the ceremonies and books were given in order to conduct [us] into the inner human being, into the true inner book from which all books have flowed. For that reason, all ceremonies, writings, and laws have been given as a memorial, remembrance, [and] testimony, for awakening and direction into the inner ground. And in truth, if we had remained inner human beings and still lived in accordance with the spirit; to this day we would be in need of no books, just as the prophets needed none. For what the simple ones read aloud or heard through the oral voice, the same things were heard and read in the true inner book of the heart. Therefore what has been written of the prophets is only written on account of our blindness and weakness and as a warrant, testimony, cognizance of all that was in us, as well as for a memorial. As often as one overcomes the outer hindrance and goes in to God, in oneself, one finds sufficient light and knowledge and knows more than all books. But inasmuch as we cannot always be inner human beings, like the prophets, some things are written down with letters, as a memorial for us and a remembrance and for the awakening and encouragement of others and to convince others in [the event of] disagreement, so that they may be brought to the inner ground, to the true living book. But many remain outside, cleaving to the shadow, to the shell, [and] do not desire to go further inward to the being and core itself.

✦ • ✦

CHAPTER SEVENTEEN

On the twofold contemplation or judgment of scripture by the outer and by the inner human being

Scripture and all judgments have two aspects: one the way a thing is before God, and one the way it appears to and is termed by human beings; on the one hand, the way it is signified inwardly in the spirit and in the inner being before God, [and] on the other hand, the way it is signified in the outer [world] before the human being. Thus Solomon calls all the worldly wise ones fools, for that is what they are before God. Paul calls these same fellows fools and wise ones (1 Cor 1[:19–20], 2[:14], 3[:18–19]), as they are called by the world and as they think and seem to themselves. Therefore, these two things do not contradict one another, even though the one says wise and the other says fools. The one calls them as they are before God, the other as they are before and are called by the world. Theophrastus says that God needs nothing, effects nothing, exercises nothing, and so on. So says Mercurius [Hermes Trismegistus]: God effects, exercises, needs all things. These two are not against one another, for the one speaks of God as he is *absolutely*, understood in and of himself. In that case he is inactive, affectless, and so on. The other speaks of God in regard to the creature, [God] who effects, exercises, and uses all [things] in all, and no creature can move without [this] God. Thus, the scripture says that a Christian cannot sin or die, and elsewhere that a Christian can do nothing but die and sin; both are true and not a lie in accordance with how one regards and judges it. The first is true in accordance with the inner human being and spirit; the second is true of the outer human being and the flesh. Two [parties] often conflict with one another and are [both] right, and are thus conflicted, united, or one. Thus scripture is bright and clear and is God's word. Scripture is dark and murky and a dead letter. Both are true and a lie. The first is true [for] to a faithful illuminated heart, scripture is God's word, and [a] good, pleasant testimony and bright and clear. But to an unilluminated, unbelieving heart it is dark and murky and a dead letter, a poison and death. Thus, the human being has no free will after the fall, and the human being does have a free will after the fall. Both are true and a lie.[79] The first is true and also a lie. It is true that the human being has no free will to convert himself of his own powers, *non est volentis neque currentis etc.* [Rom 9:16, Vulgate]. It is not within the will or action of the human being to be able to convert when he wants. It is a lie that the human being should not have a free will to say yes or no to the preceding grace of God, to abandon himself or to resist, and so on. Accordingly, that the human being has a free will is also true and a lie. It is true, for the will must, in a passive manner, bear and suffer God's grace. For against one's will God forces no one. But it is a lie that the human being has a free will, to convert oneself by one's own powers. Thus, nothing can be spoken or said that does not have a twofold aspect or judgment. From this, there arise such opposing judgments, the one in accordance with the spirit and God, the other in accordance with the flesh and human being. Therefore, one cannot speak about a thing *absolutely* correctly or incorrectly; for what one says about it is true and untrue, namely, in accordance with the way one looks at and judges it. For that reason, no one should be trapped in a statement.

According to the way one sees and judges a thing, it is true or false, and it is too bluntly said about all things when one speaks or wants to speak of them *absolutely* in a single way and fashion, on account of the two aspects that all things have, the one in accordance with human eyes, the other in accordance with God's judgment, the one before the translation and rebirth. Therefore, it is too short-sighted, when one insists on compelling, forcing, or defying [one's opponents], whether one is on one side of a dispute or the other. For example, [when one argues] that the human being is corrupted *accidentally*, and that sin is an *accidens*; and that the human being is substantially corrupted [and] sin is a *substance*. Both are true and a lie. The human being is accidentally corrupted, and sin an *accidens*, if one thus considers the soul. [One can consider] how sin arises from the will, and all sin is only in the will, and without the will no sin can happen. In this regard, sin is an *accident*, for the soul remains the soul and the will has only become broken and [has] not [been] lost.

However, when one regards the fruit of sin, that the body is corrupted, then it is not true; then sin is no *accident*, but rather a substance; for *substantialiter* [in terms of substance], the human being is corrupted in body. The entire body has been lost to the human being through sin, and thus too the *renascentia* [rebirth] is substantial and physical. For the human being receives a new celestial body out of Christ. Thus, that sin is a substance is true and a lie. It is true when one regards the effect or fruit of sin, that the substance of the body must entirely perish and that the worms eat it. In this regard, corruption is no *accident*, but rather [there is] also an essential renewal. But it is a lie when one considers the root of sin in the will. In that, sin is an *accident* and not a substance. For neither the will nor the soul have ceased to be in their substance. The will has simply become broken and not lost, and thus the rebirth or renewal is also only an *accident*; the new heart, courage, sense, and so on, is only brought about in accordance with aptitude. God does not create a new soul or heart, in the way that he creates a new celestial body, and so on. Whoever proceeds in accordance with the new birth is an inner human being. For the outer [human] is daily diminished, and whoever lives in accordance with the old birth is an outer human being, for the inner [being] is diminished by the lust of the flesh.

✦ • ✦

CHAPTER EIGHTEEN

Whence one customarily seeks and takes judgment

Whoever neither knows nor understands a thing (that is, whoever does not have the understanding or the eye within), must believe what others say, speak, and write, and must abide by this. So, for example, let us say that there is a city that has a miscreant in prison and does not know what to do to him. The city puts out an inquiry in the seats of lay justice and asks those who have experience of jurisprudence, and these answer based on the [code of] Justinian that one should behead the miscreant. The city abides by the answer, beheads the miscreant, and lets the jurists have the responsibility. But if we were Christians, we could see with our own eyes what is to be done and would not need to believe the answer of Justinian.[80] That's the way it happens with the worldly scholars: They ask others about this or that article, and whatever is reported to them by [other] people they believe. Now, although the proper and true fundamental judgment concerning all objects must flow out from within, from the eye (for as the eye is, so is the judgment taken), nonetheless there are those who do not want to know or recognize such things. For that reason they claim to take and draw their judgment either on the persuasion and opinion of others or from the simple letter of scripture. For all those who place their faith in the human being, and not in the inner sense in the spirit, expect to take and fabricate their judgment from the respect and authority of their superior teachers, and they say: Because this man has written this and believed it, for that reason do I also want to believe and opine as he does; he cannot be wrong. And because everyone for love of his teachers has selected a scribe for himself, and concocts out of this respectability and persuasion a belief for himself, it follows that faith is divided into so many sects (although the true faith is and remains only one). Others do not want to depend on the human being this way, and instead they take their judgment from the letter of scripture. Because it sounds so or so, for that reason they want to believe about their proposed articles, and whoever thinks differently is a heretic; and those who depend on the letter can never come to agreement with one another. For it is ambidextrous, and everyone can use it for himself as he will. This is why so many schisms and sects have arisen. The third [group] believes to please no one; [its members] draw their judgment not from the dead letter but rather from the faith of the spirit through the inner living sense in the heart. These remain undeceived; they are rocks; their house is built not on sand, but rather on Jesus Christ. And those are the Christians to whom it is said: Test the spirits, to see whether they are from God; whoever does not have the spirit of Christ, is not your kind (1 Thess 5; Rom 8[:9]; 1 Cor 13).

Oh, God, you true light, you not only shine in me from within, you also give me a firm prophetic word upon which I can count, as if on a light, which shines there in a dark place until the day dawns or the morning star rises in my heart (2 Pet 1[:19]). Lord, let your light break through the darkness, then my eye will be illuminated through your Word in me so that I will see, feel, and taste the truth. Thus, I will not believe so as to please anyone or draw my judgment from other people's respectability. Nor will I use the scriptures falsely in order to seduce others, but rather take the same as a testimony and exercise and make use of [them] in accordance with the spirit. Amen.

✦ • ✦

CHAPTER NINETEEN

That no one should take or make a judgment based on other people's persuasion or consideration, for it would be taken in from without and against the light of nature

The judgment through which one sees and knows what is true or false and [through which] one does no one injustice is nothing other than the true, saving faith, or Christ dwelling within us through faith (Col 1[:4]; 2 Cor 13[:5]; Rom 8[:9]). But inasmuch as the true faith renews, sanctifies, purifies, cleanses, justifies, and illuminates the heart, it is truly a living sense, feeling, seeing, hearing, touching, and tasting, so that I can joyously die thereafter, and it is not a dead, concocted phantasy. It follows from that that all those who put their faith in books and the respectability of teachers without any inner sense and experiencing in the spirit have no faith and no right judgment either. For how is it possible that I should see with the eyes of another, or hear with the ears of another, and taste with the tongue of another? Faith is an essential sense, seeing, feeling, and hearing in the inner human being.

For that reason it [faith] cannot be drawn from persuasions of people or the respectability of the writers. For even if your teacher, doctor, or writer had believed and written correctly, it would not help you if you did not sense and taste it in your heart. It is worth nothing to believe based on persuasions, nor is it good enough to say he was such a man, he had the Holy Spirit, he cannot be wrong. Submit it to the test beforehand whether it is true; it would be a sour task and difficult for you to prove such things. What is Cephas? Who is Apollo? Who is Paul?—asks the Apostle.[81] Who is this one or that one? They are human beings. God, God, God alone is the one who effects faith and gives us the judgment to test all spirits and writings.

Oh, eternal God and Creator, you have given to all alike the eye, ear, tongue, and so on of the spirit, that they shall see the truth and not believe based on persuasions so as to please anyone. But there are many who willfully let these [organs] be put out and stopped up; many let their tongue of the inner human being be tainted and soiled by venom and dirt, so that they can neither see, nor hear, nor taste. Oh, God, you sole light, illuminate my eye! Oh, God, you single understanding, open my ear! Oh, God, you highest purity, wash off my tongue of the inner human being. Then I will see, hear, [and] taste, with the prophets and the faithful Abraham, the day and the power of Christ within me, and not believe in order to please anyone. Amen.

✦ • ✦

CHAPTER TWENTY

That one should not draw the judgment in knowing all objects from the letter of scripture

Whoever takes his judgment from the letter of scripture and not from the Holy Spirit builds his faith on sand and must remain uncertain in all matters. The true judgment (as has been said) is the true faith, and faith is the true knowledge of God in Christ; such knowledge is the judgment and the touchstone for distinguishing false and true. Whenever judgment or faith is supposed to be taken from the letter of scripture, it is as if knowledge would flow out of the object, which is impossible, as will be shown in the following chapter. Scripture, read and used without the spirit, is ambidextrous: Everyone can use and lead it any way one wills against one's enemy and opponent. For each and every sect can meet its opponent with scripture; it can be turned like a waxen nose.[82] Thus, on one side the one sect says: Watch out for false prophets, false teachers. And so against that the other sect answers back: Watch out for false prophets. It may be that both [sects] are from the devil. Nevertheless, they can turn scripture against one another, like two whores in one house, whereby each claims to be justified, and there is nothing good about either, and so on. Christ says against the Pharisees:

You are children of the devil; you are of the devil. The Jews also say against Christ: Now we see that you possess the devil, and so on. Thus one sect also says against the other: *Quid Christo cum Belial?* What does Christ have to do with Belial? And everyone employs scripture for himself and against his opponent. Whoever wants to judge or test who it is that is right or wrong must have an eye; [that is,] he must have faith. Two face off against one another. The one says: They will hate, persecute, damn, [and] hereticize you on my account. The other one can make the same statement and cite the same [passage from] scripture. And each believes that this passage applies to him alone, no matter how false that might be. For the worst heretic of all can patch and cover himself with scripture, like Adam with fig leaves. For that reason no one will judge or know what is true or false, unless he has the spirit of Christ, the true judgment, within himself; for a sick person cannot make himself healthy by looking in the mirror, but rather by means of the medicine that is Christ himself by means of his spirit and power in us. Scripture is a mirror; it shows to you what you are, beautiful or horrid, sick or healthy, but it doesn't make you that. For that reason you cannot take judgment or faith from the letter of scripture; rather, in the word or the spirit you must seek and await it.

Oh, God, you true light, you have given me your word or spirit for life, so that I should walk in it as if in a single light. You have also given me scripture as a testimony to the light within me, so that I should turn inward again to the true inner human being, out of whom I ran away through disobedience. Effect the true faith through your spirit in me so that the day will dawn and the bright morning star rise in my heart. Then, I will prove my judgment and testimony of the spirit in all constancy and lead and conduct others without any error through the use of scripture to the truth. Amen.

VALENTIN WEIGEL

✦ • ✦

CHAPTER TWENTY-ONE

That knowledge does not proceed and come from the thing known, from the object, but rather from the knower himself

If I am to see a thing, I must have an eye; if I am blind, I cannot see. If I am to hear, I must have hearing in me; if I were deaf, I could not hear. If I am to taste and to distinguish tastes, then all these things would have to be in me; if not, I could not sense what is cold or warm, sweet or sour. From that, it is proven beyond contradiction that knowledge flows not from the object or thing vis-à-vis, but rather from the one who looks at and knows it, that is to say, from the eye and not from the object. *Cognitio* [cognition] comes from the *cognoscente* [the knowing one] and not from the *cognoscibili objecto* [knowable object]. *Iudicium* [judgment] must come from the *iudicante* [the one who does the judging] and be in the *iudicante*, and not [come] from the *iudicando objecto* [object to be judged]. Those are two different things: *judicans* [judging faculty] and *judicabile* [that which can be judged] or *iudicatum* [object of judgment]. The one is an *activum*, which is active, the other is a *passivum*, which is passive.

But if the judgment or knowledge is supposed to proceed from the *objectum* and not from the eye itself, it must necessarily follow that ten who judge or see one single *objectum* all receive or take the same and undivided judgment or knowledge of it, which is hardly the case. For just as often as an eye [looks at it], even that often does a particular knowledge or judgment of the single *objectum* [result]. So many heads, so many judgments; so many readers, so many senses: [all of] which would not happen if the knowledge of judgment came out of the *objectum* and into the eye. In accordance with the way one brings one's eye [to bear] on the object, that same way does one know, see, and judge the same. If the eye is truly bright within you, then your knowledge or judgment will be truly bright and without error. But if your eye is defective and dark, then your seeing, knowing, and judging will also be false and unjust. There-fore, just as you apply an eye, in the [same] way will you see and judge the *objectum*. From that it is concluded that all knowledge comes from within through the eye into the *objectum* and not from the *objectum* into the eye. Experience and the light of nature testify to this. For God has called forth all things from the inner conceal-ment [in]to the light, from the spiritual into the outer, physical [realm]. For that reason all visible things must be seen, known, and judged by the invisible spirit.

Oh, God, you invisible, concealed Creator, who sees all things in yourself from within before they emerge, you who have created all the angels as well, so that they, like you, see all things from within in themselves; you are the seeing, knowing, and judging in each one. You have called all things from the invisible into the visi-ble [realm], to be a tangible object. Oh, illuminate our dark hearts, so that we will not deny the eye that you have given us; then we will have to affirm that all knowledge flows out of the eye into the object, and all judgment must come, not from the *objectum* but rather from the *iudicante* [one who does the judging], and then will we be saved from many errors and delivered.

✦ • ✦

CHAPTER TWENTY-TWO

*That the object does not bring in the judgment or knowledge
from outside into the knower is proven
with Holy Scripture*

Not in vain does the Lord say in Matthew 6[:22–23]: If your eye is light, so will your entire body be light; and conversely, if your eye is dark, your body will be dark. That means as much as: If your heart is illuminated in faith, you can read the scripture well, for it will be in agreement with your heart; and your whole exegesis will flow out of the spirit, [and] out of the true eye. Conversely, if you are faithless, then your eye is dark and all your reading and interpreting is false; it proceeds only from the letter, and you will lead yourself and others with you astray into the eternal darkness. Some say that scripture is bright and clear and would conclude from that that one must take one's faith or the knowledge of Christ from it. But they don't say for whom it is bright and clear, namely, to the pure, faithful, God-instructed hearts. To the faithless it is obscure and dark and remains concealed and covered up. Therefore, in accordance with the kind of eye you bring to bear on Holy Scripture, so you will regard it (as has often been said). If you put on blue-tinted glasses, then objects will seem to you blue, though they are not blue. If you put on red-tinted glasses, all objects will appear red, though they are not red.[83] If you have no understanding through the spirit, scripture will appear to you divided and against [itself], though it is unitary in spirit. Therefore, if you want to use scripture with fruit and usefulness, then the knowledge or judgment must be in you beforehand, and flow out of your eye of the spirit, and not flow only from the object inward. Take an example. The Bible is a unitary, invariant object (as we have so often said up to now). Now let there be one hundred readers present and each takes his under-standing out of his own head. I say each out of his head: that means from his eye, and not from the object. If it were the case that the judgment or knowledge came from the object and not from the illu-minated, faithful eye or reader, then certainly all of the one hundred readers would take or receive a uniform, undivided understanding of all articles from the thing vis-à-vis or object, yet it is not so. Rather, it happens as they say: *Quot homines tot sensus*, as many human beings as there are, that's how many heads there are. Therefore, to our own sorrow, we are shown that knowledge or judgment is in the knower or *iudicans* [judging one] and not from the *objectum*. See, that is the way it goes with all those who through the letter impose themselves as judges of heresy, though they have a blind eye and lack the testi-mony of the spirit, deny their eye, so that in accordance with their eye's nature, which is dark and opaque, they regard and condemn Christ and all his followers as the devil and tempter.

Oh, God, you have given to us all in the beginning a pure and clear eye, by giving us of your spirit so that we should not conduct ourselves in accordance with the flesh, externally, but rather in accordance with the inner human being. However, because we deviated and became external, worldly people, and forgot about the treasure within, so have you given us also that which was hidden in us, letting it be written into the letters as a testimony, consolation, warning, instruction, and so on. Oh, break forth within us, you true light! Open up the understanding to us through your spirit, which dictated and wrote scripture. Then we will not seek in vain with the Antichrist for the judgment from the letters, as if from the object, but instead see the light in your light from within, with great joy and jubilation, and take and use Holy Scripture as a precious gift, as testimony. Amen.

✦ • ✦

CHAPTER TWENTY-THREE

That faith alone is the right judgment, and the knowledge of God, and the testing of spirits

Just as the saving faith is or brings with it all virtues, and everything that can be called good, so too it is the compass, criterion, the measuring rod, [and] yardstick for measuring the heavenly Jerusalem with its inhabitants. Don't be surprised that I say that faith is all things, that it is the judgment by which all sects are known and judged, [that] it is the eye through which all spirits are tested and seen. Whoever has faith has Christ and all things in Christ. Whoever has faith, of which the foundation is firm and unmoving, his faith is not built upon sand but upon a solid rock. For inasmuch as the true faith is not a human work, but rather a work and gift of God, God effects all that is good in the surrendered human being; for God gives himself to the heart through faith, so that he dwells in the human being, and that is called Christ. Such faith or Christ dwelling in us translates the human being from nature into grace; it renews, sanctifies, purifies, justifies, and illuminates the human being, so that he becomes a new creature, created through Christ for good works, so that the human being is no longer himself but instead God's. Every faithful human being has been delivered from himself and surrendered unto God; God thereby knows himself in the human being. From such a knowledge of God comes the judgment of all objects: Scripture is thereby taken as testimony—for it agrees with the heart—and such a one does not need to believe against his heart. Indeed, whoever forces himself to faith, and believes against his heart, only persuades himself that he is faithful, and yet is not. What is missing is the very best, namely, the testimony of the spirit. That is why such a one cannot test the sects, for he does not have the spirit of Christ (Rom 8[:9]). Therefore, let everyone first test himself, whether he is faithful, whether he has the indwelling Christ (2 Cor 13[:5]). Whoever does not [have him] lacks the measuring rod or yardstick for testing the spirits, to know the objects, to read scripture, and to distinguish truth from lies. Conversely, whoever does have the same has the eye to see all objects, with a pleasing distinction; he likewise has the measuring rod, to separate lies from truth. For whoever wants to know what is false and crooked must first of all recognize what is straight and true; and all of this is accomplished by faith, from which the judgment proceeds about all objects without any error.

Oh, God, you eternal truth, you hate lies. Oh, God, you eternal life, you vanquish death. Oh, God, you true light, you drive out the darkness. Effect through your spirit in me the saving faith, so that I will be illuminated in my eye to see and distinguish the false and the right, to avoid darkness and death, and to know in truth all spirits, [discerning] whether they are from you.

Amen.

✦ • ✦

C H A P T E R   T W E N T Y - F O U R

**That one should not seek nor can one find the testing
of spirits in external books of human beings,
but rather in the spiritual book of the heart
from within, and [by] taking Holy Scripture
as a testimony of this**

Before I came to the beginning of the true faith, and also [when] I believed along with the others so as to please the crowd, I was often very worried about this or that article [of faith] and would have liked to know on what I should have built [my belief]. I took up the books of many authors [and] read through them. But no satisfaction came to me. My heart was more and more uncertain. I could find neither ground nor truth. I regarded and considered our miserable darkness, the skirmishing, groping, and going astray. I found so many beliefs and sects now, even among those who claimed to be certain of their thing and ground, and [who] wanted to secure their protection from Holy Scripture. I beheld what a confused Babel was among us. Where the one spoke of faith, the other wanted to have works. Where the one spoke of fruits, the other would recognize nothing but a concocted faith. The third said that the sacraments were necessary for faith or for salvation. The fourth asserted that one must first take faith from the sacraments. The fifth considered that faith had to precede the sacraments. Otherwise they would not be effective or useful. The sixth said that the true faith in Jesus Christ alone makes just and saves, nothing else, no matter what. For that, he was called an Enthusiast and Sacramentarian.[84] I saw thus how one denounced the other to the worldly authorities, imprisoning, exiling, and the like, on account of original sin, free will, the person of Christ, and so on; and there was such a going astray and skirmishing for the sake of heaven, into which no one wanted to enter, even as [such things still] are going on in this present year 1578, and with no end in sight. And as I was so uncertain and sorely worried, with inner sighing to God and praying: Oh, God and truth, be told how we walk in darkness; it is as if the blind had been aroused against one another to do battle in darkness, where one as readily strikes his best friend and strikes at his throat as if [he were] an enemy. Let your Word shine to me, Lord, so that I, along with others, will be saved from this wilderness of darkness. As I thus called and prayed to the Lord, grace was visited upon me from above. For a book was shown to me that delighted me and illuminated my heart, so that I could judge and know all things [and I] could see more clearly than if all teachers in the entire world had instructed me with their books. For from it all books had been written from the beginning of the world, and this book is in me and in all human beings, in the great and the small, in young and in old, in the learned and the unlearned. But few indeed could read it. Indeed worse still, many of the worldly wise rejected and denied it [and instead] adhered to the dead letter that is outside them and neglect the book of life that is within them.

I thank you, God, you strength of my life and you light of my heart, that you make me more learned than all my teachers and book writers, that you show me the real book in my heart, through which I can read with certainty Holy Scripture that has been given to me as a testimony. For I behold it in accordance with the being and spirit that is in me and not in accordance with the shadow and dead letter that is outside me. Turn me inward, Lord, to find you within myself, that I will find and confess that the one faith is the criterion and touchstone for reading scripture and for judging all sects and spirits.

✦ • ✦

CHAPTER TWENTY-FIVE

That this book is God's word, or kingdom, or wisdom in all human beings, and [that it] has various names

What a precious treasure it is to have, know, and recognize this book is indicated in chapters seven and eight of the Book of Wisdom. Now this book is not only in me but in all human beings, excluding none. For if not for this book, no human being in the entire world would live. It is the life of all human beings and is their light that always shines in the darkness. It is the word of God. For just as all people have been created through the word or through wisdom, so too all people must be sustained and live in the word and through the word. This word is the wisdom of God in the human being; it is the image of God in the human being; it is the spirit or finger of God in the human being; it is the seed of God, the law of God, Christ, the kingdom of God, the book of life, and so on. These things can be proven by John 1: that God's Word, spirit, light, seed, Son, and so on, are one and the same thing. God is the Word, and the Word is the life of human beings, and the life is the light of human beings, and [it] illuminates all human beings who come into the world [John 1:1, 4, 9–10]. Everything that is said of God is he himself and is indistinguishable from his being. Thus God is himself the will, and the will of God is the immutable law of God in the human being, written by the finger of God into the heart. From that it follows that God's law, God's word, God's will, God's seed, God's mind, image, Christ, spirit, finger, God's kingdom, and so on, are one and the same thing and is in all human beings. For that reason, wherever the law of God is, there too is God's will, word, kingdom, and Christ; as he said to the faithless Pharisees: "The kingdom of God is within you" [Luke 17:21]. I say this on account of those who say that God's law may well be in all human beings, but not God's word, spirit, or kingdom, and so forth. Though, however, it is in all, in the evil and the good, in the learned and the unlearned ones, and all have life from it, nevertheless, human beings do not want to know or see it (John 1[:5], John 14[:17]). In these times there is no help from the false teachers or scholars who cannot read this book, who deny it, and who hinder the truth with their injustice (Rom 1[:18]). This kind places faith in the human being and accepts with fierce protectiveness what others have believed and written, though they have not seen it or sensed it through the spirit. That is why it happens that they speak of faith as a blind person speaks of color. For that reason, you people who care in your hearts about salvation, take note and read what I write. You will recognize that I am writing to you the truth. The reason is because you have the spirit of Christ dwelling within you (Rom 8[:9]). For that reason you must acknowledge that I write from the book, word, spirit that is in me and in you. For it is a spirit and is in all (Wis 11 [cf. Sap 12:1]). In the pious, he is praised; in the godless he is blasphemed.

Oh, Lord God and Father, you are yourself the word and the spirit in me, that is, out of you proceeds the word and spirit, the light and the life; you are in me and in all human beings. You wanted all human beings who come into the world to be illuminated by you, but few indeed want to surrender and give themselves to you. Rise within me, you bright morning star, and let day break forth. Then I will convince people that we all alike have this book within us. Simply see to it that we read and understand it properly. Amen.

✦   •   ✦

C H A P T E R   T W E N T Y - S I X

Why the inner book or word has become visible and external, and how [this occurs] in three ways

This book or word lies concealed in the heart, it lies concealed in the letter of scripture, and [it] is also concealed in the flesh. It becomes manifest and is placed before the eyes and ears in three ways. First, [it is revealed] through the stone tablets, on which the sum of the entire scripture is framed in letters. Second, it is revealed in the flesh, for the Word has become flesh, and life has appeared and become bodily. Third, it becomes visible or manifest through the office of the oral sermon in the entire world. God's Word is revealed and visible, *scriptione in tabulis, in incarnatione* [by writing in tablets, in incarnation], through the human genesis [of Christ], *praedicatione* [by the sermon], through the office of the spirit. All of this comes from the invisible spiritual [realm] into the visible, external, physical [realm] from within outward, and if the word and life were not in us, then it would not have been inscribed in letters. If the word and life were not in us, it would not have appeared physically by taking on human nature. If the word, life, and light were not within us, it could not be preached. Indeed, if it were not within us, no human being could read or understand scripture. If it were not in us, no one would be drawn by the voice of the Father to Christ, and no one would come to Christ. If it were not in us, it would be preached for nothing; one would have to preach until the Final Day, yet it could not be preached into [people]. For that reason it is preached: because it is in us. For that reason it is accepted by the faithful: because it is in us. For the same reason the faithless and contradictors are judged and damned: because it is in them. If it were not in them, they could not be damned or judged. If we had remained in paradise, we would have had no need of any scripture or external sermon, as even now the infants have no need of these things and yet are the most adept for the kingdom of God. But inasmuch as we have been driven out of paradise and have become external, worldly people, and have lost the body and the Holy Spirit, thus it has become necessary to be reborn of Christ. For we must have a new celestial body with Christ of the Holy Spirit; the old one belongs to the worms. Therefore, because of our blindness and weakness, the inner word has been framed in scripture, and on account of the new body from heaven, the Word has become flesh, in which eternal life is found; in order that this new birth through Christ should become known to the entire world, it must be preached publicly. Because the inner word has become external and visible, it follows that the spirit and understanding is in us and the letter outside of us. Likewise, the understanding of the word is in us, but the preached word, with its sound, outside of us. Only Christ, God and human being, the entire person, who is made manifest in scripture and sermon, is in the faithful also with his flesh and blood, for which reason too he has told us to eat in his memory.

Oh, Lord God and Father, you have indeed written for us with your finger in the book of life, so that we should not seek it externally, on paper or in the flesh in this place or that, but rather await it in us. Yet, inasmuch as human beings could not read the book, and were also in need of the body from heaven, you placed it visibly before our eyes and ears, in scripture, in the flesh, in sermons. Arouse and illuminate us from within, so that we will not remain at the letter, or seek Christ on earth, but instead in the inner Jerusalem, which is above, and unite us with him as new creatures, using the visible, until we at last behold you, Father, in the Son, with all the infants, which is the book of life within us. Amen.

✦ • ✦

CHAPTER TWENTY-SEVEN

That the short, trifling, worthless joy of the world hinders and cancels the eternal, infinite treasure

The eye looks at physical things and is delighted by them: the inner eye looks at God in the Sabbath [of the soul] and is delighted in the highest. Just as one's little finger, if it is held in front of one's eye, prevents one from seeing a city or a high mountain, so also does the contemptible, brief pleasure of the world prevent the eternal, infinite treasure from being seen or sensed. Oh, God, I lament to you often that a brief, transient, temporal, and contemptible delight and joy hinders us in the great, everlasting treasure of the new birth, which is sweeter than honey and honeycomb. Oh, if only we could compare the sweetness of all the world with only one little drop of divine sweetness, we would confess that the world's entire joy, pleasure, and delight is [like] the deepest sadness, misery, and sorrow. If we do not recognize this in this time, it must be experienced and confessed in that other world to our eternal sorrow, where they will say: What was of the good I received there [in the world], now I will be tormented. Oh, if only we could compare the temporal, brief joy with the eternal, unending torment, it would certainly drive us to the Sabbath, in order to place our hope in God and learn to await him. To the eternal inner treasure no one comes except by way of surrender, obedience of faith, or Sabbath of being silent in stillness.

There are three crude hindrances that prevent us and block the way to the eternal great good. First, there is the crowd of all scholars, who seek their pleasure and edification in arts, languages, [and] adeptness in reading, writing, disputing, poetry, [and] church music; they could not live if they did not seek their paradise in such things. Among all the worldly scholars, not a one is found who takes a single hour of Sabbath, in order to contemplate divine things on Sunday *in silentio sacro* [in sacred silence]. They are very far from the kingdom of God, with their studies, books, writings, and are so fulfilled with arts that God would not even have so much [space] as a needle's point to work within them.

The other bunch that avoids the Sabbath is the common lot, through its physical labor and crafts. They don't take enough pause to be able to hear and consider God's word on Sunday, so they could keep or celebrate the Sabbath, but instead they spend the Sabbath either with temporal worries or work or with useless chatter, going for walks, talking pointlessly, delights of the body, eating, drinking, and whatever evil things they are inclined to do. Whatever is their work on the days of the week, they complete the same on Sunday. God has commanded to work six days; on the seventh we should stop with [what pertains to] the body, and turn our hearts into the inner Sabbath. Oh, what a brief time and pleasure do we look upon and miss [thereby] the eternal infinite treasure.

The third bunch that prevents itself and keeps itself from the Sabbath, in which one must achieve the eternal treasure, are all those who live in the pleasures of the flesh, as in eating, drinking, playing, banqueting, dancing, paying for rounds in taverns, and so on, socializing all week long, and most of all on Sunday. Oh, how does a brief, contemptible pleasure keep us away from the long, great, infinite joy of heaven! The Sabbath is necessary, and for that very reason God instituted the seventh day, so that we should concern ourselves with divine things, with hearing, reading, contemplating, praying, and finally waiting in silence for God within

211

ourselves. Whoever does not do that, whether learned or unlearned, will not come into the kingdom of God, into peace.

✦ • ✦

CHAPTER TWENTY-EIGHT

That one must learn of God in this time and not wait for heaven to do so

The literalist theologians, those who have diminished the spirit, have risen up, in order to remain in their pleasure and creatural activity, and should not need to die unto themselves in the Sabbath. They have made a liar of Christ, as if he had not correctly quoted the prophets when he said in John 6[:45]: It is written in [the books of] the prophets that they will all be instructed by God; whoever would hear and learn from the Father should come to me. They understand this word as being about the future world; they want to wait *ad aeternam academiam* [for the eternal academy], thinking that in heaven there will be universities with professors and the like. In sum, they confirm that one should not learn God's word from God, but rather from the human being; they postpone the anointing of all Christians, about which [it] is written in 1 John 2[:20].

However, that Christ and the prophets are speaking of this time and not of the other world is clear and evident enough from these long chapters.

For, first of all, it is certain that one does not take or read one's understanding out of the Bible; it wasn't written for them, but rather for those who have their understanding within them, to convince their opponents.

Second, it is also true that no natural human being can have understanding from himself. Were one to try to gain faith in an active manner by reading, it would be entirely in vain, as has been proven.

Third, it must necessarily be conceded and granted that there is a supernatural passive knowledge of truth, in which the human being is silent and remains still. For this, one must obtain

212

understanding through prayer, as they themselves admit; one must ask God for understanding, so that he reveals for us to see what is in scripture. To ask, however, means to wait for God in spirit and truth, to hear from the Father, to learn from the Holy Spirit, as supernatural knowledge requires. One cannot learn it from natural powers or from the letter of scripture. So let it be as it may: One must return inward and seek the source from which scripture flowed. That is to say, we must hear and learn it from the spirit in a quiet Sabbath. We have been created for calm or for the Sabbath; the calm is the eternity that remains and does not pass away.

Oh, God, what are we human beings doing? We have left behind calm and thrown ourselves into temporal restlessness. What we could have kept and what would remain with us without end, that [is what] we leave behind; and what cannot remain and must soon cease and cannot be retained, that [is what] we desire to own, [as we do] all temporal things from which we can learn nothing permanent. Where something could be found, that we leave, namely, the calm or eternity, and that from which nothing can be kept, as active time, that [is what] we pursue and disappear with it. Oh God, when and how are we to come from such temporal restlessness into the quiet Sabbath, where all things can be possessed eternally, and so on?

✦ • ✦

CONCLUSION TO THE READER

That I have filled so many chapters with so many words and written so many words about a single subject—this has happened because of [our hope of] at last convincing our opponents who deny the inner testimony of the spirit or the anointing in us all (1 John 2[:20]), in which the entire ground rests, and that we might become wise and abandon human teachings and adhere only to Christ and remain so, in order that we would not have to be wretchedly blown hither and yonder by every wind of doctrine. Therefore, favorable reader, do not be annoyed that a single matter has been treated with so many words, [that it has been] repeated and [so] often restated. It happened of necessity, in order to lead us all with one another to the inner testimony, so that we recognize that judgment or knowledge does not come to people from without, from books, as from the object, but rather from within outward, as both lights sufficiently testify that all proceeds from within outward and not from without inward, and so forth.

Read through this little book often and ask God for [its] understanding, so that you can defeat, with few words, all the worldly scholars, and overcome all universities with a scornful defense, like little David the great, tall Goliath. For it is certainly true that what is now high and mighty in the eyes of the world will soon be low enough, and what is scorned shall be raised up and honored.

יְהוָֹה [God]

Written in the year 1578
at Zschopau in Meissen

✦ · ✦

Notes

1. The technical term *Spiritualism* is unrelated to the *spiritism* of séances; and it is only very generally related to *spirituality* (to the same degree that all forms of inner religiosity are expressions of spirituality). Though Luther applied the term *Geisterei* as a pejorative against such contemporary dissenters as the Spiritualist Sebastian Franck, the concept came into its own in the writings of modern scholars such as Harnack, Hegler, and Troeltsch. Though the term has been subjected to scholarly criticism, Troeltsch treated Spiritualism as an ideal type, contrasting it with the Baptist or Anabaptist in Reformation history. Where the Baptist emphasizes baptism, the letter of the Bible, and the lawlike aspect of the Sermon on the Mount, the typical Spiritualist deemphasizes the sacraments, elevates spirit above letter, and embraces the inner freedom and free movement of the spirit. Where the typical Baptist adheres to a firmly organized church that practices exclusion, the typical Spiritualist instead emphasizes a universal, invisible church that knows no boundaries. See Ernst Troeltsch, *Die Soziallehren der christlichen Kirchen, Gesammelte Schriften*, vol. 1 (Tübingen: Mohr, 1923), 863–64, 898; cf. J. F. G. Goeters's article, "Spiritualisten," in *Religion in Geschichte und Gegenwart* (Tübingen: Mohr, 1962).

2. See Jürgen Hübner, *Die Theologie Johannes Keplers zwischen Orthodoxie und Naturwissenschaft* (Tübingen: Mohr, 1975), 108–9. Like the Humanist author Nikodemus Frischlin, Kepler refused to sign the Formula of Concord because of its angry condemnation of other believers such as Sacramentarians, Catholics, and Calvinists.

3. Cf. Günter Wartenberg, "Die Entstehung der sächsischen Landeskirche von 1539 bis 1559," *Das Jahrhundert der Reformation in Sachsen*, ed. Helmar Junghans (Berlin: Evangelische Verlagsanstalt, 1989), 71, 74.

4. In addition to the adiaphoristic dispute, other doctrinal divisions arose, so that the Gnesio-Lutherans became factionalized among

215

themselves. The Nuremberg reformer Andreas Osiander, an early opponent of the Interim, broke ranks with the other resisters by proclaiming
the doctrine of an indwelling *iustitia essentialis*. He incurred the condemnation of almost all Lutheran theologians. The Philippist theologian
Johann Major brought upon himself the fierce rebuttal of Flacius, Amsdorf, and the Gnesio-Lutherans when he argued that good works proceed-
ing from faith are necessary for salvation. A so-called antinomian
controversy over the "third use of the law" caused another split among the
Gnesio-Lutherans themselves. The so-called synergistic controversy
revolved around the question whether the human will can cooperate in
effecting a conversion to faith, as Melanchthon and his fellow Philippists
taught. The Crypto-Calvinist controversy concerned the question of
Christ's invisible but real physical presence in the bread and wine of communion. Christ's real physical presence in communion was resolutely
affirmed by Gnesio-Lutherans; Philippists entertained qualifications that
put them closer to the Calvinist position. For a brief account of the Gnesio-
Lutheran Controversies, see *The Oxford Encyclopedia of the Reformation*
(Oxford: Oxford University Press, 1996).

5. See the Select Bibliography for the titles of Pfefferl's edition
(PW) of Weigel's works.

6. See the Select Bibliography for the list of works by volume of
the Zeller edition (ZW) of Weigel.

7. Zwey schöne Büchlein / Das Erste / Vom Leben Christi…Das
Ander / Eine kurtze aussführliche Erweisung… (Newstatt: Knuber,
1618), 45.

8. See in the Classics of Western Spirituality series, Jacob Boehme,
The Way to Christ, trans. and intro. Peter Erb, preface by Winfried Zeller
(New York: Paulist Press, 1978); Andrew Weeks, *Boehme: An Intellectual
Biography of the Seventeenth-Century Philosopher and Mystic* (Albany, N.Y.:
State University of New York Press, 1991).

9. Anna Ovena Hoyers, *Geistliche und weltliche Poemata* (Amster-
dam: Elzevier, 1650), 164–65.

10. Bernard McGinn, *The Flowering of Mysticism: Men and Women in
the New Mysticism—1200–1350* (New York: Crossroad, 1998), 12–13.

11. On the idolization of Luther in Weigel's time, Robert Kolb wrote:
"Luther's status as an extraordinary instrument of God's proclamation of His
Word to his people became amply confirmed among Lutherans by 1577. He
himself had insisted that Scripture alone could set forth and evaluate all
the teaching of the church; yet his followers viewed him as a 'living voice

of the gospel,' and one of particular authority because of his God-given role in ending 'the dark night of error' under the medieval papacy....Cyriakus Spangenberg [a Gnesio-Lutheran, whom Weigel at one time criticized] 'demonstrated in a series of sermons why Luther should be regarded as a contemporary Paul, Elijah, or John, a prophet, a confessor, the angel destined to bring God's special message for the End Time to the earth'" (Robert Kolb, "'Perilous Events and Troublesome Disturbances': The Role of Controversy in the Tradition of Luther to Lutheran Orthodoxy," in *Pietas et Societas: New Trends in Reformation Social History* [Essays in Memory of Harold J. Grimm], vol. 4, *Sixteenth Century Studies*, ed. Kyle C. Sessions and Phillip N. Bebb [Ann Arbor, Mich.: Edwards Brothers, 1984], 181, 189).

12. That Weigel is arguing a case made by Luther himself is evident from the latter's *Against the Celestial Prophets (Wider die himmlischen Propheten)*: Christ's words in Luke 17:21 are associated there not only with the issue of the nature of the presence of Jesus, but also with the significance of ceremonies for the attainment of salvation. Thus Luther wrote: "It is a very different thing whether I speak of Christ or of Christ's body and blood; for when the Evangelist says, 'Here or there is Christ' and the like, it is said of the entire Christ, that is, of the kingdom of Christ, as is forcefully made evident by the text of Luke 17[:21], where he states: 'The kingdom of God does not come with external gestures; nor will one say, look, look there it is,' which the other Evangelists thus discourage: Here or there is Christ—this is as much as saying: 'Christ's kingdom does not stand in external things, places, times, persons, works,' but rather, as he puts it himself: 'The kingdom of God is within you'; from which it does not follow that Christ is nowhere, but rather that He is everywhere and fulfills everything (Eph. 1). But he is not bound to any place in particular, so that he would have to be there and nowhere else, as those pretend who would not allow our conscience to be free, but rather bind it to special places, works, and persons." Cf. *Werke* (Weimar edition), 18, 211.6–18 (my translation).

13. Weigel could draw support for this notion from Jesus' blessing of the children in Matthew 19:13–15, Mark 10:13–16, and Luke 18:15–17.

14. Martin Luther, "Sermon on the Gospel of St. John," chapters 1–4, in Pelikan, *Works*, 22:27.

15. Ibid., 22:28.

16. Valentin Weigel, *Gnothi seauton*, PW 3:99.

17. Luther, "Sermon on the Gospel of St. John," 22:225.

18. Kurt Flasch has performed a valuable service to scholarship by discussing the importance of Sermon 1 (on John 1: *In principio erat verbum*)

with its observation that the ineffable, infinite, and unknowable deity is called by various names by the various peoples and tongues *Nominatur humanis diversis vocibus, diversis linguis diversarum nationum, licet nomen suum sit unicum, summum, infinitum, ineffabile et ignotum* (*Nikolaus von Kues. Geschichte einer Entwicklung. Vorlesungen zur Einführung in seine Philosophie* [Frankfurt/Main: Klostermann, 1998], 22).

19. See Winfried Zeller, "Eckhartiana V. Meister Eckhart bei Valentin Weigel. Eine Untersuchung zur Frage der Bedeutung Meister Eckharts für die mystische Renaissance des sechzehnten Jahrhunderts," *Zeitschrift für Kirchengeschichte* 3 series, 57: vol. 3/4 (1938): 309–55.

20. Meister Eckhart, *Deutsche Werke*, ed. Josef Quint (Stuttgart: Kohlhammar, 1971). Henceforth DW.

21. See Eckhart, *Quasi vas auri solidum ornatum omni lapied pretioso*, DW 1:493.

22. See below, Weigel, *On the Place of the World*, 112. I am indebted to Bernard McGinn for pointing out that this view, while it is possibly attributable to Eckhart, is certainly characteristic of Eriugena.

23. See Andrew Weeks, *Paracelsus: Speculative Theory and the Crisis of the Early Reformation* (Albany, N.Y.: State University of New York Press, 1997), 92–93.

24. Eckhart, DW 1:156 *(Quasi stella matutina)*.

25. Eckhart, DW 1:34, "Were the spirit constantly united with God in this power, the human being would not age" *(Wære der geist alle zît mit gote vereinet in dirre kraft, der mensche enmöchte niht alten)*.

26. Sebastian Franck, *Paradoxa ducenta octoginta* (Ulm: Varnier, 1534), 1v.

27. Cf. Nicholas of Cusa, *On the Vision of God*, chap. 7 ("With my sensible eye I see [the nut-tree] as tall and wide, colored, and heavy with branches, leaves, and nuts. And then with the eyes of the mind I perceive that this tree existed in the seed, not as I look at it now, but virtually"), cited from Nicholas of Cusa, *Selected Spiritual Writings*, trans. and intro. by H. Lawrence Bond, preface by Morimichi Watanabe (New York: Paulist Press, 1997), 245. (Thanks are due to Bernard McGinn for pointing out the affinity of language with *On the Vision of God*.)

28. Martin Luther, "Lectures on Genesis, Chapters 1–5," *Works*, vol. 1, ed. Jaroslav Pelikan (St. Louis: Concordia, 1958), 68 ("In the remaining creatures God is recognized as by His footprints; but in the human being, especially in Adam, He is truly recognized, because in him there is such

wisdom, justice, and knowledge of all things that he may rightly be called a world in miniature"). The original has the Greek word mikrokosmos.

29. Luther, *Lectures on Genesis*, 46.

30. See Weigel, PW 3:83, and *De Vita Beata*, 2.

31. See PW 4:52 (footnote 7). Pfefferl points to similar passages and calls attention to Eckhart's sermon on the conversion of Saint Paul in the *Basel Tauler Edition*.

32. See Martin Brecht, "Einleitung" and "Das Aufkommen der neuen Frömmigkeitsbewegung in Deutschland," in *Geschichte des Pietismus*, vol. 1, *Der Pietismus vom siebzehnten bis zum frühen achtzehnten Jahrhundert*, ed. Martin Brecht (Göttingen: Vandenhoeck & Ruprecht, 1993).

33. See Vulgate, Matthew 13, on the good seed and the weeds (or tares).

34. Cf. *The Theologia Germanica of Martin Luther*, trans., intro., and commentary by Bengt Hoffman, preface by Bengt Hägglund (New York: Paulist Press, 1980), chap. 47, p. 136 ("Hell is and consists of self-will").

35. The misleadingly called "Chronicle of Heretics" *(Ketzerchronik)* is contained along with the other chronicles in Sebastian Franck's world history, the *Chronica, Zeytbuoch vnd geschychtbibel* (1st ed. [Strasbourg, 1531]; 2d ed. [Ulm, 1536]). Actually, it is an alphabetical catalog of heresies, *Chronica der Römischen Ketzer*, prefaced by the author's suggestion that the heretics might well be the true Christians: "You should not think, my reader, that I regard all those as heretics, about whom I have told here [and] counted among the enumeration of heretics; judge that by means of the Chronicle [itself]...for if I were to judge, I would perhaps turn the judgment around and canonize and count among the number of the saints many of those who are denounced here as heretics." ("Dv solt nicht darfür haben/ mein leser/ das ich alle die für ketzer acht/ die ich hie erzöltet/ in das zalbuoch der ketzer geschriben hab/ das vrteil durch die Chronik...dan solt ich vrteylen/ ich würde villeicht das spil vmbkören/ vnd deren vil canonisieren/ vnd in der heiligen zal setzen/ die hie für Ketzer ausgeruefft"—*Chronica*, 1531, lxxxi verso).

36. The German word *Unfrieden*, "unpeace," cannot be translated without a certain awkwardness. The passage from Matthew contains "the sword," obviously in a metaphorical sense.

37. "Diximus, Pax, et non est pax; promisimus bona, et ecce turbatio" (Bernard of Clairvaux, *De consideratione libri quinque ad Eugenium III*, *lib. II, cap. 1* [Migne, *Patrologia Latina* 182:743]). Henceforth PL.

38. In citing this passage Weigel indicated that one will know true from false teachings by the fruits they bring. Even more relevant to the metaphors of the rock is Matthew 7:24–25.

39. Weigel uses the term *knighthood* but is perhaps thinking of 1 Timothy 1:18, where Christians are instructed to fight the good fight.

40. Weigel is quoting from Franck's *Chronica* (1531), ccix verso.

41. The sixth general council of the church was held in 680–81 in order to resolve the Monothelitic Controversy. Eastern Emperor Constantine IV, who presided over the opening sessions, was remembered for moderation, religious tolerance, and a relative acceptance of the position held by Rome (see Andreas N. Stratos, *Byzantium in the Seventh Century (668–685)*, vol. 4, trans. Harry T. Hionides [Amsterdam: Hakkert, 1978], 4).

42. A frequent argument for the inner authority and inner being of the divine world is made by Weigel by citing this older translation of Luke 17:23, "The Kingdom of God is within you." Though this may appear as if it were a trademark of dissenting Spiritualism, much the same point was made by Luther on the basis of the same passage from Luke (see n. 12).

43. In denying that the Adamic fall from grace affected the substance *(Wesen)* of the human being and affirming that what was corrupted was "accident" rather than "substance" *(Wesen)*, Weigel takes sides on this point of doctrine against the Gnesio-Lutherans, Matthias Flacius Illyricus, and Cyriakus Spangenberg, whose view of complete corruption was rejected by the framers of the Formula of Concord (see Andrew Weeks, *Valentin Weigel (1533–1588): German Religious Dissenter, Speculative Theorist, and Advocate of Tolerance* [Albany, N.Y.: State University of New York Press, 2000], 92–93).

44. The comparison of the world with an egg, intended to account for the stability of the world in the age before the discovery of the power of gravity, is found not only in Paracelsus who was probably Weigel's immediate source but also in Johannes Reuchlin's *On the Art of the Kabbalah* of 1516 (cf. trans. Martin and Sarah Goodman. Lincoln: University of Nebraska Press, 1983, 101), as well as such older sources as the cosmology in Hildegard of Bingen's *Scivias*. Weigel seems to have borrowed here from the Paracelsian late work, *Astronomia Magna oder die ganze Philosophia sagax der grossen und kleinen Welt*, which compares the earth to an egg yolk in albumen; the latter is the "chaos" of air in which the world is suspended. See *Sämtliche Werke*, ed. Karl Sudhoff, Div. 1, vol. 12 (Munich: Oldenbourg, 1929), 322.

NOTES

45. Similary, chapter 19 of Jacob Boehme's first work, *Aurora* (1612), proclaims the discovery that the "true heaven" is not identical with the heavens above the earth.

46. Weigel refers here to a land of winter rather than to Ireland. "Hibernia" is used in the same sense by Paracelsus in *Fragmentum libri. De sagis et earum operibus*, in Paracelsus, *Schriften*, vol. 14, ed. Karl Sudhoff (Munich: Oldenbourg, 1933), 7.

47. The works of Petrus Apianus (1495–1552), a cosmographer and mathematician at the University of Ingolstadt, on astronomy and cosmography were influential. His *Cosmographiae Introductio, cum quibusdam Geometriae ac Astronomiae principiis ad eam rem necessariis* of 1524 and 1525 contained maps of America, apparently based on the ground-breaking map of Waldseemüller.

48. Weigel draws extensively on Sebastian Franck (1499–1542), whose *Weltbuch: spiegel vnd bildtnisz des gantzen erdbodens von Sebastiano Franco Woerdensi in vier buecher/ nemlich in Asiam/ Aphricam/ Europam/ vnd Americam/ gestelt vnd abteilt* (1534) described the four parts of the world, including America. Franck's book also cited Petrus Apianus.

49. Weigel takes this etymology from Franck's *Weltbuch* (p. 5 recto: "Aphrica (welche die Griechen Libiam nennen) hatt/ wie Josephus lib. anti. anzeyget/ von Afro einem auss den nachkummen Abrahe den nammen"). Presumably, this is a masculine form from the name of Aphrah, "dust," mentioned in Micah 1:10.

50. See above, Franck, *Weltbuch* (1534).

51. The precise reference to Paracelsus is not clear. Weigel seems to have borrowed especially from the late work *Astronomia Magna oder die ganze Philosophia sagax der grossen und kleinen Welt*, which contains passages that recognize the natural symbolism of the earth suspended like an egg yolk in albumen. The latter stands for the "chaos" of air in which the earth is suspended (see Sudhoff's division, 12:322). Elsewhere, Paracelsus's *Philosophia de generationibus et fructibus quatuor elementorum* states, "The element air is assigned to no other thing, except to be as a house of the other three elements, to hold the same, each one in its own room" (Sudhoff, 13:15).

52. Weigel's thoughts on the paradoxes of infinitude are usually close to Nicholas of Cusa; however, this passage appears to echo Luther, who reflected as follows: "Nothing is so small but God is still smaller, nothing so large but God is still larger, nothing is so short but God is shorter, nothing so long but God is still longer, nothing is so broad but

God is still broader, nothing so narrow but God is still narrower, and so on. He is an inexpressible being, above and beyond all that can be described or imagined" (*Weimarer Ausgabe*, 26:339, my translation).

53. "Mercurius" is presumably Hermes Trismegistos, the legendary author of the *Emerald Tablet*, whose fame and relevance to the pristine theology had been in currency since Marsilio Ficino.

54. Here the reference is to Pr. 38 ("In illo tempore missus est angelus Gabriel" [DW 2:233, cf. 680]).

55. Weigel is referring to his first major theoretical work, *Gnothi seauton* (1571).

56. Here Weigel is referring to the nature theory of Paracelsus, according to which the substance of all things consists of the three principles of sulphur, mercury, and salt. Since the *limus terrae*, or clump of earth from which Adam was made, contained the three principles—indeed since it contained *in nuce* all things—the human being is a microcosm; self-knowledge therefore entails knowledge of the world.

57. Here Weigel is close to the thinking of Cusanus, as in the latter's *On the Vision of God*, chap. 7. See reference in n. 27 above.

58. See *The "Theologia Germanica" of Martin Luther*, trans., intro., and commentary Bengt Hoffman, preface Bengt Hägglund (New York: Paulist Press, 1980), 136 ("Thus this world is a precinct to Eternity. That is why we may safely call it a paradise").

59. Anicius Manlius Severinus Boëthius, *The Consolation of Philosophy*, trans. and intro. Richard Green (Indianapolis, Ind.: Bobbs-Merrill, 1962), Bk. 2, Prose 1, p. 21.

60. After the summary of chapter 16, the remaining chapters of Weigel's work shift from the contemplation of place to an ascending meditation upon metaphysical or mystical themes. If the exposition appears repetitive, it demonstrates a breadth and compositional skill combining an orthodox Christology (see p. 134) and Lutheran doctrine of grace (p. 109) with diverse literary and mystical sources. Thus, the second paragraph of chapter 26 (p. 134) skillfully mingles the geometrical symbolism of Cusanus with reflections drawn from Franck's *Paradoxa* (see *Paradox* 21) and, in the process, redeems an allusion made by Franck to chapter 42 of the *Theologia Germanica*. To the very end of his treatise, the *Theologia* is of signal significance. Weigel closes (p. 142) with the inaugural reference to the complete superseding the incomplete from the *Theologia* (ch. 1; cf. Saint Paul's dictum in 1 Cor 13:10). The allusion sounds a solemn note of finality,

rounding out both Weigel's synthesis and his mystical-eschatological vision in *On the Place of the World.*

61. The rare Latin compound *omnicapax* occurs in the translation by Ambrosius Traversari of Pseudo-Dionysus the Areopagite's *On the Divine Names* (*De divinis nominibus*). See *Dionysiaca*, 1 (Desclee de Brouwer & Cie, 1937), 484 (*sedes omnicapax, omnia contenta una praecellenti connexioni...*).

62. Here Weigel is echoing a tradition of geometrical symbolism best known through the work of Nicholas of Cusa, though of far older origin. A common trope of this symbolism describes the divine ubiquity as an infinite circle whose center is everywhere and whose circumference is nowhere, that is, not within the universe of created beings (see Dietrich Mahnke, *Unendliche Sphäre und Allmittelpunkt* [Halle/Saale: Niemeyer, 1937]).

63. In this chapter Weigel takes sides in a watershed scientific dispute of his century between the nature theorists, who sided with Aristotle's views (cf. *Meteorology*, bk. 1, chaps. 9–12), and those who favored the views of Paracelsus, as expressed for example in his *De Meteoris, Schriften*, vol. 13, 144 ("Also verstandent nun von den sternen, wie sie in ihrem element standen, und wie sie mit irem element eingeleibt sind und wie sie frücht sind gleich den beumen auf erden"). At root, what was involved was a clash between a view of nature that accorded it a relative autonomy and one in which the creation of nature out of nothing prevailed.

64. One should compare this with Cusanus's view that God is in all things and all things in God through the Word as Mediator: "God, therefore, is all things in all things, and all are in God through this Mediator" (see *On Learned Ignorance, Nicholas of Cusa, Selected Spiritual Writings* [New York: Paulist Press, 1997], 192). This has as its corollary that all things are in all things: "Therefore, to say that 'each thing is in each thing' is not other than to say that 'through all things God is in all things' and that 'through all things all are in God'" (ibid., 140).

65. Here Weigel is drawing upon Genesis 2:7 ("Formavit igitur Dominus Deus hominem de limo terrae..."); however, the context suggests that the phrase should also be read in connection with Paracelsus's understanding of supernatural forces present in the elements, such as the earth. Cf. Hartmut Rudolph, "Hohenheim's Anthropology in the Light of His Writings on the Eucharist," in *Paracelsus: The Man and His Reputation, His Ideas and Their Transformation*, ed. Ole Peter Grell (Leiden: Brill, 1998), 193–96.

66. Matthew 6:22–23 ("The eye is the lamp of the body. If your eyes are good, your whole body will be full of light. But if your eyes are bad, your whole body will be full of darkness").

67. The teaching of the threefold eye is attributed to Hugh of St. Victor (without referring to a specific work) in *Gnothi seauton* (see PW 3:71 n. 3; Pfefferl offers as a possible source Hugh's *De sacramentis,* in PL 176:329). Variants or equivalents of the three ways of seeing are also found in Cusanus and Augustine, authors also known to Weigel.

68. The *limbus* is a concept drawn from Paracelsian speculative thought. Comparable to the quintessence, it is a supernatural, spiritual material of creation from which the eternal body and eternal world are fashioned. *Limbus* pertains to the creation before the fall and after the resurrection (see Rudolph, "Hohenheim's Anthropology in the Light of His Writings on the Eucharist.")

69. See Paracelsus, *Werke,* vol. 13 *(Liber de Imaginibus),* 383–84. In a passage reminiscent of Augustine's application of the Trinity to the mental faculties, Paracelsus compares the mind *(gemüt),* faith *(glaube),* and "the perfect imagination that comes from the stars" ("die perfecte imagination, die von den astris kompt") to the "divine trinity" ("dem trinitato deo"). Of special relevance to the spiritualism of Weigel is the fact that, while it is through mind that we come to God and through faith to Christ, it is through the imagination that we come to the Holy Spirit.

70. I am translating Weigel's *das gezweyte* as "alterity." Cusanus, in chapter 9 of *De Coniecturis,* writes similarly "de unitate et alteritate." I agree with Pfefferl that this is the most probable source for Weigel (PW 8:31 n. 1).

71. Weigel has little to say about cabala. Here his interest is guided by Paracelsian usage and thinking in positing a realm of supernatural agency that is not divine. According to Paracelsus, the imagination can operate upon the external world. That this is so paradoxically serves to reinforce the boundary between faith, on the one hand, and miracle or magic, on the other, by suggesting that the supernatural is not necessarily the divine.

72. See n. 12 above on Luther's use of this passage in relation to Weigel's.

73. See *Meister Eckhart: Teacher and Preacher,* ed. Bernard McGinn, with the collaboration of Frank Tobin and Elvira Borgstadt, preface by Kenneth Northcott (New York: Paulist Press, 1986), part 12, 270: "The eye in which I see God is the same eye in which God sees me" (p.224).

74. See Zeller, "Eckhartiana V. Meister Eckhart bei Valentin Weigel," 59ff.

75. Cf. Franck, *Paradoxa ducenta octoginta,* 92–93.

76. See n. 65 above.

77. *Spiraculum* is a term used by Paracelsus in the same context with *limus terrae*. It signifies the vital life breathed by God into Adam and also a divine spirit or principle within the human being.

78. See Paracelsus, *Werke*, in Sudhoff, 13:287–334.

79. Here, Weigel attempts to resolve the opposing positions taken during the "synergistic controversy" (over whether the human being does or does not exercise free will in conversion) into paradox, so that the positions agree on the higher plane of reality upon which opposites are resolved in God and understood by the illuminated understanding. His thinking reflects the paradoxes of Nicholas of Cusa and Sebastian Franck.

80. The Justinian code prohibiting readministration of the sacrament of baptism provided the legal pretext for condemning Anabaptists to death.

81. Weigel is referring to 1 Corinthians 1:12–13 and 1 Corinthians 3:5, 22 (Paul's admonitions to maintain Christian unity).

82. I am indebted to Bernard McGinn for pointing out that this is a famous analogy attributable to Alan of Lille.

83. See *On the Vision of God*, in Bond, *Nicholas of Cusa: Selected Spiritual Writings*, 243 ("So indeed the eye of the flesh, while peering through a red glass, judges that everything it sees is red or if through a green glass, that everything is green"). I am indebted to Bernard McGinn for calling my attention to this passage.

Select Bibliography

I. WORKS BY VALENTIN WEIGEL

The first attempt at a critical edition began appearing in print in 1962 under the name of Will-Erich Peuckert. It was carried on by Alfred Ehrentreich (volume 4 only) and, as the most productive editor, Winfried Zeller. The second attempt, now in progress under the editorship of Horst Pfefferl, is based on a more extensive examination of extant materials. The new critical edition is appearing under the auspices of the Akademie der Wissenschaften in Mainz. Volume 3 *(Gnothi seauton)*, volume 8 *(Der güldene Griff)*, and volume 4 (Weigel's writings on prayer) are now available (see Horst Pfefferl, "Die kritische Ausgabe der 'Sämtlichen Schriften' Weigels," *Chloe. Beihefte zum Daphnis* 24, 1997). This new edition will also incorporate (with some revisions and a more comprehensive scholarly commentary) all the works that appeared in the Zeller edition, as well as several writings considered partially but not completely authentic. Each volume will include an introduction and an extensive apparatus of notes and text variants.

The two editions are referred to here as the Zeller (ZW) and the Pfefferl (PW) editions of Weigel. A further, collected edition of considerable importance is that of Siegfried Wollgast. Though based in part on inferior texts *(Gnothi seauton* and *Der güldene Griff* are cited here only in the Pfefferl edition), the Wollgast edition retains its value as a one-volume compendium of the most important writings, facilitated by modernized German spellings, and with

226

helpful commentaries by a ground-breaking historian of early modern German philosophy. Beyond these three editions I have included the individual works that appear in this study but which could not be cited as yet from any of the modern editions. The eulogy for Martha von Ruxleben, which was the only work that appeared in print during Weigel's lifetime, has been published as an appendix to Opel's *Valentin Weigel*.

Three Weigelian writings were translated and published in seventeenth-century England: *Of the Life of Christ* (London, 1648, presumed authentic); the *Astrologie Theologized* (London, 1649); and *A Brief Instruction of the Way and Manner to Know All Things* (translated by Benjamin Furly, 1664). Only the first of the three is regarded by scholars as authentic. The other two are presumed to be imitative.

A. Zeller-Peuckert Edition (ZW)

Sämtliche Schriften. Edited by Will-Erich Peuckert, Winfried Zeller, Alfred Ehrentreich, and Horst Pfefferl. Stuttgart-Bad Cannstatt: Frommann Verlag, 1962f. This incomplete edition is divided into seven *Lieferungen* (installments).

Installment 1. *Vom Ort der Welt*. Afterword by Will-Erich Peuckert (1962).

Installment 2. *Von der Vergebung der Sünden oder vom Schlüssel der Kirchen*. Afterword by Winfried Zeller (1964).

Installment 3. *Zwei nützliche Tractate, der erste von der Bekehrung des Menschen, der andere von Armut des Geistes oder wahrer Gelassenheit* (1570), *Kurzer Bericht und Anleitung zur Deutschen Theologie* (1571). Edited and Afterword by Winfried Zeller (1966).

Installment 4. *Dialogus de Christianismo* (1584). Edited and Afterword by Alfred Ehrentreich (1967).

Installment 5. *Ein Büchlein vom wahren seligmachenden Glauben, wie Adam in uns untergehen und sterben müsse und Christus dargegen in uns *solle auferstehen und leben* (1572). Edited by Will-Erich Peuckert and Winfried Zeller, and Afterword by Winfried Zeller (1969).

Installments 6–7. *Handschriftliche Predigtensammlung* (1573–74). Edited by Will-Erich Peuckert and Winfried Zeller, with the collaboration of Horst Pfefferl and Martin Quiring, Foreword by Winfried Zeller (1977, 1978).

B. Pfefferl Edition (PW)

Vol. 3. *Vom Gesetz oder Willen Gottes* (shortly after 1570), *Gnothi seauton* (1571?).

Vol. 4. *Büchlein vom Gebet* (around 1572), *Gebetbuch* (after 1575), *Vom Gebet* (1610?), *Vom Beten und Nichtbeten* (undated).

Vol. 7. *Von Betrachtung des Lebens Christi* (1574), *De vita Christi* (after 1573), *Vom Leben Christi* (1578).

Vol. 8. *Vom judicio im Menschen* (1575), *Der güldene Griff* (1578).

C. Wollgast Edition

Ausgewählte Werke. Edited and Introduction by Siegfried Wollgast. Stuttgart: Kohlhammer, 1977. (*Gnothi seauton*. Newenstatt: Knuber, 1615; *Vom Ort der Welt*. Stuttgart: Frommann, 1962; *Der güldene Griff*. Halle, 1613; *Die Predigt vom armen Lazarus*, from *Kirchen oder Hauspostill*. Newenstatt: Knuber, 1617; *Dialogus de Christianismo*. Stuttgart: Frommann, 1967).

D. Other Editions by or Attributed to Weigel Cited in This Study

(The publisher, Knuber, and place, Newstadt and its variants, are fictional designations that appear on many of the early Weigelian or pseudo-Weigelian publications.)

> *Libellus de Vita Beata, non in Particularibus ab extra quærenda, sed in Summo Bono intra nos ipsos possidenda. Item Excitatio Mentis de Luce & Caligine.* Halle: Joachim Krusicken, 1609.

SELECT BIBLIOGRAPHY

Kirchen Oder Hauspostill. Newenstatt: Knuber, 1617, 1618.

Von Betrachtung desz Lebens Christi / vnnd wie Christus zu vnserm Nutz erkennet werden / in fünff Capitulen verfasset. (Printed in the compilation *Philosophia Mystica,* II, 5.) Newstatt: Knuber, 1618.

II. BIOGRAPHICAL AND BIBLIOGRAPHICAL

Anonymous. "Chronicon Weigelianvm, und umständliche Nachricht von Val. Weigeln und dessen Schrifften." In *Unschuldige Nachrichten von Alten und Neuen Theologischen Sachen, Büchern, Uhrkunden, Controversien, Veränderungen, Anmerckungen, Vorschlägen, u.d.g.* Leipzig: Braun, 1715.

Arnold, Gottfried. *Unparteyische Kirchen- und Ketzer-Historie / Vom Anfang des Neuen Testaments Biß auff das Jahr Christi 1688.* Frankfurt: Thomas Fritsch, 1700.

Gorceix, Bernard. *La Mystique de Valentin Weigel (1533–1588) et les origines de la théosophie allemande.* Dissertation. Paris: 1972.

Israel, August. *M. Valentin Weigels Leben und Schriften. Nach den Quellen dargestellt, mit Weigels Bildnis und einer Nachbildung seiner Handschrift.* Zschopau: Raschke, 1888.

Kawerau, Gustav. "Israel, August, *M. Valentin Weigels Leben und Schriften*" (book review). In *Theologische Literaturzeitung* 13:24 (1888): 594–98.

Lieb, Fritz. *Valentin Weigels Kommentar zur Schöpfungsgeschichte und das Schrifttum seines Schülers Benedikt Biedermann.* Zurich: EVZ-Verlag, 1962.

Opel, Julius Otto. *Valentin Weigel. Ein Beitrag zur Literatur- und Culturgeschichte Deutschlands im 17. Jahrhundert.* Leipzig: T. O. Weigel, 1864. Appendices include 1. Materials from Weigel's studies in Leipzig, 2. Weigel's printed "Eulogie for Marthe von Ruxleben," 3. Documents on the dismissal of Biedemann, and 4. Charges against a Weigelian pastor in Worms.

Pertz, Ludolf. *Beiträge zur Geschichte der mystischen und ascetischen Literatur. Erster Beitrag: Geschichte des Weigelianismus, unter Benutzung auch handschriftlicher Quellen. Zeitschrift für historische Theologie* 27, NF 27 (1857): 3–94.

Pfefferl, Horst. *Die Überlieferung der Schriften Valentin Weigels.* Inaugural dissertation. Marburg/Lahn, 1991.

———. "Christoph Weickhart als Paracelsist. Zu Leben und Persönlichkeit eines Kantors Valentin Weigels." In *Analecta Paracelsica. Studien zum Nachleben Theophrast von Hohenheims im deutschen Kulturgebiet der frühen Neuzeit,* edited by Joachim Telle (*Heidelberger Studien zur Naturkunde der frühen Neuzeit,* 4). Stuttgart: Steiner, 1994.

———. "Die kritische Ausgabe der 'Sämtlichen Schriften' Valentin Weigels. Ein neues Konzept für die zu Unrecht vernachläßigte Edition theologisch-philosophischer Texte des 16./17. Jahrhunderts." In *Chloe* (Supplement to *Daphnis*) 24 (1997): 577–87. (*Editionsdesiderate zur Frühen Neuzeit, Beiträge zur Tagung der Kommission für die Edition von Texten der Frühen Neuzeit).* Part 1. Edited by Hans-Gert Roloff.

———. "Das neue Bild Valentin Weigels—Ketzer oder Kirchenmann? Aspekte einer erforderlichen Neubestimmung seiner kirchen- und theologiegeschichtlichen Position." In *Herbergen der Christenheit (Jahrbuch für deutsche Kirchengeschichte* 18 [1993/94]: 67–79).

———. "Die Rezeption des paracelsischen Schrifttums bei Valentin Weigel. Probleme ihrer Erforschung am Beispiel der kompilatorischen Schrift 'Viererlei Auslegung von der Schöpfung.'" In *Neue Beiträge zur Paracelsus-Forschung.* Edited by Peter Dilg and Hartmut Rudolph. *Hohenheimer Protokolle* 47 (1995): 151–65.

———. "Valentin Weigel und Paracelsus." In *Paracelsus und sein dämonengläubiges Jahrhundert. (Salzburger Beiträge zur Paracelsusforschung)* 26 (1988): 77–95.

———. "Zur Wirkungsgeschichte des Paracelsus am Ende des 16. Jahrhunderts. Neue Aspekte zu einem Kantor Valentin Weigels."

SELECT BIBLIOGRAPHY

Nachlese zum Jubiläumskongreß. 500 Jahre Paracelsus. Vienna: Österreichischer Kunst- und Kulturverlag, 1995.

Reichelius, Johannes Gottlob. *Vitam, Fata et Scripta M. Valentini VVeigelii, ex genvinis monvmentis comprobata atqve a complvribvs naevis ac lapsibvs pvrgata.* Dissertation. Wittenberg, 1721.

Schiele, Fritz. "Zu den Schriften Valentin Weigels." *Zeitschrift für Kirchengeschichte* 48, New series 11 (1929): 380–89.

Walch, Johann Georg. *Historische und Theologische Einleitung in die Religions-Streitigkeiten, Welche sonderlich ausser der Evangelisch-Lutherischen Kirche entstanden* (Vierdter und fünffter Theil). Jena: Meyers Erben, 1736.

Weeks, Andrew. *Valentin Weigel (1533–1588): German Religious Dissenter, Speculative Theorist, and Advocate of Tolerance.* Albany, N.Y.: State University of New York Press, 2000.

Zeller, Winfried. *Die Schriften Valentin Weigels. Eine literarkritische Untersuchung.* Berlin: Ebering, 1940; reprinted Vaduz: Kraus, 1965.

III. SELECTED CRITICAL LITERATURE ON WEIGEL AND WEIGELIANISM

Baring, G. "Valentin Weigel und die 'Deutsche Theologie," *Archiv für Reformationsgeschichte* 55/1 (1964): 5–17.

Bosch, Gabriele. *Reformatorisches Denken und frühneuzeitliches Philosophieren. Eine vergleichende Studie zu Martin Luther und Valentin Weigel.* Inaugural dissertation (Giessen), 1998.

Brecht, Martin. "Das Aufkommen der neuen Frömmigkeitsbewegung in Deutschland." In *Der Pietismus vom siebzehnten bis zum frühen achtzehnten Jahrhundert,* edited by Martin Brecht. Göttingen: Vandenhoeck & Ruprecht, 1993.

Carriere, Moriz. *Die philosophische Weltanschauung der Reformationszeit in ihren Beziehungen zur Gegenwart.* Zweite vermehrte Auflage. Part 1. Leipzig: Brockhaus, 1887.

VALENTIN WEIGEL

Dülmen, Richard van. "Schwärmer und Separatisten in Nürnberg (1618–1648). Ein Beitrag zum Problem des 'Weigelianismus.'" *Archiv für Sozialgeschichte* 55/1 (1973): 107–37.

Ehrentreich, Alfred. "Valentin Weigels religiöser 'Dialogus' als literarische Schöpfung." *Zeitschrift für Religions- und Geistesgeschichte* 21 (1969): 42–54.

Goldammer, Kurt. "Friedensidee und Toleranzgedanke bei Paracelsus und den Spiritualisten" (Part 2: "Franck und Weigel"). *Archiv für Reformationsgeschichte* 47/2 (1956): 180–211.

Koyré, Alexandre. *Mystiques, spirituels, alchimistes du XVIe siècle allemand.* Paris: Gallimande, 1971.

Längin, Heinz. "Grundlinien der Erkenntnislehre Valentin Weigels." *Archiv für die Geschichte der Philosophie* 41 (1931): 435–78.

Maier, Hans. *Der mystische Spiritualismus Valentin Weigels.* Gütersloh: "Der Rufer" Evangelischer Verlag, 1926.

Ozment, Steven E. *Mysticism and Dissent: Religious Ideology and Social Protest in the Sixteenth Century.* New Haven, Conn.: Yale University Press, 1973.

Steiner, Rudolf. *Mysticism at the Dawn of the Modern Age.* Translated by Karl E. Zimmer. Introduction by Paul M. Allen. Edgewood, N.J.: Rudolf Steiner Publications, 1960.

Wentzlaff-Eggebert, Friedrich-Wilhelm. *Deutsche Mystik zwischen Mittelalter und Neuzeit. Einheit und Wandlung ihrer Erscheinungsformen.* Third extended edition. Berlin: de Gruyter, 1969.

Wollgast, Siegfried. "Valentin Weigel." Chapter 9 in *Philosophie in Deutschland zwischen Reformation und Aufklärung, 1550–1650.* Berlin: Akademie Verlag, 1988.

———. "Valentin Weigel und Jakob Böhme. Vertreter einer Entwicklungslinie progressiven Denkens in Deutschland." In *Protokollband. Jakob-Böhme-Symposium (Görlitz 1974).* Göritz: Rat der Stadt Görlitz, 1977.

———. "Valentin Weigel und seine Stellung in der deutschen Philosophie- und Geistesgeschichte." In *Vergessene und Verkannte. Zur Philosophie und Geistesentwicklung in Deutschland zwischen Reformation und Frühaufklärung.* Berlin: Akademie Verlag, 1993.

———. "Grundlinien oppositionellen weltanschaulich-philosophischen Denkens in Deutschland zwischen 1550 und 1720." In *Wegscheiden der Reformation. Alternatives Denken vom 16. bis zum 18. Jahrhundert,* edited by Günter Vogler. Weimar: Böhlaus Nachfolger, 1994.

Zeller, Winfried. "Eckhartiana V. Meister Eckhart bei Valentin Weigel. Eine Untersuchung zur Frage der Bedeutung Meister Eckharts für die mystische Renaissance des sechszehnten Jahrhunderts." *Zeitschrift für Kirchengeschichte* 3 series 8, 57: Heft 3/4 (1938): 309–55.

———. "Der ferne Weg des Geistes. Zur Würdigung Valentin Weigels." In *Theologie und Frömmigkeit. Gesammelte Aufsätze.* Edited by Bernd Jaspert. Marburg: Elwert Verlag, 1971.

———. "Der frühe Weigelianismus—Zur Literaturkritik der Pseudoweigeliana." In *Theologie und Frömmigkeit. Gesammelte Aufsätze.* Edited by Bernd Jaspert. Marburg: Elwert Verlag, 1971.

———. "Valentin Weigel und die Augsburgische Konfession—Zu einem neuen Weigel-Autograph." In *Theologie und Frömmigkeit. Gesammelte Aufsätze.* Edited by Bernd Jaspert. Marburg: Elwert Verlag, 1971.

IV. Selected Literature Relevant to Mysticism and Tolerance

Edwards, Mark U., Jr. *Luther and the False Brethren.* Stanford, Calif.: Stanford University Press, 1975.

———. *Luther's Last Battles: Politics and Polemics, 1531–46.* Ithaca, N.Y.: Cornell University Press, 1983.

Gericke, Wolfgang, ed. "Introduction," *Sechs theologische Schriften Gotthold Ephraim Lessings.* Berlin: Evangelische Verlagsanstalt, 1985.

VALENTIN WEIGEL

Grell, Ole Peter, and Bob Scribner, eds. *Tolerance and Intolerance in the European Reformation*. Cambridge: Cambridge University Press, 1996.

Hegler, Alfred. *Geist und Schrift bei Sebastian Franck. Eine Studie zum Spiritualismus in der Reformationszeit*. Freiburg im Breisgau: Herder, 1892.

Jones, Rufus M. *Spiritual Reformers in the Sixteenth and Seventeenth Centuries*. Kessinger Pub. Second edition. Boston: 1959.

Kamen, Henry. *The Rise of Toleration*. New York: McGraw-Hill, 1967.

Kühn, Johannes. *Toleranz und Offenbarung*. Leipzig: Meiner, 1923.

Lecler, Joseph. *Toleranz und Reformation*. New York: Association Press, 1960.

Lutz, Heinrich, ed. *Zur Geschichte der Toleranz und Religionsfreiheit*. Darmstadt: Wissenschaftliche Buchgesellschaft, 1977.

Mensching, Gustav. *Tolerance and Truth in Religion*. Translated by H. J. Klimkeit. Tuscaloosa, Ala.: University of Alabama Press, 1971.

Paulus, Nikolaus. *Protestantismus und Toleranz im sechszehnten Jahrhundert*. Freiburg im Breisgau: Herdersche Verlagsbuchhandlung, 1911.

Schultze, Harald. *Lessing's Toleranzbegriff. Eine theologische Studie (Exkurs II. Lessings Verhältnis zum Spiritualismus)*. Göttingen: Vandenhoeck & Ruprecht, 1969.

Weeks, Andrew. *German Mysticism from Hildegard of Bingen to Ludwig Wittgenstein: A Literary and Intellectual History*. Albany, N.Y.: State University of New York Press, 1993.

Index

Abacus regionum (Apianus), 78, 81, 82, 83

Adam, 110, 113, 137, 151–52, 191

Amsdorf, Nikolaus von, 14

Anabaptists, 2, 3, 9

Andreae, Jakob, 18

Antichrist, 45, 58, 181

Apianus, Peter, 78, 81, 82, 83

Aristotle, 151

Arndt, Johann, 38

Augustine, St., 40, 91–92

Baptism, 3, 9, 24–25, 26

Basler Tauler-Druck, 33

Bible, 30, 198–99, 201–3; Lutheranism and, 2, 11–12; Franck and, 4; Weigel and, 25, 27–28, 44

Boehme, Jacob, 20, 38, 48

Boëthius, Anicius Manlius Severinus, 36–37, 102, 116

Book of Concord, 11–12, 18

Brecht, Martin, 45

Büchlein vom Gebet (Weigel), 39–40

Calvin, John, 2, 11

Calvinism, 41

Catholicism, 13; Council of Trent and, 11; Weigel and, 2, 48

City of God (Augustine), 91

Confessionalization, 5, 6, 11

Consolation of Philosophy (Boëthius), 36–37

Corner, Christopher, 27

Council of Trent (1545–63), 11

Creation, 27–28, 38, 42, 43–44, 97–98, 151–52,

Crypto-Calvinists, 41

Cusanus, 32–33, 37, 48

De Docta Ignorantia (Cusanus), 33

De Pace Fidei (Cusanus), 33

De Vita Beata (Weigel), 19, 39

De Vita Longa, 35

Devil, 88, 95, 102–4, 110–13,

136–37, 138; as good, 34;
  see also Hell
Dialogus de Christianismo
  (Weigel), 18–19, 20
Dualism, 3, 6–7, 31

Eckhart, Meister, 28, 32, 33–36,
  38, 40, 48, 95; image,
  concept of the, 30, 334
Erasmus, 11

Faith, 26, 203–4, 205;
  justification by faith, 1, 2,
  13–14, 16, 23, 205
Flacius Illyricus, Matthias,
  13–14, 39
Formula of Concord (1577),
  11–12, 15, 18, 42, 43
*Fourfold Interpretation of the
  Creation* (Weigel), 28
Franck, Sebastian, 2–3, 4–5, 8,
  36, 48, 78

Gebetbuch (Weigel), 39–40
Genuine Lutherans, 14
Gilly, Carlos, 19
Gnesio-Lutherans, 14
Gnothi seauton (Weigel), 30, 38,
  39
Golden Grasp, The. See *Güldene
  Griff, Der* (Weigel)
Güldene Griff, Der (Weigel),
  15–16, 19–20, 28, 42,
  43–47, 48; text, 145–214

Heaven, 54, 101–2, 105–7,
  121–42

Hell, 88, 95, 101–4, 106, 113,
  117–20, 133–37
Heresy, 41, 55, 57
Hermes Mercurius,
  Trismegistus, 95, 192–93
Hildegard of Bingen, 48
Hoyers, Anna Ovena, 21
Hugh of St. Victor, 37

Image, concept of the, 34–35,
  38, 110–12
Infinitude, 9, 96, 98–101

Justification by faith, 1, 2,
  13–14, 16, 23, 205
Justinian, 195

Kant, Immanuel, 10
Karlstadt, Andreas, 24
Kepler, Johann, 12
Knowledge, 145–214; in
  heaven, 125–28; natural
  knowledge, 158–60, 161,
  162, 169–75, 178–81, 184;
  supernatural knowledge,
  158–60, 161, 178–84;
  threefold knowledge, 39,
  156–57, 162–65; twofold
  knowledge, 160–62,
  192–95

Laity, 14–15, 23
Leipzig *Interim*, 13–14
Lucifer. *See* Devil
Luther, Martin, 10–11, 23,
  38–39; and Catholicism, 2;
  Christology, 24; divine

omnipresence and
omnipotence, 28–29, 40;
dualism, 31; "imputed
justification," 26; laity, 23;
Ninety-Five Theses, 10, 23;
paradox of freedom and
bondage, 31; prayer,
39–40; *Theologica
Germanica*, 27
Lutheranism, 1, 13–31, 32, 38,
39, 45; *sola scriptura*, 11–12

"Magisterial Reformation," 2
Majoristic controversy, 16
Manuscript Collection of Sermons
(Weigel), 40–41
McGinn, Bernard, 22–23
Melanchthon, Philipp, 13
Mercurius. *See* Hermes
Mercurius, Trismegistus
Müntzer, Thomas, 2–3, 5, 10
Mysticism, 15, 22, 24, 26–27,
32, 44

Neoplatonism, 3, 7, 28, 45, 47
Nicholas of Cusa. *See* Cusanus,
Nicholas
Nicolai, Philipp, 38
Ninety-Five Theses (Luther), 10,
23

Oetinger, Christoph, 38
On the Bound Will (Luther), 29
On Christian Freedom (Luther),
31
On the Foundation of Wisdom
(Paracelsus), 189–90

On the Life of Christ (Weigel), 20
On the Place of the World
(Weigel), 28, 34, 42–43,
44; text, 65–142
Osiander, Andreas, 45

Paracelsus, 7, 22, 35–36, 38, 45,
48, 89, 104, 192–93;
"elemental spirits," 35;
image, concept of the, 30,
34, 35; imagination, 164;
macrocosm and
microcosm, 22; sidereal
spirit, 39; wisdom, 189–90
Paradox, 36, 40, 46
Paradoxes (Franck), 36
Pascal, Blaise, 9
Paul, St., 25, 30, 31, 108, 115
Peucer, Caspar, 41
Pfefferl, Horst, 19, 45
Philippists, 14, 41
Pietism, 6, 8, 45
Plato, 3, 32
Prayer, 39
Prayer Book (Weigel), 39–40
Protestant Reformation. *See*
Reformation

Quietism, 1

"Radical Reformation," 2
Real presence, 2
Reformation, 9, 10–11, 23, 49
Religious tolerance, 5, 41, 55;
Eckhart, 32
Rosicrucians, 20

Sacraments, 3, 16, 205; *see also* Baptism

Salvation by faith. *See* Justification by faith

Satan. *See* Devil

Schleiermacher, Friedrich, 46

Schmalkaldic League, 13

Schwenckfeld, Caspar, 2–3, 4–5, 8, 11, 45

Scriptures. *See* Bible

"Sermon on the Good Seed and the Weeds" (Weigel), 41; text, 53–61

Shakers, 47

Short Report and Introduction to the "Theologia Germanica," A (Weigel), 27, 32, 37, 38

Sidereal spirit, 38, 39, 164

Small Book on the True and Saving Grace, A (Weigel), 17–18

Sophia Christiana, 36, 95, 126, 127, 128

Spiraculum vitae, 38, 39, 188

Spiritism, 1

Spiritualism, 1–8, 9

Tauler, Johannes, 28, 32, 33, 185

Theologica Germanica, 27, 32, 33, 37–38, 46, 179, 182; equivalent alternatives, 28, 47; image, concept of the, 30; paradise, 100

Tolerance. *See* Religious tolerance

Trinity, 35

Two Useful Treatises… (Weigel), 16–17, 24–25, 32, 33

Weickhart, Christoph, 19

Weigel, Valentin, 9–21, 47–49; Christology, 4; coincidence of opposites, 33; denunciation and response, 17–18, 21, 31; early life, 12–13; "imputed justification," 26; marriage and family, 17; negative theology, 36; pastorate, 12, 17–18, 19; threefold world as threefold heaven, 40–42; *see also* specific headings, e.g.: Creation; Religious tolerance; and titles of individual works, e.g.: *Güldene Griff, Der* (Weigel)

Weltbuch (Franck), 78, 79

Williams, George, 2

Wisdom. *See* Knowledge

Wollgast, Siegfried, 45

Zeitbuch und Geschichtsbibel (Weigel), 4

Zeller, Winfried, 36, 45

Zwingli, Ulrich, 2, 11

Other Volumes in This Series

Abraham Isaac Kook • THE LIGHTS OF PENITENCE, LIGHTS OF HOLINESS, THE MORAL PRINCIPLES, ESSAYS, LETTERS, AND POEMS

Abraham Miguel Cardozo • SELECTED WRITINGS

Albert and Thomas • SELECTED WRITINGS

Alphonsus de Liguori • SELECTED WRITINGS

Anchoritic Spirituality • ANCRENE WISSE AND ASSOCIATED WORKS

Angela of Foligno • COMPLETE WORKS

Angelic Spirituality • MEDIEVAL PERSPECTIVES ON THE WAYS OF ANGELS

Angelus Silesius • THE CHERUBINIC WANDERER

Anglo-Saxon Spirituality • SELECTED WRITINGS

Apocalyptic Spirituality • TREATISES AND LETTERS OF LACTANTIUS, ADSO OF MONTIER-EN-DER, JOACHIM OF FIORE, THE FRANCISCAN SPIRITUALS, SAVONAROLA

Athanasius • THE LIFE OF ANTONY, AND THE LETTER TO MARCELLINUS

Augustine of Hippo • SELECTED WRITINGS

Bernard of Clairvaux • SELECTED WORKS

Bérulle and the French School • SELECTED WRITINGS

Birgitta of Sweden • LIFE AND SELECTED REVELATIONS

Bonaventure • THE SOUL'S JOURNEY INTO GOD, THE TREE OF LIFE, THE LIFE OF ST. FRANCIS

Carthusian Spirituality • THE WRITINGS OF HUGH OF BALMA AND GUIGO DE PONTE

Catherine of Genoa • PURGATION AND PURGATORY, THE SPIRITUAL DIALOGUE

Catherine of Siena • THE DIALOGUE

Celtic Spirituality •

Classic Midrash, The • TANNAITIC COMMENTARIES ON THE BIBLE

Cloud of Unknowing, The •

Devotio Moderna • BASIC WRITINGS

Early Anabaptist Spirituality • SELECTED WRITINGS

Early Dominicans • SELECTED WRITINGS

Early Islamic Mysticism • SUFI, QUR'AN, MI'RAJ, POETIC AND THEOLOGICAL WRITINGS

Early Kabbalah, The •

Elijah Benamozegh • ISRAEL AND HUMANITY

Elisabeth of Schönau • THE COMPLETE WORKS

Emanuel Swedenborg • THE UNIVERSAL HUMAN AND SOUL-BODY INTERACTION

Ephrem the Syrian • HYMNS

Fakhruddin 'Iraqi • DIVINE FLASHES

Other Volumes in This Series

Francis and Clare • THE COMPLETE WORKS
Francis de Sales, Jane de Chantal • LETTERS OF SPIRITUAL DIRECTION
Francisco de Osuna • THE THIRD SPIRITUAL ALPHABET
George Herbert • THE COUNTRY PARSON, THE TEMPLE
Gertrude of Helfta • THE HERALD OF DIVINE LOVE
Gregory of Nyssa • THE LIFE OF MOSES
Gregory Palamas • THE TRIADS
Hadewijch • THE COMPLETE WORKS
Henry Suso • THE EXEMPLAR, WITH TWO GERMAN SERMONS
Hildegard of Bingen • SCIVIAS
Ibn 'Abbād of Ronda • LETTERS ON THE ṢŪFĪ PATH
Ibn Al'-Arabi • THE BEZELS OF WISDOM
Ibn 'Ata' Illah • THE BOOK OF WISDOM AND KWAJA ABDULLAH ANSARI: INTIMATE CONVERSATIONS
Ignatius of Loyola • SPIRITUAL EXERCISES AND SELECTED WORKS
Isaiah Horowitz • THE GENERATIONS OF ADAM
Jacob Boehme • THE WAY TO CHRIST
Jacopone da Todi • THE LAUDS
Jean Gerson • EARLY WORKS
Jeremy Taylor • SELECTED WORKS
Jewish Mystical Autobiographies • BOOK OF VISIONS AND BOOK OF SECRETS
Johann Arndt • TRUE CHRISTIANITY
Johannes Tauler • SERMONS
John Calvin • WRITINGS ON PASTORAL PIETY
John Cassian • CONFERENCES
John and Charles Wesley • SELECTED WRITINGS AND HYMNS
John Climacus • THE LADDER OF DIVINE ASCENT
John Comenius • THE LABYRINTH OF THE WORLD AND THE PARADISE OF THE HEART
John of the Cross • SELECTED WRITINGS
John Donne • SELECTIONS FROM DIVINE POEMS, SERMONS, DEVOTIONS AND PRAYERS
John Henry Newman • SELECTED SERMONS
John Ruusbroec • THE SPIRITUAL ESPOUSALS AND OTHER WORKS
Julian of Norwich • SHOWINGS
Luis de León • THE NAMES OF CHRIST
Margaret Ebner • MAJOR WORKS
Marguerite Porete • THE MIRROR OF SIMPLE SOULS
Maria Maddalena de' Pazzi • SELECTED REVELATIONS

Other Volumes in This Series

Martin Luther • THEOLOGIA GERMANICA

Maximus Confessor • SELECTED WRITINGS

Mechthild of Magdeburg • THE FLOWING LIGHT OF THE GODHEAD

Meister Eckhart • THE ESSENTIAL SERMONS, COMMENTARIES, TREATISES
AND DEFENSE

Meister Eckhart • TEACHER AND PREACHER

Menahem Nahum of Chernobyl • UPRIGHT PRACTICES, THE LIGHT OF
THE EYES

Nahman of Bratslav • THE TALES

Native Mesoamerican Spirituality • ANCIENT MYTHS, DISCOURSES,
STORIES, DOCTRINES, HYMNS, POEMS FROM THE AZTEC, YUCATEC,
QUICHE-MAYA AND OTHER SACRED TRADITIONS

Native North American Spirituality of the Eastern Woodlands •
SACRED MYTHS, DREAMS, VISIONS, SPEECHES, HEALING FORMULAS,
RITUALS AND CEREMONIALS

Nicholas of Cusa • SELECTED SPIRITUAL WRITINGS

Nicodemos of the Holy Mountain • A HANDBOOK OF SPIRITUAL
COUNSEL

Nil Sorsky • THE COMPLETE WRITINGS

Nizam ad-din Awliya • MORALS FOR THE HEART

Origen • AN EXHORTATION TO MARTYRDOM, PRAYER AND SELECTED
WORKS

Philo of Alexandria • THE CONTEMPLATIVE LIFE, THE GIANTS, AND
SELECTIONS

Pietists • SELECTED WRITINGS

Pilgrim's Tale, The •

Pseudo-Dionysius • THE COMPLETE WORKS

Pseudo-Macarius • THE FIFTY SPIRITUAL HOMILIES AND THE GREAT
LETTER

Pursuit of Wisdom, The • AND OTHER WORKS BY THE AUTHOR OF THE
CLOUD OF UNKNOWING

Quaker Spirituality • SELECTED WRITINGS

Rabbinic Stories •

Richard Rolle • THE ENGLISH WRITINGS

Richard of St. Victor • THE TWELVE PATRIARCHS, THE MYSTICAL ARK,
BOOK THREE OF THE TRINITY

Robert Bellarmine • SPIRITUAL WRITINGS

Safed Spirituality • RULES OF MYSTICAL PIETY, THE BEGINNING OF
WISDOM

Sharafuddin Maneri • THE HUNDRED LETTERS

Other Volumes in This Series

Shakers, The • TWO CENTURIES OF SPIRITUAL REFLECTION
Spirituality of the German Awakening, The •
Symeon the New Theologian • THE DISCOURSES
Talmud, The • SELECTED WRITINGS
Teresa of Avila • THE INTERIOR CASTLE
Theatine Spirituality • SELECTED WRITINGS
'Umar Ibn al-Fāriḍ • SUFI VERSE, SAINTLY LIFE
Vincent de Paul and Louise de Marillac • RULES, CONFERENCES, AND
 WRITINGS
Walter Hilton • THE SCALE OF PERFECTION
William Law • A SERIOUS CALL TO A DEVOUT AND HOLY LIFE, THE SPIRIT
 OF LOVE
Zohar • THE BOOK OF ENLIGHTENMENT

The Classics of Western Spirituality is a ground-breaking collection of the original writings of more than 100 universally acknowledged teachers within the Catholic, Protestant, Eastern Orthodox, Jewish, Islamic, and Native American Indian traditions.

To order any title, or to request a complete catalog, contact Paulist Press at 800-218-1903 or visit us on the Web at www.paulistpress.com